CRIME
CULTURE &
VIOLENCE

Understanding How Masculinity
and Identity Shapes Offending

DR KATIE SEIDLER

www.
AUSTRALIANACADEMICPRESS
.com.au

First published in 2010
Australian Academic Press
32 Jeays Street
Bowen Hills Qld 4006
Australia
www.australianacademicpress.com.au

National Library of Australia Cataloguing-in-Publication entry

Author:	Seidler, Katie.
Title:	Crime, culture and violence : understanding how masculinity and identity shapes offending / Katie Seidler.
Edition:	1st ed.
ISBN:	9781921513565 (pbk.)
	9781921513572 : (ebook : pdf)
Subjects:	Crime--Social aspects--Australia. Violence--Social aspects--Australia. Violent offenders--Attitudes.
Dewey number:	364.994

Cover photograph by © istockphoto.com/credhumv. Cover design by Maria Biaggini.

To Margaret,
for being an inspiration.

contents

acknowledgments

I would like to thank Dr Daphne Hewson, who was gracefully willing to take on the supervision of this research more out of faith in me rather than any knowledge or interest in crime and criminals. This research challenged her at times, but more importantly, she was able to challenge and extend me and my thinking, and this made the journey so much richer. I also want to thank Dr Greg Noble for his interest, energy, commitment and motivation, even when confronted by different disciplines and different institutions. He was always willing to help, and his continued interest and assistance has enabled this project to come to fruition.

I could not have completed this research without the assistance of the offenders I interviewed. I want to thank them for their time, commitment and honesty in assisting me by telling me their stories. I hope I have done them justice; I have endeavoured to do so.

To all the staff of the NSW Department of Corrective Services who helped facilitate this research through my visits to jails, thank you.

I also want to think Dr Chris Lennings for his assistance in reviewing the chapters for this book. His feedback and continued guidance and support have been invaluable to me.

Lastly, I need to thank the qualitative research group at Macquarie University — Gayle, Alison, Tracey, Jamie, Janet and others who have come and gone. The team support you have provided me with has been invaluable, especially as qualitative research is still very new to Macquarie and the institutional support for our work is not always obvious.

1

why I wrote this book

I HAVE BEEN PRACTISING as a clinical and forensic psychologist for almost 15 years in New South Wales, Australia and most of my work has been with males (juvenile and adult) in custody for sex and violent crimes. I find my work fascinating and I always have. It is challenging, interesting, demanding and confronting. In particular, I enjoy the challenge of engaging offenders to consider and enact change, ultimately making them better people, thereby protecting potential victims and reducing the cost to the community. I also find it a challenge to work within the criminal justice system at a time in history when the public sentiment is generally against offering treatment to offenders. Often no one wants to hear what I have to say. Further to this, I recognise that we live in a complex society, especially here in modern multicultural Australia and I believe that this has created certain pressures on people, at least some of which may contribute to crime. Therefore, my platform has been to push greater responsibility for crime, both for offenders and for the community, so that we, as a society, may address the factors that contribute to crime and violence, thereby creating a safer society with greater opportunities for people, who will generally be happier and more fulfilled.

Living in a multicultural society has brought issues of race and culture to the fore in many Australian's minds and this is reflected by the media and other social institutions. This has also implicated crime. The debate about crime and culture is a complex one and I don't think we understand the relationship between crime and culture, if any, particularly well. Some believe that being of a certain race or cultural group predisposes you to a particular type of criminal behaviour. Some are aware that particular ethic groups are over-represented in our prison system and they wonder why this is. Some are wondering whether culture or ethnicity has become a motivation for crime. The truth is we don't really know.

Through my work, I have become particularly interested in how offenders from different cultures both commit and account for their crimes. Over the years, I have worked with many offenders whose stories about crime reflected on issues of culture, and this motivated me to embark on research exploring the relationship between culture and crime. I believe there is a need to understand these issues separate from the public frenzy around crime and ethnicity, and this understanding has many implications for various aspects of our criminal justice process, from policing to court dispositions to forensic treatment. However, the relationship between crime and culture remains unclear, and I believe it is important not to get bogged down in the public perception of any link between these concepts, and to take an inquisitive position on whether there is, in fact, a connection between cultural experience and criminal violence. Through this process we may uncover important issues surrounding crime and culture that we should not shy away from.

Several years ago, as I was thinking about these complex concepts, I was excited to receive two separate referrals to assess clients for court that highlighted for me crucial issues in relation to culture and crime. The first client was an Anglo–Australian male, who was being sentenced for an assault and attempted robbery where he had tried to steal the handbag of a woman, he claimed, because he was drunk and on drugs and needed money to feed his drug habit. When she resisted him, he was both verbally and physically abusive to her, presumably because she interfered with his ability to meet his needs and achieve the desired outcome. As such, the offender's motives in offending were seemingly selfish. Further to this, although this offender came from a specific, indeed the dominant, cultural background in Australia, we would not normally think of his behaviour in 'ethnic' terms. The other client was a young man from a Vietnamese cultural background who had fled his home country on a boat with his family to avoid the fragile political and social conditions. He had arrived here as a primary school-aged child and not long afterwards, drifted into a 'gang' of youths from the same ethnic background. He had been involved in a situation where one of his 'gang' identified two people as members of a rival Asian gang. He and some others attacked these men and one of the victims died as a result of stab wounds. It turned out to be a case of mistaken identity in that the victims were not known to the offenders, thus making the situation all the more tragic.

I thought about why the offenders did what they did and whether, in all the hype about Asian gangs of late (at least in Australia), their cultural or ethnic background had anything to do with their crime, as many might claim. I wondered why the second offence was so easy to conceptualise in ethnic terms, whereas the first was not. I wondered whether a history of racial marginalisation might have contributed in some way to a sense of victimhood for the second offender, or to a situation in which he felt that using violence was his only option to rectify the situation. I also wondered about the meaning of the criminal behaviour for both offenders. Was it about belonging or not belonging? About achieving certain important personal or social goals? About feeling powerful and as if they had some agency? Was it about getting back at society? I was restrained from exploring these issues by my job, which at the time was to assess these young men for the purposes of sentencing at court. However, the questions and curiosity remained in that there were issues around identity and social connectedness in relation to violence and crime that needed addressing. Naturally, 'identity' is not just about ethnicity or culture, but also involves questions of class, gender and sexuality, as well as many other important aspects. The connections between these different aspects of identity also intrigued me, particularly in relation to their connection with crime and violence.

Based on my clinical experience and years of pondering these issues, I think that if I had been able to ask these young men the questions I had wanted to, both of them would have had different stories, not only about themselves and their 'group' (social network/culture), but also about their crimes. In a sense, I suspect they would have attributed different meaning to their criminal behaviour and this would have also reflected different understandings of identity and relationship, which I believe is a function of cultural experience.

Offence and Offender Characteristics

Consider the offence and offender characteristics that you can obtain from the brief information contained in official statements about the offending of these men (deliberately ignoring personal and psychological characteristics — both for the sake of brevity and confidentiality).

Offender 1

- Anglo–Australian
- Young
- Drug addicted and under the influence of both alcohol and drugs during offence
- Committed the offence alone
- According to the offender, the victim was chosen because of circumstance — that is, she was there, she was alone and she looked like an 'easy target'
- Offender said he needed money to buy drugs
- Violence was used just enough to attempt to meet his needs and thereby not excessive

Offender 2

- Vietnamese
- Young
- Drug-addicted but not particularly under the influence of drugs during the offence
- Committed the offence with others

- Was a member of an Asian gang
- Offender claimed that the victims were targeted for a specific purpose related to the gang
- Use of force was excessive and retaliatory

There are differences between these offenders and their crimes, even on such superficial analysis. Since that time, I have seen many offenders whose stories reflect similar differences and this seems most poignant in cases of *interpersonal offending*. That is, offending where at least two people are involved — an offender and a victim. In order to commit offences, one must override the 'normal' social boundaries that exist. These boundaries are harder to transgress when another person, or a victim, is involved. In this situation, not only must social boundaries be negotiated, but also human and moral boundaries because, in some way, the offender must rationalise the pain they cause to the victim. There are different criminal needs that come into play when you are dealing with a victim; a human being rather than an object. For example, if you compare the robbery of a clothes store and a bag snatch, both might be committed to gain money, but in the second situation, a person has to be chosen to snatch the bag from, rather than stealing from a shop, which is far less personal. The offender might choose someone who appears rich or someone who looks weak or vulnerable. In any case, they have to think about people and about what kind of person they wish to perpetrate the crime on as well as what kind of person they can rationalise hurting and thereby cope with emotionally. In this way, interpersonal crime involves some 'relationship' between the offender and the victim, however long that relationship lasts or however distorted it is in the mind of the offender. In this sense, interpersonal crime is going to load on ideas about relationships and thereby necessarily also ideas about Self and about Other in a psychological sense. I am curious about how these ideas relate to cultural experience and how this, in turn, impacts on crime and specifically criminal violence, especially in relation to perceptions and experiences of ethnicity. This is what this book sets out to explore.

2

crime in context

CRIME HAS LONG BEEN a major concern in Australian society. As a colony whose express purpose was as a dumping ground for the overflowing population of English prisons and hulks, it is hardly surprising that government authorities and social commentators have constantly worried about the moral and social consequences of the birth of modern Australia. As well as the class dimensions of this concern, there was some preoccupation with the 'racial' nature of crime in Australia — first with the concern regarding the Irish presence, and then with the growing Indigenous 'problem' (Grabosky, 1977). However, since the huge influx of non-English-speaking migrants into Australia after the close of World War II, crime and ethnicity have been increasingly melded in political and media discourse. Migrants are often blamed for bringing crime into this country and this issue has a long history in both the research and media within Australia. The public consensus has been that migrants — whether they be Asian, Middle Eastern or, more recently, African and Pacific Islander — are more heavily involved in crime than their 'real' Australian counterparts, despite equivocal statistical evidence from both arrest and incarceration data (Hazelhurst, 1987; Mukherjee, 1999).

This perception is partly shaped by the social and political history of 'White Australia' and its long-standing fears of foreign invasion (Burke, 2001). Despite the relatively successful adoption of policies of multiculturalism in Australia, these fears have not abated, but often taken new forms. While multicultural practices have majority support in Australia, it is often qualified and ambivalent (Ang, Brand, Noble, & Wilding, 2002), and multiculturalism has been subject to intense criticism for much of the past decade, particularly in the wake of the extremist political party One Nation's success in the 1990s. Consequently, many white 'Australians' continue to see migrants as not only different from 'us', but often arriving from cultures that are perceived as having histories of violence and crime. Specific migrant groups are, therefore, seen as 'Other' to much of mainstream Australia. These Others are often then made scapegoats for a range of social problems, including crime (Saxton, 2003; Teo, 2000; van Dijk, 1987, 1993). In many cases this amounts to the 'criminalisation' of entire ethnic communities (Poynting et al., 2004).

At the same time, however, ethnicity is a factor in many social domains in a culturally complex nation such as Australia and this would include crime. To argue that much of the 'criminalisation' of ethnic minorities is ideological does not diminish the often significant ways in which cultural difference plays out within criminal activity, the courts and prisons. This is, in part, pressing because of the perceived overrepresentation of some groups within the prison system and because of the use of the 'cultural defence' in criminal cases (Sheehan, 2006). Research that carefully examines the significance and complexity of the relationship between ethnicity and crime is, therefore, sorely needed and this is one small contribution to this.

This book aims to explore criminal violence, including sexual violence, in culturally situated ways, taking a more complex approach to the exploration of culture and crime in contrast to simplistic discourses that locate blame for crime in culture. Crimes of violence that are interpersonal in nature, such as murder, often entail questions of identity and relationship, and this is one pathway through which cultural experience can influence criminal behaviour. This book aims to explore the experience of male violent offenders, including exploring their understandings of their crimes, their motivations and rationalisations for their actions, and how these relate to issues of identity, community and responsibility for these men. Through this analysis of violent crime, a richer understanding of violence and its motivations is offered by extending existing theory to suggest that the criminal is a 'culturally situated actor'. This approach has implications for clinical practice, for criminological theory, for the criminal justice process and for the community as a whole.

It has become a key tenet of social theory that people construct their identities (socially, personally, physically and symbolically) by making reference to Others who are different, both with respect to personal characteristics and cultural practices, and this is as relevant in a discussion of crime as anywhere (Lupton, 1999c; Reynolds & Turner, 2001). Linking crime and identity is significant in two key ways. On the one hand, representations of criminality are an important way in which 'mainstream' society constructs a sense of itself. On the other hand, as suggested, criminal activity often involves a performance of identity on the part of the offender.

Constructing an Other ('them') is a common process by which people make sense of and understand their social world and is particularly salient under conditions of anxiety caused by unfamiliarity or a lack of understanding (Lupton, 1999b), or in situations in which the characteristics of the Other bring into relief the values of the majority (Staub, 1988). Socially and politically, this other can be utilised in the service of maintaining the dominance of the majority and this is achieved through judgments being made about individuals on the basis of how closely they represent the 'us', which becomes the gold standard that is 'taken for granted' (Oktar, 2001).

Australian national identity is often constructed not so much by what is 'Australian', but by what is 'not Australian' (Jakubowicz et al., 1994), and sociocultural institutions, such as the media, play an important role in the construction of this identity. Often, this identity is constructed in reference to issues of race and this then becomes the social criteria according to which minority groups are systematically disenfranchised and disempowered within the community (Hazelhurst, 1987). Over time, this construction of identity becomes part of the available social discourse, not only about the characteristics of certain cultural groups, but also about their role in causing particular social ills, such as crime. This discourse forms the foundation for the social perception of the links between culture and crime, and such discourses are more likely to be mobilised under anxiogenic social conditions. So, for example, it is perhaps no coincidence that over the past few years, during a period of social anxiety about cultural conflict, international terrorism and so on, we have seen increasing reportage about 'race rape' in relation to Muslim men, violent gangs of Pacific Islanders, Asian drug gangs and so on. All of these events have consequences for how these communities are publicly represented as a whole and not just with respect to the individuals concerned. People are scared of crime and of criminals; however, increasingly, this fear is manifesting in fear of members of particular cultural groups and, again, this is reflected by the media. Through this process, members of minority communities in this country become increasingly marginalised and disenfranchised, in addition to which, they become conceptualised as a threat to the dominant sections of society (Collins, Noble, Poynting, & Tabar, 2000; Saxton, 2003), utilising resources inappropriately, occupying valuable space, taxing social resources and, importantly for the present purposes, perpetrating crime (Mackey, 1999; Winkel, 1990).

Such community fears inform theoretical notions of 'risk', which serve to pinpoint discrete targets for anxiety and chaos in complex modern society, of which crime is only one (Lupton, 1999b). What is considered to be a risk is culturally determined (Lupton, 1999c) and, with respect to crime, it relates to one's perception of their position in the community, in addition to the perceived likelihood of being victimised, performing certain available discourses on blame and responsibility (Hope & Sparks, 2000). Such risks are culturally shared and based on collective moral narratives that serve political, social and cultural functions, often utilised in the service of constructing the Other (Lupton, 1999b; 1999c). This occurs through the normalising effects of risk. In other words, referencing notions of risk allows people to define what is normal and acceptable and, by definition, what is abnormal and unacceptable (Mackey, 1999). This is often the essentialised (and racialised) Other. By placing the burden of responsibility onto the Other, such scapegoating also means that the 'mainstream community' can have a diminished sense of responsibility for such crimes (Collins et al., 2000).

Lupton (1999a) showed in her Australian research that people's fear of crime tends to be projected onto the socially constructed character of the 'unpredictable stranger'; the image of whom is someone other than the Self, someone different both in form and character and, therefore, both unknown and unsafe. Lupton adds that this unpredictable stranger then becomes the repository for community fear, not only about crime, but about social disorder and disintegration, including such social issues as poverty, drug use and family breakdown. This unpredictable stranger is often translated into an essentialised ethnic Other because, as Poynting, Noble, Tabar, and Collins (2004) point out, it is important for community fears to be as specific as possible, so that people have something to focus on in order to deal with their fear and restore some sense of agency or control over the perceived social threat (see also Colombo & Senatore, 2005). In this sense, fear then has a face.

In Australia, like other developed nations, crime is a topic receiving increasing public interest and, given increasing public fear about crime, people are looking for protection and a greater sense of security. The community wants to know why crime is happening and who is to blame. All too often we hear stories about crime that blame migrants; profiles of criminals at large are offered in ethnic terms and whole sections of our community are being stigmatised as criminals. We are living in a time of public frenzy about ethnic crime and, particularly, about ethnic violence. Yet, how much do we really know about the role cultural background plays in the motivations and justifications for offending? How does ethnicity play out in relation to criminal behaviour, including acts of rape or murder?

An exploration of the stories of convicted male violent offenders suggests that violence is, in part, a performance of identity and meaning, as well as a way of gaining social capital or esteem, which can be understood through the rubric of 'culture'. However, criminal violence also often appears to involve complex links between ethnicity, class, gender and many other aspects of identity. For those offenders from more individualist cultures, identity was framed by personal need and self-interest, whereas for those offenders from cultures prioritising collectivism, the identity performed through criminal violence not only served self-interest, but also strengthened group identity and facilitated cultural pride. Of particular importance is the effect of fragility in identity that can often occur for migrants, and this was often constructed in cultural terms. Offenders' stories also often implicated culture in explaining the motivations and justifications for criminal violence, drawing on community discourses about crime that blame culture.

The Outline of the Book

The primary focus of this book is an exploration of offenders' accounts for their criminal violence. A number of convicted and incarcerated adult male violent offenders, from various ethnic cultural communities, were interviewed about their offending. These interviews focused on issues relating to the offenders' understanding of and motivations for their criminal violence, in addition to their cultural experience and values.

Chapter 3 is an overview of the general theories of criminal behaviour, with a focus on violence, in order to set the scene for the current state of knowledge about crime. This chapter provides a basic framework for current understandings of criminal behaviour, with a view to focusing on crime as a social construction, shaped by available sociocultural discourse, which, in turn, is also influenced by the experience of culture.

Chapter 4 discusses the relevant literature on culture. For the purposes of this book, culture is conceptualised as a dynamic process, which is socially constructed and experienced differently by different people, even within the one community. It cannot be reduced simply to ethnicity or geographic location.

Chapter 5 introduces the offenders whose stories are central to this book.

As stated earlier, understanding criminal violence from a cultural perspective, particularly focusing on interpersonal relationships, draws on discourses of identity, relationship and masculinity, and these issues will form the foundation for Chapter 6 on identity. This chapter is a collection of related subchapters, which discuss separate aspects of identity, including that pertaining to ethnicity, criminality and masculinity. Specifically, an analysis of how identity, as contextualised in culture, is related to the performance of criminal violence will be offered. An important issue raised in this chapter relates to the fragility of identity and how this may have specific effects on the performance of criminal violence.

Chapter 7 reviews offenders' accounts of the meanings of their criminal violence. Specifically, it is suggested that offenders' motivations for criminal violence is understood as a function of cultural experience. In other words, it is suggested that offenders from group-oriented (collectivist) cultures offend for group-oriented reasons, whereas those from cultures prioritising individualism offend for individual reasons. This is a novel idea within criminological theory and extends 'taken for granted' knowledge about crime and violence to suggest that offenders are culturally situated in their behaviour, an understanding of which adds significantly both to criminological theory, as well as increasing the responsivity of forensic treatment and improving aspects of the criminal justice process.

Issues of identity, masculinity and culture are salient in offenders' accounting for their criminal violence. These accounts are designed, in various ways, to navigate issues of responsibility and accountability, primarily to alleviate guilt and maintain positive self-image, both publicly and privately. The next chapter focuses specifically on the ways in which offenders navigated agency and responsibility for their criminal violence. Much of the offenders' work in this area is consistent with that in the literature. However, this chapter will highlight how offenders suggest that crime is behaviour that occurs when some theoretical threshold has been breached in the presence of extraordinary circumstance. Invoking this notion of a threshold breach allows offenders to navigate responsibility by suggesting that crime is irrational and uncontrollable, therefore, removing agency and diminishing guilt. Further, this chapter will extend current thought by situating culture within discourses of agency, exploring how participants drew on cultural meanings as a way of navigating responsibility.

The conclusion provides a summing up in the context of extant criminological theory, offering a novel and more nuanced understanding of crime and criminals within the context of culture. The implications in relation to policing, offender management and rehabilitation within the criminal justice system will then be explored.

In summary, this book is about crime and culture, and it is hoped that it will challenge existing understandings about crime and about the 'taken for granted' relationships between culture and crime that operate in the Australian community.

3

a review of what we know about crime

The Crime Literature

THERE ARE MANY THEORIES that seek to explain the genesis and mainte-nance of criminal behaviour, some of which have focused on individ-ual pathology, some of which have examined sociocultural influences and others that seek to combine factors from a variety of sources. The aim of this chapter is to set the stage in terms of criminological under-standing for the chapters that follow. Further, this provides a context for current understandings of criminal behaviour that have informed the development of theory and practice in this field, as well as con-tributing to available community discourse about crime and criminals.

Biology

Very early theories of criminal behaviour explored notions of inherent 'evil' in a spiritual sense, whereby criminals were suggested to behave in certain ways due to their 'innate' amorality (Hopkins Burke, 2005). From this tradition, there have been various attempts to explain crim-inal conduct as the expression of a biological tendency to crime.

Recent research has, in fact, demonstrated reliable links between various biological and neurological markers and antisocial behaviour, including violence. Specifically, it has been shown that criminals are more likely to exhibit frontal and temporal lobe abnormalities (Raine & Buchsbaum, 1996), reduced levels of the neurotransmitter serotonin (Moore, Scarpa, & Raine, 2002) and lower levels of physiological arousal (Raine & Liu, 1998). Gender has also been implicated causally in crime, with the suggestion that being male predisposes one to antisocial behaviour (Towl & Crighton, 1996). However, there are also a range of potentially confounding factors in examining gender's influence on crime, including the socialisation of males (Smith, 1992), and the sociocultural discourses available on masculinity that contribute to crime (Messerschmidt, 1993).

Another significant theory about the causation of crime that highlights biological factors is that of Wilson and Hernstein (1985, as cited in Farrington, 1996), and this work extended other earlier research that focused purely on congenital factors. Wilson and Hernstein suggested that individuals differ with respect to their innate propensity to crime. The likelihood that a person would engage in antisocial conduct was a function of this propensity, in addition to an analysis of the costs and benefits associated with offending, as mediated by the cognitive variables of conscience and intelligence (such as planning, reasoning skills, and so on). This would include weighing up the material gain likely to be obtained from crime, with the risks associated with potential punishment or social ramifications from criminal conduct. As such, these authors asserted that a biological predisposition may be influenced by variables associated with the psychology of the individual.

Psychology

There are a variety of psychological theories that seek to explain criminal behaviour as a function of individual psychopathology and these theories refer to personal vulnerabilities, such as personality, impulsivity or low intelligence (Farrington, 1996), the experience of mental illness or psychological disorder (Vermeiren, 2003), or a poorly developed sense of moral reasoning (Palmer, 2003). A psychological approach to crime considers that criminal behaviour results from the complex interaction between intraindividual vulnerabilities and environmental factors that facilitate criminal opportunity. Psychological theories of crime and violence then seek to highlight a range of relevant 'risks' in a psychological sense and the impact of these risks is suggested to be additive in contributing to the expression of crime or violence.

Psychodynamic theories assume that criminal behaviour occurs as a result of the interplay between a weak superego and an underdeveloped ego, which is then unable to inhibit the instinctual desires of the id (Andrews & Bonta, 2007). As such, the offender is motivated to seek immediate gratification, which is expressed through hedonistic, selfish and otherwise criminal behaviour.

Psychological understandings of crime suggest that antisocial behaviour occurs when a person has failed to develop appropriate inhibitory mechanisms through socialisation. Learning theory suggests that criminal behaviour, including violence, is shaped through a process of reinforcement and punishment, which ideally encourages socially appropriate behaviour and extinguishes inappropriate or deviant behaviour. Social learning theory (Bandura, 1986) extends this; highlighting that social motivations may also act as both reinforcers and punishers for behaviour, and that modelling occurs within the social context that shapes behaviour in important and socially relevant ways. With respect to violence specifically, according to this framework, the actions of others are interpreted as threatening, which loads on particular social expectations and obligations that are then translated into aggression through the social modelling and reinforcement of such behaviour as an effective problem solving strategy. In this way, violence (and crime) may be viewed as a solution to complex psychosocial concerns, rather than being inherently problematic (Downes & Rock, 2003).

One significant individual theory on crime is Hirschi's social control theory from the late 1960s (see Hirschi & Gottfredson, 1995). This theory states that those children who develop delinquent and antisocial behaviours are those who are less attached to conventional social goals and activities, such as education and future employment prospects. These children tend to be less focused on sociomoral conventions or expectations and, therefore, breach social rules by engaging in crime due to limited investment in maintaining social mores. In other words, they don't want the same things in life that most others do and, hence, they engage in crime because it is non-mainstream and acquisitive in nature, allowing them to obtain the goods that would not otherwise be available to them without the conventional route of education and employment.

According to social control theory, people will become antisocial if important 'barriers' are absent, and these relate to positive self-esteem and the presence of a prosocial network of attachments, both to individuals and also to relevant social institutions. Gottfredson expanded Hirschi's original work and developed the general theory of crime (Gottfredson & Hirschi, 1990). This theory states that the most salient individual factor relating to engagement in crime is low self-control. This refers to the extent to which individuals are vulnerable to the temptations of the moment and are, thereby, impulsive. Impulsive people are suggested to be more likely to take risks, have low cognitive and academic skills, be egocentric, lacking in empathy, and have a short time focus. Low self-control thereby makes it difficult for people to defer gratification, and criminal behaviour often results from the need for immediate reward, in addition to the fact that such people tend to be insufficiently influenced by the possible future painful consequences of offending. Gottfredson and Hirschi argued that crime is part of a larger category of deviant acts, including drug and alcohol abuse, gambling, and promiscuity, which were all argued to be behavioural manifestations of the key underlying theoretical construct of low self-control.

Most psychological theories assume that there is an underlying personality construct associated with antisociality, which may also be referred to as criminal potential (Farrington, 1996). This trait contributes to the development of antisocial attitudes and a tendency to associate with antisocial peers, which are considered important in the onset of criminal behaviour. Using this concept of antisociality as a foundation, Andrews and Bonta (2007) developed the theory of the psychology of criminal conduct (PCC). PCC highlights the role of antisocial tendencies and influences in shaping criminal behaviour, which is also seen as a function of the interplay between such personality variables and sociocultural factors, including work/study opportunities, stable/positive relationships and substance abuse. In this way, PCC seeks to represent a comprehensive psychological approach to crime that highlights a range of variables, including biological, sociocultural, existential and cognitive/behavioural, in the development of such behaviour.

Ward (2002) developed an alternative psychological approach to understanding criminal conduct, including violence, which is interesting and directly informs treatment and risk management initiatives with offenders. Ward proposed that people are motivated to live 'good lives', which allow them to achieve basic primary goods that are inherently beneficial to human beings. Primary goods may be biological in nature and related to the basic survival needs of an organism, such as food, water, sex, and so on. Strictly speaking, from a behavioural perspective, sex is not a biological need, as failure to have sex does not result in damage to the organism. However, sex is frequently referred to as a biological need in the same vein that hunger, thirst and sleep deprivation are. According to Ward, such needs may also relate to the Self, referring to the desire for autonomy, relatedness and competence. Last, primary goods may also refer to the social life, by which Ward suggests individuals are motivated to achieve social and family support, relevant work and study opportunities or appropriate recreational activities.

According to Ward, being able to live 'good lives' allows people to achieve identity and meaning. However, conversely, being unable to attain these necessary goods is hypothesised to lead to psychological distress, which in turn motivates the adoption of alternative, often maladaptive, means of meeting substitute needs. Crime is one such strategy. Further to this, and importantly for the present purposes, this model allows for the influence of culture as necessary goods are assumed to be mediated by social learning experiences that, to a large extent, are shaped by culture.

In sum, psychological explanations of crime highlight the importance of individual variables in shaping criminal behaviour. Both the community as a whole and the media specifically, have tended to prefer explanations of crime that focus on the individual (Ericson, Baranek, & Chan, 1991; Tunnell, 1998), thus ignoring the social conditions that may give rise to criminal behaviour. However, much of the recent important theoretical work in understanding criminal behaviour has highlighted the role of sociocultural factors in the development and maintenance of antisociality.

Sociocultural Factors

Another theoretical understanding of criminal behaviour posits that it occurs as a result of economic and social 'strain', coupled with a lack of positive social supports (Colvin, Cullen, & Ven, 2002). Staub (2003) argued that social conditions that frustrate the attainment of basic psychological needs are conducive to both crime and violence, as are the complexities of navigating society from a position of political, economic and social disadvantage (e.g., Winlow, 2001), including minority group status (Collins et al., 2000). Further to this, Mukherjee (1999) stated that the greater the extent of social disorganisation present in a community, the greater the likelihood of criminal activity within that community, and this is seen in the case of many disadvantaged communities within this country.

The most salient contribution in this area is that of strain theory (Merton, 1966). Strain theory asserts that society acts to progressively exclude low class members from resources and opportunities, and this creates 'strain'. These socially disadvantaged people are then forced to find different (and often antisocial) ways of achieving their goals (see also Taylor Gibbs & Merighi, 1994). In this way, society presents the same images of success to all its members, regardless of social standing (such as owning cars and expensive brand clothing) and according to this theory, if these ideals cannot be gained legitimately, they must be gained illegitimately, that is, through crime. In this way, crime becomes normalised in various areas of society, contributing to the development of criminal subcultures (Ferrell, 1999).

Balancing Risk and Protective Factors

Whatever theory one operates on in relation to understanding criminal behaviour, clinically, the propensity to antisociality and violence is conceptualised along a continuum of risk and protective factors (Farrington, 1991; 1996). Risk factors are those that increase the likelihood of crime occurring, and protective factors are those that inoculate people against developing antisocial tendencies or engaging in such behaviours. Some of these risks are *static* and, therefore, historical, and others are *dynamic,* implying that they are changeable, responsive to treatment and indicative of an offender's current life situation (Andrews & Bonta, 2007). There has been a great deal of research in this area and, as a result, there is a general consensus in the field about common risk and protective factors that need to be considered in determining the risk an individual poses both in relation to violence and generalised criminality, and these have been operationalised within commonplace risk assessment tools that have been used in the forensic field. For example, the Level of Services/Case Management Inventory (Andrews, Bonta, & Wormith, 2004). This is a structured risk assessment guide designed to assist professionals in management and treatment planning with offenders. In addition to identifying salient risk factors, this instrument also includes considerations of issues that may enhance treatment planning and service delivery within the forensic field. Salient risks rated in this instrument include previous criminal behaviour, behaviour in custody, mental health concerns, active substance abuse and antisocial peers.

Intraindividual risk factors that have been shown to be associated with criminal behaviour include the presence of mental illness or substance abuse (Vermeiren, 2003) and particularly early conduct disorder or oppositional defiant disorder. Further to this, poor attachment to caregivers has also been demonstrated to have a predictive relationship to later psychosocial problems, including antisociality (Kobayashi, Sales, Becker, Figueredo, & Kaplan, 1995), as has immature moral reasoning (Palmer, 2003) and antisocial attitudes (Loeber et al., 2002).

In addition to the sociocultural risk factors outlined earlier (e.g., poverty and social disadvantage) that contribute to the criminalisation process, there is also a considerable body of research identifying risks within the immediate social and familial environments of offenders. Specifically, those who engage in criminal behaviour are far more likely to have come from family environments where they were exposed to harsh parenting practices (Vermeiren, 2003), parental substance abuse (Hudson, 2005) or criminality (Loeber et al., 2002). Moreover, the families of offenders are also likely to have poor discipline and inconsistent boundaries (Quinn, Sutphen, & Marcia, 1994), and to be low in cohesion (Bischof, Stith, & Whitney, 1995). It is also common for such families to have experienced discord, with the absence of one or both parents (Bor, Najman, O'Callaghan, Williams, & Anstey, 2001), in addition to being entrenched within socially disadvantaged subcultures, including exposure to unemployment and poverty (Winlow, 2001).

The majority of this literature has focused on identification of risk factors associated with engaging in criminal behaviour. Protective factors, thereby, are the converse of these risk factors and include secure attachments, lack of abuse history, positive experiences of community living, prosocial attitudes, psychological stability and relative social advantage.

On the basis of the theories reviewed earlier, various factors have been implicated causally in criminal behaviour and these include biological factors, individual psychopathology and social variables. Hopkins Burke (2005) has summarised the main theoretical movements in this domain. He stated that the first wave of criminological theory rested on the 'rational actor model', which suggested that people are rational and act on free will and will engage in antisocial behaviour if the deterrents against this are insufficient and the rewards for crime too great. Second, there was the 'predestined actor model', which examined factors extant both within the individual or their immediate personal and social environment that may cause the person to engage in crime and about which they have little control. The most recent wave in criminological theory has emphasised the 'victimised actor model'. This asserts that people make decisions to behave in certain ways that may be perfectly rational for them but that through sociocultural processes, including social disadvantage and lack of political and social power, the underprivileged sections of the community are criminalised according to the definitions of deviance set by the privileged (Ferrell & Sanders, 1995b; Presdee, 2000).

Definitions of Deviance

Although the literature is equivocal about the causes of crime, more recent work in this area suggests that criminal behaviour in general, and violence in particular, are socially constructed phenomena that are considered deviant and outside of conventional social norms, and for which punitive responses are required (Cohen, 1972; Heath, 1984). Further, rational choice theories of crime suggest that in a rational society everyone will act according to reason, including criminals (Hopkins Burke, 2005). Therefore, any act that is deemed to be irrational is outside of understanding and tends to be labelled evil or deviant. As such, crime is subject to discourse and comes to be defined and understood within the social and cultural conditions of any given community (Ferrell, 1999), which are then enshrined within the legal system and criminal codes that govern behaviour in that community. What is understood as constituting criminal behaviour is then variable, subject to change over time and in response to social demand and available discourse.

Deviance is a relative term that does not have an independent existence outside of social discourse and, therefore, in order for something to be deemed deviant, it must be interpreted as such by members of the community (Adler & Adler, 1994). There are commonalities between communities in terms of acts that are considered deviant, such as murder and sexual abuse (Smith & Pollack, 1994). However, outside of these acts, societies will differ in what they consider deviant and this tends to be defined according to the agendas of the powerful and dominant sections of the community (Presdee, 2000). This is a process referred to as criminalisation.

Changes in social structure, organisation and practice that have occurred throughout recent history have also shaped the discourses available in relation to understanding deviance (Foucault, 1975, as cited in Davidson, 1999). Essential to understanding these discourses is Michel Foucault's analysis of power. According to Foucault, important changes in social structure have brought about subsequent transformations in the dynamics and operation of power. He understood power as being a decentralised foundational process or force dispersed throughout society and operated on by all members of a community (White, 1992). In this sense, people were understood as agents of power and control, but they also came to be shaped by the experience of this same power and control, and this has implications for the development of personal, social and collective identity (Barker, 1998). This shaping occurred through the process of 'normalisation', whereby individuals developed operating frameworks for understanding social expectations and norms. According to Foucault, a norm was an element according to which power was established and deemed legitimate. The establishment of norms allowed for the identification, measurement and quantification of deviance from the accepted, and this process was hypothesised to be perpetuated by the workings of state institutions including prisons, hospitals, schools, factories or other large apparatus of social control and order (Rouse, 2005).

Foucault thus argued that power was positive, dynamic and constitutive of experience, according to which people shaped their identities, lives and experiences, and it was through this process that power
could have global effects. The operation of power also included reference to deviance or abnormality, in response to which social control
was desired. Social control is a means by which deviance is contained
or curtailed and it is intimately related to the practices of power
(White, 1992). Social control is ostensibly an organised response to
the occurrence of deviant behaviour, such that this behaviour is minimised or controlled, and the practice of social control has become
infinitely more complex and taken for granted in postmodern developed communities (Innes, 2003), which are becoming increasingly
focused on control by the state. This complexity in social control has
been manifest in the increasingly rigid and draconian strategies that
have been instituted in police forces within developed democratic
nations in recent years. Such policing strategies (e.g., sex offender regis-
ters) allow the community to feel safer; however, alarmingly they are not
associated with any tangible reduction in risk and, rather, may, in fact,
increase risk by placing greater stress and 'strain' on offenders (Petrunik,
2002; Wilson, Picheca, & Prinzo, 2007a, 2007b; Seidler, 2010).

The most salient example of perfected power (and social control)
is arguably the panopticon (Barker, 1998; Flynn, 2005). This was an
architectural design of a prison, whereby the cells of inmates were
placed circularly around the observation room of guards. The design
and lighting of the prison was such that prisoners in their cells could
not see into the observation room and, therefore, could not tell when
they were being observed. As such, the panopticon provided an ever-
present threat of surveillance, even when surveillance did not occur,
rendering the actual exercise of power meaningless. In this way, the
power of the individual prisoners was reduced, but the more generalised power of society (vis-a-vis the guards) as a whole was increased.
Of course, the power of society was, in fact, invisible and became
internalised within the individual, who monitored the exercise of this
power on an ongoing basis. Foucault argued that this was an example
of how people can become responsible for maintaining their own discipline, subject to the power of the 'normalising gaze' (White, 1992),
according to which people judge themselves and their behaviour. The
suggestion is that the extant norms of any society will have a similar

political and powerful effect in 'normalising' behaviour and creating the desire to exclude or reduce deviance. It is through this process that Foucault suggests that society has become ever more complex with respect to efforts at policing and social control. According to Innes (2003), this complexity has become intimately connected with the occurrence of criminal behaviour, which has comprised a target for the focus of social risk and concerns about social disorder or disintegration (see also Lupton, 1999b). Again, this is manifest in the greater emphasis on law and order in public policy that developed communities have seen in recent years.

Criminal behaviour is considered an example of socially constructed deviance according to this philosophical approach. However, what of violence particularly? Foucault argued that there were subtle differences in the exercise of power and violence, which he defined as being concerned with the direct application of force over another (Barker, 1998). Specifically, he argued that violence assumes the target person does not have the ability to act autonomously and is, therefore, bowed to the will of the person enacting the violence. Therefore, the victim is powerless and the violent behaviour is considered deviant because it is nonmainstream and outside of the norms of what is acceptable conduct in society. However, the exercise of power, in contrast, is also involved in the attempt to control and manage behaviour and individuals according to this approach, although the exercise of power, by definition, assumes the possibility of choice and the opportunity for resistance on behalf of the targets of that power, whereas violence does not.

With respect to the criminal justice system, which is primarily responsible for the management of deviance in this society, there is assumed to be an inherently knowable 'truth' of crime (Foucault, 1975, as cited in Davidson, 1999), which the criminal justice process is designed to elicit from the offender. In other words, the criminal justice process is supposed to be designed to encourage offenders to disclose the truth about their offending behaviour. However, it is suggested that the criminal justice process, as it is currently exercised, obfuscates the relative truth of criminal behaviour as experienced by the offenders themselves.

Further to this, the criminal justice system is designed to identify notions of abnormality and dangerousness, which are themselves socially constructed phenomena that have their foundations in understandings of norms and practices of power, according to Foucault. The power that tends to be specifically exercised over deviants and criminals is that of exclusion, rejection and exile as manifest in criminal justice sanctions or punishments, and it is worth noting that these are also the exercises of power typically applied to ethnic minority groups (Innes, 2003) who have tended to be targeted as 'folk devils' responsible for much of the criminal behaviour that impacts on society (Taylor Gibbs & Merighi, 1994). Currently, in Australia, this is most salient for people from Islamic or Middle Eastern communities (Collins et al., 2000). However, the labelling of evil in relation to crime obscures the real social and cultural forces that contribute to deviance in the first place, thus maintaining the status quo and allowing the dominant mainstream to avoid responsibility for the causes of or solutions to crime. In this sense, power has political effects that often serve to reinforce marginalisation through the exclusion of anything or anyone constructed as deviant or otherwise abnormal.

Crime and Culture

Culture has traditionally been overlooked in understanding crime. Presdee (2000) has written a great deal about the cultural basis of crime, contributing to the development of a new field known as cultural criminology. According to Presdee, crime is contextualised within culture, which in turn provides the foundation from which to understand that which is criminal. This understanding is generally framed within the dominant discourses of any given community, such that criminalisation tends to affect those who are also socially marginalised. Criminal behaviour then becomes the means by which those in positions of social disadvantage seek to express themselves and get their needs met (Ferrell, 1998a; Winlow 2001). In this way, for many, the performance of crime is an attempt at communicating anti-establishment ideals, in addition to resistance to the effects of social marginalisation (Poynting et al., 1994).

Presdee (2000) suggested that cultural criminology is interested in the social and cultural context in which the criminalisation process occurs and crime is performed. An understanding of this context is considered essential to understanding the meaning of criminal behaviour and the purpose for the offender of engaging in crime. Through this process, the ways in which social institutions, including the media and other organised networks such as the criminal justice system, come to shape criminal behaviour is also important. Hence, criminal behaviour is considered to implicate all areas of a society, including its cultural discourses and, therefore, crime is not only about criminals but about all members of a given community and is, therefore, inherently cultural. Locating responsibility for crime solely with offenders, therefore, doesn't make sense. Rather, it can be argued that crime is a community-based problem, the solutions for which will only come from the community as a whole and, hence, seeing crime as located in community and culture is essential.

It has been argued that, over time, crime becomes stylised and framed within symbolic shared meanings that have their origin in culture (Ferrell, 1999) and these processes themselves may also become criminogenic (Kane, 2004), thus perpetuating the crime cycle. This, for example, may be evident in gang subcultures where crime itself can have meaning in terms of identity and belonging. The concept of crime is therefore dynamic and socially constructed, and can have both political and ideological impacts.

Crime, Individualism and Multiculturalism

Modern western societies are inherently individualist in their foundation and this will be discussed in more detail in the following chapter. Important for the present discussion is the fact that modernisation and individualism, in addition to the competitiveness and disconnection that such culture encourages, have been linked to criminal behaviour (Colvin et al., 2002; van Dijk, 1999). Given the salience of social disadvantage, poverty, unemployment and social disorganisation highlighted earlier, it is not surprising that modern western societies have higher crime rates than their pre-industrial neighbours, where there is less social inequality, focus on consumerism and material wealth (Westen, 1985). Particular types of crime that have become more salient in recent times, along with the rise of international capitalism, include transnational crimes, such as drug/arms/organ trafficking, terrorism and corporate crime (Newman, 1999). This has changed the face of criminal behaviour and added a new international dimension to what was previously a more local phenomenon.

Many powerful western individualist nations are also multicultural and the migrant sections of such communities are typically also exposed to relative social disadvantage, made more complex by the demands on migrants of having to adjust to the dominant culture and this has also been linked to crime (Taylor Gibbs & Merighi, 1994; van Dijk, 1987).

Australia is a multicultural country and, with the exception of New Zealand, is more European in its foundation than it is like its closer neighbours in Asia and Oceania (Fisher & Sonn, 2002). This has to some degree shaped perceived cultural discourse in this country and thereby has also influenced the available discourse around crime, as well as other social concerns. In Australia, crime has become ethnicised in public discourse (Collins et al., 2000; Poynting et al., 1994) and, therefore, the public, as well as the media and other social institutions, are asking questions about the link between culture and crime, which often seeks to causally attribute crime to ethnic status. This is inherently unhelpful and implies 'taken-for-granted' assumptions about culture/ ethnicity and crime that may be unfounded.

Multiculturalism has generally been embraced by much of Australia and consequently most people in this country lead ethnically and culturally hybrid lives. However, it appears that there are, nonetheless, specific difficulties for many people of migrant descent in establishing identity and belonging, particularly when they are from non-dominant cultures (Ang et al., 2002; Ang, Brand, Noble, Sternberg, 2006), and this may also impact on the experience of social marginalisation and, therefore, crime.

Crime Statistics

So what is the evidence that migrants are more involved in crime than those from dominant sections of the community?

According to Mukherjee (1999), official crime statistics from Australia, in addition to other dominant western countries such as Europe, North America and New Zealand, show that members of some migrant groups are overrepresented within the criminal justice system. For example, Mukherjee reported that between 1996 and 1997 in the state of Victoria, the following numbers of offenders were processed and these data are specifically focused on the countries of most interest to this research, with a particular emphasis on violent offending (Table 1.1).

Table 1.1

Country	Number	Violent offenders	Percentage of ethnic population of Australia
Australia	107,321	13.9%	3.3%
Asia (Cambodia, China, Malaysia, Vietnam)	4014	9.4%	3.5%
Lebanon	738	15.7%	5.3%

Further to this, Corben (2006) reported that of all inmates in New South Wales correctional centres (including those on periodic detention) in 2006, 19.9% were of Aboriginal or Torres Strait Islander descent, 22.2% were born overseas and 16.7% came from non-English-speaking backgrounds. Moreover, of those inmates born overseas, 2.2% were Pacific Islanders, 2.7% were Middle Eastern and 7.3% were born in Asia. These groups of inmates far exceeded those from other countries, with the exception of north-western Europe (also including the United Kingdom) at 2.4% and south-eastern Europe at 2.3%, who were likely to be of Anglo descent. The predominance of Pacific Islanders, Middle Easterners and Asians in this sample is generally consistent with Hazelhurst's (1987) data from 10 years earlier (nationwide); however, both sets of data are confounded by the fact that they do not identify those born in New Zealand who are of Pacific Islander descent.

Data available from the Australian Bureau of Statistics' 2001 Census suggests that in New South Wales, people born in Asian countries comprise 4.6% of the population, with Middle Easterners and Pacific Islanders (including those born in New Zealand) at 1.7% and 2.08% respectively. Therefore, there is some evidence that these groups of people are overrepresented within the criminal justice system, at least in New South Wales.

Despite the claims that minority groups are overrepresented within the criminal justice system, this is not marked, as the aforementioned statistics show. Furthermore, there are other issues that potentially confound making interpretations from these statistics about meaningful differences between ethnic groups and crime. There is reliable evidence that minority groups are more likely to be surveilled, targeted and arrested by police in dominant western countries (e.g., Innes, 2003). Therefore, minority group members are more likely to be brought to the attention of criminal justice representatives and they are also more likely to be processed (found guilty) by this system than their counterparts from the dominant Anglo-Saxon sections of the community. This will conflate statistical evidence on crime rates and ethnicity. It is also worth noting that the research in this area, linking crime rates to ethnic groups, is statistical in nature and, therefore, does not tell us anything meaningful about any relationship between crime and culture/ethnicity.

4

a working definition of culture

DEFINING CULTURE IS COMPLEX and there are varied definitions of culture in the extant literature, many of which use the terms race, ethnicity and culture interchangeably, thus confusing the picture further. In search of a definition of culture, commencing with dictionaries, the following were the most interesting and useful understandings of the word culture. First, from *Merriam-Webster's Medical Dictionary* (2002), culture is 'all the knowledge and values shared by a society', including:

The totality of socially transmitted behaviour patterns, arts, beliefs, institutions, and all other products of human work and thought.

The predominating attitudes and behaviour that characterise the functioning of a group or organisation.

The integrated pattern of human behaviour ...

The customary beliefs, social forms and material traits of a racial, religious or social group.

The attitudes and behaviour that are characteristic of a particular social group or organisation.

According to the Random House *Webster's Unabridged Dictionary* (1997), culture is 'the sum total of ways of living built up by a group of human beings and transmitted from one generation to another'.

It is important to note that these definitions of culture do not focus merely on ethnic status but rather highlight that culture is something that develops within groups of people with certain shared characteristics (including race, but also religion, and so on). While useful as a base to work from, these definitions fail to capture the complexities of culture from a psychological perspective in terms of how culture is experienced and maintained both by individual people and communities.

Culture as Performative

Bruner (1990) stated that culture gives meaning to a person's actions by placing them within an 'interpretive system' that allows people to understand their behaviour through reference to shared myths, traditions, beliefs and languages. In this sense, culture is performative and associated with the production of social meaning (Jakubowicz et al., 1994). That is, culture is socially constructed, as realised through people's behaviours and their beliefs, rather than being a theoretical notion invisible to people that participate in it. In this sense, culture shapes meaning and experience, but it is also, in turn, constructed by these factors in a relationship of mutual influence (Staub, 1988). Therefore, culture is not static, but rather, is expected to shift gradually over time and with social change and context.

Wetherell and Potter (1992) argue that the social construction of culture is based on the past; past experiences, past traditions and past values that are transmitted through generations in order to define the present expression of culture. Culture is thereby seen as something that the present generation should preserve for the future. In other words, culture is maintained by the performance of culture, both at the individual and community level.

Culture as Constitutive

In the same way that culture is active and can be seen to be performed in the interactions, behaviour and language of particular groups of people, culture is also constitutive of experience. That is, through culture, meaning is constituted by reference to shared understandings that contextualise and construct the behaviour and interactions of individuals. Bruner (1990) refers to these systems of understanding as folk psychologies and individual members of cultures are suggested to internalise these folk psychologies at a young age, such that the later experiences and choices of that person within their community are shaped.

Bond (2004) takes a more pragmatic view of culture in suggesting that all cultural systems represent a series of rules and expectations about how resources shall be divided and social problems solved. In this sense, culture determines how society shall operate. Similarly, Westen (1985) understands culture as the 'arbiter' between competing needs. That is, culture determines which needs will win out in any conflict between the needs of an individual versus the needs of a group (e.g., family, community). Further, at the individual level, these rules and expectations are seen to shape the behaviour of people into consistent patterns, so that a shared understanding develops between members of any given culture. Over time, these patterns then form implicit values and norms, in relation to which social interactions are conceptualised (Woo, 2004). In this sense, culture is understood to have ramifications for all levels of a society's operation.

In summary, culture is created by shared social values, stories and meanings, but it is also an active agent; acting on the community by influencing how people are understood and treated, and also in constituting relationships between individual people and groups of people. For example, rich and poor, black and white (Staub, 2003). Ostensibly then, culture has something to say about who we are, how we relate to one another, what we want and what we can expect in life. Culture can thus be seen as an ideological tool (Oktar, 2001), impacting on various aspects of a society, including the economic and political systems that exist within a given community.

A Cultural Psychology

Traditional anthropological notions of culture are difficult to extend to the psychological arena and, over the years, various attempts have been made to broaden psychological theory to include notions of culture. Cole (1997) provides a succinct synthesis of aspects of culture and psychology in proposing a cultural psychology that recognises (a) the need and ability of humans to live within the medium of culture as ostensibly definitional; and (b) that culture is both shaped by and shaping of our psychological experience, such that it is difficult to formally separate notions of Self and environment in understanding psychological phenomena. Cole proposes a cultural psychology that has the following characteristics:

- that action mediated through context is emphasised
- that historical, ontogenetic and microgenetic factors are understood to influence psychological understanding
- that analysis should be grounded in everyday life
- that mind as a concept is co-constructed through the joint activity of people
- that individuals are acknowledged as being active in their own development, although they do not always act in ways that are entirely of their own choosing
- that the nature of mind is emphasised, in an interpretive sense, in understanding action, rather than reducing explanation to simplistic cause and effect dynamics
- that the contributions of other human science methodologies, such as anthropology and biology, be embraced within the domains of psychological inquiry and theory.

A cultural psychology, such as that offered by Cole, is important because it allows for a greater breadth of knowledge to be brought to bear on concepts that are situated in action and in culture, but are interpreted within the framework of psychology.

Discourse Communities

A concept akin to the notion of culture is that of a 'discourse community' (Little, Jordens, & Sayers, 2003). A discourse community is essentially a group of people who share common beliefs and a common language and who, therefore, share in the performance of particular discourse. By definition, this has nothing to do with ethnicity or race. Discourse communities might be cultural groups, sporting groups or professional groups of people, for example, who conform to particular ways of being based on shared understandings, which, in turn, shape available discourse within the group. Obviously, these discourse communities are not *essentially* a person's identity but rather, relate to individual relationships and identities at particular points in time and with respect to the membership of particular groups. Being consistent with the group in expression (linguistically and behaviourally) is integral to ongoing membership of that group and people will construct narratives on the basis of the shared discourses within that community (or group), in such a way that the group's interests are maintained. This may be an explicit or an implicit process.

Discourse communities are constitutive of particular aspects of identity and have both political and ideological implications through being created by and operating in discourse (De Cilla, Reisigl, & Wodak, 1999). Similarly, Potter and Wetherell (1987) stated that the discourses available within a society will also be shaped by the cultural discourse communities available within that society and, therefore, the relationship between culture and discourse is also reciprocal.

The concept of a discourse community is helpful, because it highlights the fact that membership of a cultural community constructs identity in such a manner that language and behaviour are also shaped. A discourse community prizes certain values and these become unspoken norms, which exert power over the members participating in that community, thus constructing their identities and relationships. An example of this would be the influence of the gang exerted over gang members to behave in certain ways, including using similar language when communicating with one another and dressing in certain ways.

In the past, popular ideology focused on race or ethnicity as the determinant of culture and the criteria by which to distinguish between peoples, often invoking social judgments of worth and legitimacy (Tajfel, 1978). For example, black has traditionally been seen as somehow less than white. However, race is also a socially constructed phenomenon and, solely based on phenotypical characteristics of people, does not go far enough in explaining the differences in how individuals perceive, construct and participate in culture. As such, of late there has been a shift away from race or ethnicity as definitive of culture. Rather, the discursive notion of culture has come to replace the use of race as the ideological tool for the social construction of relationships between peoples and communities (Wetherell & Potter, 1992). In this way, culture is one example of a discourse community and ethnicity or race is one way in which people may chose to perform culture. However, culture is more than ethnicity and may be invoked according to other criteria, such as sexuality, religion, profession and so on.

Differences in Culture

A common categorisation of (ethnic) culture is between what has been termed individualism and collectivism, and this is important in understanding ethnic aspects of cultural experience. Crudely speaking, individualist cultures are understood as those belonging to the modern, developed western world, whereas collectivist cultures are assumed to belong to the lesser developed East. There are many differences between these two conceptions of culture, which have been theoretically assumed and empirically demonstrated to have different effects on many aspects of individual, interpersonal and social functioning. In essence, the fundamental difference between individualism and collectivism lies in the construction of the Self in relation to Others (Andersen & Chen, 2002; Gardner, Gabriel, & Lee, 1999).

Individualism is seen to have developed out of the social and philosophical revolution of the Middle Ages (Westen, 1985), which to some degree arose in the context of Christianity in opposition to other more traditional religions, such as rabbinic Judaism (Sampson, 2000). During this period, there was an increasing focus on the individual, as distinct from the familial, social and institutional ties that had previously bound people and their obligations. There was a push for rationalism, for the success of mind over matter and for the achievement of a state of intellectual enlightenment that allowed a person to separate themselves from their emotional or animalistic nature (Lupton, 1999b). In this sense, individualism has been associated with modernity, urbanisation, increased mobility, capitalism and the increasing complexity of society and fragmentation in culture (Hazelhurst, 1987; Wetherell & Potter, 1992). Immigration and multiculturalism have also been linked to individualism (Triandis, Bontempo, Villareal, Asai, & Lucca, 1988), although this is perhaps less cause than effect, as the most powerful individualist nations tend to also be those with the most appealing economies and lifestyles, thus attracting migrants from other generally less-developed nations, resulting in a multicultural hybrid community.

Individualism is associated with a focus on the Self, such that autonomy, independence and self-reliance are prized. In addition, there is an emphasis on the pursuit of individual goals and the expression of personal attributes, which are understood as being stable and enduring, such that they are definitive of a person. The Self is seen as more important than the group and, while they are acknowledged to be salient with respect to social comparison and social experience, Others are seen as instrumental in the pursuit of personal goals (Sampson, 2000; Triandis et al., 1988), including validation of the Self (Markus & Kitayama, 1991). As such, relationships within these cultures tend to be more emotionally detached, transitory and superficial.

In collectivist cultures, the group is seen as taking priority over the individual, who is simply considered to be an extension of the group. People are expected to maintain tight emotional connections to the important Others around them, whose goals are seen as taking priority over those of the individual. Reciprocity and obligation are thus salient features of relationships within collectivist cultures (Rhee, Uleman, Lee, & Roman, 1995). The Self is seen as being more fluid in these cultures, with the presence of Others also having definitional importance to the Self. Further to this, although individuals are understood to possess personality attributes, including attitudes and talents, these are considered situationally determined and occurring in the context of the group within which the person is operating (Markus & Kitayama, 1991).

People within individualist cultures are likely to be members of a large number of social subgroups, although their connection to these tends to be limited, superficial and transitory. Moreover, when there is a conflict between the goals of the individual and that of the group, it is anticipated that the individual will fulfil their own needs first. In collectivist cultures, in contrast, people are likely to belong to far fewer groups and their commitment to these groups will be intense, pervasive and enduring, such that they operate under rigid conceptions of honour and obligation. It is thus the role of the individual to conform to and maintain the harmony of the group, facilitating the group's needs at the expense of their own (Triandis et al., 1988) and this is the means by which people achieve 'face' or cultural honour. For people with collectivist cultural experience, membership of these subgroups is considered to be involuntary, whereas in individualist cultures, a person may choose their membership status to various groups. As such, individuals in dominant western individualist cultures are allowed and expected to exercise choice, whereas collectivist cultures ostensibly tell people how to be, thus removing a sense of personal agency.

According to Markus and Kitayama (1991), participating in either a collectivist or an individualist culture can have a profound impact on the experience and expression of cognitions, emotions and relationships, and these differences have to do with the foundational discrepancy between what they term *independent* (individualist) and *interdependent* (collectivist) notions of Self. In other words, these authors suggest that when any event or experience directly implicates the Self, the nature of the psychological processes invoked will differ vastly according to whether one participates in a collectivist or individualist culture. One way in which this difference may manifest is in the extent to which Others are considered and prioritised. For example, Markus and Kitayama (1991) refer to anger as being an independent-oriented emotion, as it focuses on the expression of individual needs and values (see also Phillips, 1998), often at the expense of Others. This has implications for understanding crimes of violence that, for many, will be an expression of anger (Browne & Howells, 1996). Furthermore, collectivist and individualist cultures will also differ in their preferred means of behavioural control; individualist cultures tend to focus on internal mechanisms of control, such as guilt, whereas collectivist cultures operate more on shame, which is socially driven (Triandis et al., 1988).

With respect to motivations for behaviour, individualist cultures assume that people are motivated to behave in reference to their internal dispositions, which tend to focus on the strategic operation and expression of personal needs. Whereas, people in collectivist cultures are seen to operate on shared understandings of the group's goals, including the perceived thoughts and feelings of Others within the relevant in-group (Markus & Kitayama, 1991). Furthermore, the emphasis in collectivist cultures tends to be on people rather than tasks, with the reverse being true for individualist cultures (Triandis et al., 1988) and this also has implications for the motivation of behaviour, including criminal behaviour, across cultural groups.

Conventionally, (ethnic) cultures are considered to differ according to whether they are individualist or collectivist. Traditionally, this has been seen as a dichotomy, particularly in the West; however, it is possible that individualism–collectivism represents more of a continuum (Sampson, 2000). This may be especially the case within the individual who, by virtue of migrant experience, may exist somewhere between cultures and communities. Whatever the case, the degree to which a culture is individualist versus collectivist is expected to shape the definition of Self, in addition to the experience of members of that culture, including the construction of identity, relationships, the meaning of experience, and the social rules and obligations according to which the culture is performed. Although Self is the defining feature, Others are also implicated and other people are recognised as important in both collectivist and individualist cultures. However, cultures will vary in the degree to which they focus on the priority, needs and expectations of Others. This has important implications for identity, psychological processes and interpersonal behaviour, including crime.

Despite understanding culture as existing along a continuum, for the purposes of brevity and ease of identification, cultures will be referred to as being primarily individualist or collectivist in this book. This is not to ignore the complexity of culture, or to reduce culture to terms of ethnicity or race. Rather, cultures referred to as individualist will be understood as those performing the dominant narratives of individualism and vice versa for those cultures referred to as collectivist.

Culture and Crime

Culture provides a system by which to make meaning of action, thereby also allowing meaning to be made of inaction or departures from the normative (Bruner, 1990). This is particularly relevant to an understanding of violence and criminal behaviour, which is generally accepted as a 'cultural' or social aberration.

Culture is understood to influence violence (and therefore interpersonally violent crime) by creating stories about expectations, relationships and personal needs (Staub, 2003). For example, in individualist cultures, individual success and achievement is seen as a paramount endeavour. Yet, social conditions, such as poverty, high unemployment and a lack of social opportunity, may make the achievement of these more difficult. Hence, under such complex conditions, people are more likely to become frustrated and disempowered (according to their cultural values of success) and this can make violence more likely within a society.

Modern forms of individualism have been linked to a number of social ills, of which crime is one, but which also include mental illness, divorce, high levels of stress and abuse (Triandis et al., 1988). This is hypothesised to be related to the emphasis on hedonism and the pursuit of individual goals at the expense of Others. Jenkins (1990) argues that these shared understandings serve to create discourses that promote violence and restrain personal responsibility and this is evident in the excuses offenders make for their behaviour (e.g., Doherty & Anderson, 2004; James, Seddon, & Brown, 2002). Further to this, individualism serves to weaken the emotional and social bonds between people (Bond, 2004), which facilitates the dehumanising and objectifying process that justifies crime and violence (Ressler, Douglas, Burgess, & Burgess, 1993; Turvey, 1990). Individuals from collectivist cultures that engage in interpersonal violence are also seen as having lost connection with their culture and their heritage (Wetherell & Potter, 1992), which places considerable stress on the individual who is then disconnected from the Others from whom they gain their sense of identity and purpose.

In summary, culture is conceptualised as something by which people make meaning of their existence by reference to shared stories, traditions and experiences. As such, culture is greater than ethnicity or race and involves people participating in active discourse communities that may relate to a myriad of characteristics, including gender, nationality, profession or religion. Through the process of participating in culture, certain beliefs, values and expectations are created and these inform how people live their lives and perform meaning. This will be different depending on whether a culture is individualist or collectivist in nature. Crime, too, will be shaped by the cultural context and it is how this specifically relates to crimes of interpersonal violence, implicating notions of Self and Other, that this book is most interested.

5

meeting the offenders

THE GROUP OF OFFENDERS whose stories are used in this book were comprised of convicted and incarcerated violent offenders. All offenders were sentenced on charges of an interpersonally violent nature. Interpersonal violence was defined as an act of violence in which a person was deliberately targeted and hurt (e.g., murder, aggravated sexual assault, malicious wounding, assault occasioning actual/grievous bodily harm). Acts of violence that were directed against an object (e.g., bank robbery) were not included, as it was in the relationship between victim and offender that the influence of culture was anticipated to be most salient.

Offenders were either considered to belong to an individualist or a collectivist cultural group. The individualist group was comprised of people of Anglo–Australian descent, who were born in Australia, as were at least one of their parents. Collectivism was defined in relation to group-oriented cultures and offenders from Asian, Pacific Islander and Middle Eastern communities were included. These three groups were identified not as being primary or perfect examples of collectivism or group-oriented cultures, but because they are the most significantly represented in the criminal justice system of the possible collectivist cultural groups. In order to maximise the ethnic cultural experience in the collectivist groups, offenders who were either born overseas, in Asia, the Middle East or the Pacific Islands, or who were first generation Australians and whose parents were born in the aforementioned areas, were selected as potential participants in the collectivist group.

All participants were males aged between 18 and 35 years. There were 12 participants recruited; four of whom were from the individualist group and 11 from the collectivist group. Of the latter, there were four from Pacific Islander cultures, three from Middle Eastern cultures and one from an Asian culture. All of the offenders were offered the option of selecting a pseudonym to be referred to. Some took up this offer, while others referred to themselves by their first name.

Following is a brief introduction to the offenders and their stories. The voices of these men are the backbone of this book and provide an insight into criminal violence and the way in which cultural experience may shape this behaviour through identity and the process of making meaning.

Eloqui

Eloqui is a 34-year-old Anglo–Australian male, whose family go back as far as the convicts in this country. He was raised in rural Australia and described having led a fairly insular life. At the time of interview, Eloqui had served 15 years of a 19-year sentence for two counts of murder, one count of manslaughter and one count of malicious wounding. He was 20 years of age when the offences occurred. The victims were two females and a male who he knew through his work, in addition to another male who was ostensibly unknown to him.

In the period prior to the offences, Eloqui described fleeing his home town, which is located in rural Victoria, and embarking on a journey to find himself/secure his identity, particularly in light of difficult early experiences, including being the victim of sexual abuse. This journey led him to the highly masculine environment of the shearing sheds in rural New South Wales and the offences occurred in this location.

In the period directly precipitating Eloqui's offending, he encountered a number of difficult interpersonal experiences, which served to challenge his sense of identity and masculinity. These included failed sexual relationships with the female victims, in addition to identifying himself in relation to a male victim, who was held up as the epitome of masculine success, further reinforcing Eloqui's failures and inadequacies.

Eloqui clearly described a 'build-up' of depression, anger and hopelessness in the period prior to the offences, in addition to feeling lost, dislocated, and rejected. He coped with these poorly by increasing his alcohol consumption and becoming progressively more violent. Also during this period, he began having homicidal thoughts, although he did not account for why his emotional despair had translated into homicidal thoughts, rather than other potential avenues of emotional release.

In essence, Eloqui described his offending as being motivated by the desire to retaliate against others who made him feel bad about himself. Through this process, he also hoped to destroy his old identity and create something new. From participating in treatment, he felt the need to take responsibility for his criminal behaviour and make meaning out of the lives he 'destroyed' and to create a new, more stable identity as he moved towards release.

Jim

Jim is a 27-year-old Anglo–Australian man who was serving a 4-year minimum term of a 6-year head sentence for five charges of sexual intercourse without consent, one count of detain with intent to commit indictable offence and three counts of common assault. Jim was already in his parole period at the time of the interview and, although this was Jim's first jail sentence, he acknowledged a history of offending, including repeated charges for violence, which were escalating in severity and intensity in the period leading up to the charges for which he was incarcerated.

In the period leading up to the offending, Jim described a 'build-up' of emotions associated with significant life events and with which he was not coping well. The most salient of these events relates to the breakdown of a significant and long-term relationship. After 5 years in the relationship, he apparently walked in on his girlfriend having sex with his best friend and this brought about the end of the relationship.

Jim described being devastated by this experience and, although he claimed to have forgiven his partner, he then connected this experience with his engaging in casual and superficial 'relationships' with other women, which he claimed was motivated by his difficulties trusting and opening his heart again, for fear of being hurt.

Jim's account of the violent offences for which he was incarcerated suggested that the violence was a reaction to not being listened to and not feeling respected by Others. In this sense, violence was about getting his needs met and about ensuring that Others behaved on his terms. At a deeper level, it appears that Jim is someone who has great difficulties self-regulating and managing his emotional state. Violence appeared to be the only means that he had available to solve interpersonal conflict or resolve difficult emotions and, in these situations, violence was about not only controlling himself, but also controlling Others around him, so that he could achieve relative emotional stability.

Nick

Nick is a 23-year-old Anglo–Australian man, who was serving a 12-year minimum term of a 16-year head sentence for various charges, including murder, goods in custody, break and enter, armed robbery, possession of a firearm and discharge of a firearm in a public place.

Nick has a long history of antisocial behaviour and performed a well-established 'criminal' identity that has shaped a generally hedonistic and selfish lifestyle, which he believed has been easier than mainstream pathways to success. Nick discussed his offending in an almost methodical or clinical way and his explanations for the offences tended to be superficial and devoid of emotions, which was likely related to the fact that he sees crime as a lifestyle choice.

Nick's criminal behaviour was motivated by selfish desires associated with maintaining his hedonistic and nonmainstream lifestyle. In other words, Nick appeared to offend when he needed money, or wanted the property of another and he was able to justify his behaviour on the basis of self-centred needs and a lifestyle that does not conform to what he sees as 'normal' or 'right' and is, therefore, criminal.

Norm

Norm is an Anglo–Australian man, who was 34 years old at the time of interview and was serving a 5-year sentence for a home invasion and armed robbery. He had an extensive criminal career and had served considerable time in custody throughout his life.

Norm's offence involved attending the home of the victim, with two of his friends, forcing entry to the home and bashing the victim with a baseball bat. The victim was targeted with the sole purpose of physically assaulting him and Norm had not met the victim previously.

Norm's story of his offending shifted during the interview and there were two main narratives about his behaviour. The first of these involved retaliation for the physical assault on a woman who was an associate of one of his co-offenders. To justify this version, Norm drew on discourses of masculinity that paint women as incapable and inferior and needing male protection. He portrayed himself as being a morally strong and principled person whose behaviour was motivated by ethical standards for what he considers appropriate according to personal values. These principles can be seen both as part of and as distinct from the criminal principles that Norm also operated under. Norm also accounted for his offending in terms of supporting his friends and not letting them down, and this drew on notions of masculinity and criminality.

Norm's offending can be seen as part of his general commitment to important relationships. In other words, a man's relationship to his family, a man's relationship to a woman, a man's relationship to his friends and a man's relationship to the community.

Iash

At the time of the interview, Iash was 27 years of age and incarcerated for two counts of detain for advantage and two counts of causing grievous bodily harm. This was Iash's first time in custody and he was serving a 4-year minimum term of a 6-year head sentence.

Iash was born in Australia to Lebanese parents; however, culturally he identified strongly with the Lebanese community and actively disengaged and separated himself from the mainstream Australian community, which he imbued with negative characteristics. Iash described himself as being 'essentially' Lebanese and, even though during his younger years he identified with Australia as his homeland, Iash claimed that he had not been comfortable in Australia for some years, primarily as a result of what he perceived to be the global media attack on Lebanese people and the Islamic religion, in which he is an active participant.

In relation to his criminal behaviour, Iash acknowledged a long history of involvement in crime, dating back to his early teenage years. The charges that gave rise to his sentence related to two different sets of offences. The first set of offences, relating to the detain for advantage charges, were essentially described as relating to a 'business transaction'. Iash claimed that the victim owed him money and he kidnapped and 'tortured' the victim and another man in attempt to extract the money he was owed. While incarcerated, Iash was charged with two counts of grievous bodily harm, which relate to offences that he organised while in jail. Specifically, Iash organised to have some of his associates (also Lebanese) conduct a home invasion and assault several members of his extended family for allegedly threatening his ex-wife and children.

Kadr

Kadr is an Australian-born Lebanese man, who was 22 years old at the time of the interview and serving a 6-year sentence for the charges of manslaughter, affray and possession of a loaded weapon. Culturally, Kadr identified strongly with the Lebanese community. Generally, he separated from the 'Australian' culture and aligned himself with the Lebanese Muslim community. However, he also at times identified as Australian, given that he was born in this country.

Kadr's story of the manslaughter charge suggested that he and his co-offender, a long-term friend of Turkish origin, were provoked by two drunk and aggressive Anglo–Australian males who threw something at their car and made racial taunts towards them. Kadr claimed that he attempted to de-escalate the conflict; however, one of the victims tried to punch him and his co-offender, who then drew Kadr's gun and shot one of the victims. The affray and possession of a loaded weapon charges related to a separate incident when Kadr and the same co-offender were in an 'Australian' area of Sydney, when they stopped at a service station in the early hours of a morning to purchase food. According to Kadr, a group of 'Australian' youths provoked the incident by again making racial slurs and negative comments about their car and damaging the car in order to cause an altercation. Again, Kadr was adamant that he and his co-offender did not cause the incident but, when angry, merely responded by brandishing the gun to scare and intimidate the other youths.

Sammy

Sammy is a 33-year-old Turkish–Australian man, who was serving a lengthy custodial sentence for various offences. He was first incarcerated for the charges of break and enter and armed robbery. However, during the early years of his sentence, he was involved in killing another inmate and he received significant additional time for this offence.

With respect to the murder, Sammy claimed that the victim threatened him by referring to him as an informant and then challenging him to a fight within the public area of the jail yard. Both Sammy and the victim, whom he identified as 'Australian', brought along a friend for support and Sammy's co-offender was also Turkish. The two pairs of men met and were armed and, after a brief fight, the victim died after sustaining two stab wounds to the abdomen.

Genuine

Genuine is a 23-year-old Vietnamese–Australian man, who was serving a 3½-year prison term of a 5 years and 3 months head sentence for the charges of common assault, possession of an implement and possession of drugs.

Genuine came to Australia with his parents when he was 8 years of age, after fleeing Vietnam as a refugee. He alluded to how the experience of leaving Vietnam and travelling to Australia by boat was both difficult and traumatic, and he described being packed tightly on to refugee ships, much like the recent media images of illegal immigrants to this country. Possibly as a result of this experience and other negative early experiences he had in Vietnam, Genuine saw being in Australia as a privilege and a benefit, and he valued the fact that he has experience of two cultures, which he described as making him genuine.

Genuine was involved in an assault on a criminal associate, who was aligned with another (rival) gang and the offence was allegedly motivated by the desire to retaliate against a perceived wrong relating to an assault on a friend and fellow gang member.

Ngahau

Ngahau is a 23-year-old Tongan–Australian man, who was serving a 4-year minimum term of a 6-year head sentence for the charges of aggravated robbery, malicious damage, goods in custody, steal from person, and aggravated break and enter. These charges arose from two separate occasions, and all of Ngahau's offences were committed in the presence of co-offenders.

Ngahau was born in Australia, but spent most of his early years in Tonga, only to return to Australia as an adolescent. He identified as Tongan culturally and clearly performed the values of this culture in his relationships with others. Throughout the interview, Ngahau separated himself from mainstream Australia, suggesting that he is an outsider ostensibly, who has had to survive in a foreign country, with different values and a different lifestyle. To some extent, he blamed this for his criminalisation.

According to Ngahau's account, his first offence involved physically assaulting a man, whom he was told had problems with one of his friends, and his (cultural) values demanded that Ngahau perform as a loyal friend by assaulting the man. With respect to the second set of offences, Ngahau claimed that he was informed by a friend that a man at a party was badmouthing him in front of his then girlfriend. In response to this, Ngahau went to the party with his friend and physically assaulted the man he believed had been disrespectful to him. The attack on the victim was extreme and Ngahau even attempted to cut the man's throat.

Richarn

Richarn is a 25-year-old dark-skinned man who was born in New Zealand, but is of Samoan descent. He had been incarcerated for approximately 8 years for killing a taxi driver when he was 17 years of age. The offence was committed with two co-offenders, both of whom were also of Samoan descent. The taxi driver was apparently Lebanese and made racist comments towards Richarn and his co-offenders — suggesting that Pacific Islander people were poor people who tended to leave without paying their fare. Richarn articulated being strongly motivated by the desire to retaliate against what he perceived were racist comments, causing him to take umbrage on behalf of Pacific Islander peoples. After beating the taxi driver, Richarn and his co-offenders left him on the side of the road, stole his taxi and drove away, and he subsequently died as a result of his injuries.

T

T is a 24-year-old Samoan–Australian who was serving a 4-year term of a 7-year head sentence for the offences of aggravated sexual assault, armed robbery, and break and enter. The focus of the interview was on the sexual assault, in which T and four co-offenders broke into the house of the victim to search for money or property to steal in order to purchase more alcohol and drugs. While at the premises, the victim was raped, both orally and vaginally, by all five men at the same time. T handed himself in to police for the offence about 2 weeks later. None of his co-offenders have been caught and T did not disclose their identity to police.

Culturally, T identified as being Samoan. His parents are Samoan; however, T himself was born in New Zealand and migrated to Australia around the age of 3 or 4 years. Although he has returned to New Zealand, he has never been to Samoa. Nevertheless, he aligned himself strongly with Samoa, as well as internalising (and externally upholding) the values, interests, personality characteristics and fashions associated with Pacific Islanders.

Lucky

Lucky is a dark-skinned Fijian man who was 26 years of age at the time of the interview. He had served approximately 4 years of a 12-year minimum term (16-year head sentence) for the murder of a taxi driver that occurred when he was 22 years of age. The taxi driver was apparently of Indian descent.

Lucky identified strongly as Fijian. He stated that both his parents were born in Fiji, although his father reportedly had some European blood. Lucky had only arrived in Australia in 1996 as an 18-year-old man, with his mother and sisters. On the night of the offence, Lucky, his younger cousin and two friends (both of whom were also Fijian) had been out drinking at a party. They were intoxicated and had also smoked some marijuana. Lucky and his co-offenders took a taxi cab home with the victim, whom he identified directly as being Indian, and who allegedly drove them the 'long way' home rather than taking them the most direct route to their destination. Lucky was displeased about this and, on reaching the end of their journey, refused to pay the taxi driver the additional cost. An argument ensued, during which

Lucky claimed that the taxi driver manhandled his cousin in an attempt to get the extra money he was owed.

Lucky intervened at this point and began to assault the taxi driver. He made racial comments to the taxi driver as he was kicking and punching him. At some point, the taxi driver allegedly pulled out a knife, which caused the violence of Lucky and his co-offenders to escalate against the taxi driver until presumably he was incapacitated. Lucky and his co-offenders then left and fell asleep out the front of a house further down the street.

6

'I have to prove that I'm there' — identity and its relationship to criminal violence

THIS CHAPTER AIMS TO EXPLORE how the performance of criminal violence may promote particular aspects of identity that are located in complex dimensions of culture, pertaining to racial or ethnic culture, group culture, criminal culture, and masculine culture.

What is Identity?

The notion of identity has been associated with the sense of who one is (Wetherell & Potter, 1992). Through identity, a person develops a narrative or ontological understanding of the Self, which is constructed in reference to social and personal experience, in addition to cultural norms and values (Lupton, 1999b).

Human beings are inherently social creatures and experience the world in social terms, predominantly with respect to relationships and interactions with others, although the degree to which this influences identity will be shaped by culture, as discussed in earlier chapters. Identity is inherently interpersonal (Andersen & Chen, 2002) and is defined in relation to others, whether in reference to an individual or to a group (Sampson, 2000; Tajfel, 1978). As such, identity is usually comprised of two parts: that in relation to the Self (personal identity) and that in relation to Others (social identity; Brewer & Gardner, 1996). Further, identity may be constructed in multiple ways, such as by reference to gender, ethnicity, territory, culture or any other specifically salient construct (Colombo & Senatore, 2005; Connell, 1987). In this sense, identity privileges certain ways of being that will become more salient in particular contexts and in relation to the particular Others present.

Identities are constructed, negotiated and performed through talk (Burman & Parker, 1993) and are designed to have social, ideological and/or political effects (Potter & Wetherell, 1987), depending on how they are used to navigate the complexities of social interaction. Given that identity is constructed through language, it is also inherently discursive in nature and bound to historical, social and institutional factors that privilege certain identities over others (Hall, 1996). Discourse makes available certain positions for identity (Parker, 1992), which are then constantly reshaped by the social and discursive practices in which identity is implicated (Davies & Harre, 1990).

Identity I — Cultural Identity
Identity is Cultural

As discussed previously, identities are inherently cultural (Bruner, 1990) and are constructed in relation to experience, both subcultural and social. With respect to ethnic culture, individuals from group-oriented cultures are expected to prioritise Others, whereas the converse would be the case for those from cultures valuing individualism. Iash and Jim typify these differences in identity and focus. Although both these men identify the importance of Others in their lives, they account for this differently, which has its foundation in cultural understandings of Self and Other.

> Iash (Lebanese): I would go ballistic. If it's a close — one of the close-knit mates — if someone touches their sister or hurts their mother, I would go ballistic as well, you know, because this family, this close-knit group that I'm telling you about, these people are like my [emphasised] mother, they're like my [emphasised] sister, I've grown up with them ... I've slept at their house, I've ate at their table, I've broken bread with them and then for me to turn around and just see his mother or his sister get attacked and just say 'Oh well, lucky it's

not my mother', I couldn't do that, I could not do that and even my other mates couldn't do that and my cousins couldn't do that, there'd be no way they'd do that, you know?

Jim (Anglo): Because when I come in [to jail], it was all me, me, me, um … things had [emphasised] to be done the way I wanted, if we went out, it was to where I wanted to go out, you know? Um … I'm very, very protective, you know, you look at my missus the wrong way, 'I don't care mate', whack! [makes a sound like hitting someone], you know, if you insult my missus, whack! … you insult my mother, whack! [chuckles], you know, I'm very protective of my family and if I'm with a woman, she's my family … Um no hesitation whatsoever, I'm defending … my kingdom.

Iash was born in Australia, but identifies strongly with the Lebanese culture of his parents, which is collectivist in its orientation. Iash's words speak to the priority he places on Others in his life, by positioning himself in relation to these Others. He identifies the fluid nature of the boundaries around relationships, which are defined by shared experience, obligation and reciprocity. Thus, Others may be defined as 'family', even without any blood or kinship ties. In contrast, Jim was born in Australia and subscribes strongly to individualist values as a function of his White European heritage. Jim also discussed the importance of family; however, unlike Iash, Jim positions the Others in his life in relation to himself, as these people become part of his 'kingdom', which he believes he is entitled to defend. In this way, people belong to Jim and are obligated to meet his needs.

This is consistent with cultural understandings of identity discussed earlier in relation to individualism and collectivism. Specifically, people who participate in individualist cultures tend to have clearly defined selves; autonomy and independence are prized and individual identity is seen to be comprised of fixed, stable internal attributes (Markus & Kitayama, 1991; Triandis et al., 1988). Within the framework of collectivism, the boundaries around identity are fluid and flexible, and responsive to both social context and mutual obligation. The individual is seen as inherently and *essentially* a function of the salient Others with whom they are connected and, in fact, it is only in these important interactions that people can realise their identity (Brewer & Gardner, 1996; Rhee et al., 1995).

The Complexity of Ethnic Culture

Grounding identity in (ethnic) culture is useful theoretically; however, the reality is that culture is complex and confusing, and difficult to develop a relationship to, perhaps even more so for people from dominant cultural groups, for whom ethnicity is not seen as essential to public identity.

> Jim (Anglo): . . . [pause] ... I have a culture?
>
> Interviewer: Are you surprised you have a culture?
>
> Jim: Yeah I am.
>
> Interviewer: Well let's come back a step then, what does culture mean to you? When I say 'culture', what's your understanding of what culture is?
>
> Jim: (chuckles) You want me to be honest, I have no [emphasised] idea.

Jim has obviously not positioned himself in relation to culture in any concrete way and, although identity has its foundation in cultural values and experience, Jim's words highlight that culture can be 'taken for granted' that is not consciously used in developing identity. This is likely to be particularly the case for those whose ethnicity (perceived culture) is not obvious through colour (Moreton-Robinson, 2000; Sampson, 1983). As such, culture is seen as something that only belongs to the non-White and this belief is also reproduced by members of minority groups as follows.

> Iash (Lebanese): ... with Australian cultures, it's just a joke mate, the father's out the back getting drunk, the mum's in the bedroom punching cones, the daughter's rooting her boyfriend in the bedroom, the son's out there um jacking up a stolen car, taking the wheels off it ... You know, they've just got no culture there, you know, but like I wouldn't do that in my own back yard, that's what I said to you from the word go, you don't do that sort of stuff.

For Iash, culture appears to be related to the performance of moral behaviours that prioritise respect for Others and conversely, a perceived lack of culture relates more to the performance of antisocial behaviour within one's family and community. This says more about Iash's relationship with his own internalised cultural values, which he separates from those of mainstream Anglo–Australians. In this sense, even though Iash is born in Australia, he positions himself in relation to Australians, rather than as an Australian.

Culture is conspicuously lacking in the accounts of offenders from individualist cultures. This is consistent with the suggestion that culture is something that belongs to the Other, as defined in relation to the dominant majority (Moreton-Robinson, 2000). As such, for many offenders from migrant communities, who, as a result of their 'obvious' minority status, either by birth or by appearance, position themselves and are positioned by the dominant majority, in terms of ethnic culture. This implies that there is a comfort or taken for granted in identity that comes from being a member of the dominant majority. This is important in understanding the performed identities of offenders and suggests that identity cannot simply be reduced to cultural experience in developmental terms. Rather, there is a dimension of lived experience that shapes identity in the context of ethnic cultural status.

Bicultural Identity

For those offenders with migrant experience either by birth or through their parents' heritage, it appears that negotiating ethnic identity is particularly complex. It is suggested that for minority groups, ethnic identity may be constructed as lying along a continuum, where at times, identity may be positioned *with* 'Australians' and at other times, *separate from* 'Australians'. For example, Kadr, who was born in Australia to Lebanese parents, drew on his Australian and Lebanese ethnic identities variously. In this first quote, Kadr is accounting for his offending behaviour, relating to an incident where he brandished a gun and threatened a group of youths whom he perceived were making racist comments towards him and his co-offender.

> Interviewer: What happens to you [emphasised] inside as these guys are having a go at you and calling you 'wog' and 'Go back to your own country' and all that kind of stuff?

> Kadr (Lebanese): I'm just fuming, fuming up inside … I get angry and aggressive, you know what I mean? My feelings are like, who are they to do this, we're all Australians, we've done nothing wrong to these people.

Kadr identifies himself as Australian here, suggesting that he shares an ethnic cultural identity with the people who are allegedly making racist comments towards him. However, at other times, Kadr distances himself from mainstream Australia by claiming that he is not Australian, or at least he is not identified as Australian by others.

> **Kadr:** Just so they can leave me in jail for another 6 months ... But that's how they work, you know what I mean? Fuck this, but if I was Australian, nothing would happen. If I was Australian, you know, do what you want, you know what I mean?

Kadr chooses to position his cultural identity variously in relation to the particular ideological/political point that he is making at interview. In the first quote, Kadr utilises his Australian identity in the service of portraying himself as an innocent and 'hard done by' person, who was ostensibly pushed into criminal behaviour by the allegedly racist and inappropriate behaviour of others. This is related to how Kadr has sought to rationalise his criminal behaviour, both to himself and to others.

In the second quote, Kadr is claiming 'Lebanese-ness' in an attempt to mobilise his anger at the criminal justice system, which he believes has treated him unfairly. Kadr makes repeated comments about the perceived inappropriate length of his sentence, in addition to the allegedly unfair ways in which Lebanese people have been treated within the criminal justice system. This allows Kadr to maintain a sense of anger and injustice, which preserves his identity in relation to those who imprisoned him and judged him (in the literal sense of the term). To this end, he is drawing on particularly salient social and political issues that provide him with the framework for his position, such as the global, local and social ramifications of the War on Terror, in addition to other high profile events that have implicated Lebanese Muslims in recent years, such as the Skaf gang rapes and the Tampa Boat Crisis in Australia (Collins et al., 2000; Poynting et al., 2004; Saxton, 2003). These particular events have served to stigmatise Lebanese and Muslim people in this country. As such, people from Muslim or Lebanese cultural backgrounds must position themselves in relation to the socially constructed and often essentialised ethnic identities that exist in the community, and which can be both restrictive and pejorative.

Several offenders from Middle Eastern or Lebanese backgrounds made reference to feeling disconnected from mainstream Australia, at least on occasion. For example, despite being born in Australia, Iash comments that he has not felt comfortable here for some years, which he attributes to 'all this rubbish on TV ... about, you know, the rapists, about terrorism'. This has a direct relationship to Iash's criminal behaviour, as he claims not to 'shit in my own backyard' but instead, commit crimes outside of his local and cultural community. Whether or not this is accurate is not at issue. Rather, this is how Iash constructs his offending within his particular social and cultural environment, and it is this positioning that speaks to issues of identity.

> Iash (Lebanese): ... drugs and criminal activity, yeah because that's all [emphasised] we know, that's all we've been shown.
>
> Interviewer: By Australia or by Lebanon?
>
> Iash: By Lebanon, by Australia, you know what I mean, by the way we were brought into this country ... they brought us here for my father and mother to work, to be peasants, because they needed slaves ... That's all it was, they needed someone to do the bodgy jobs that nobody else wanted to do ... So basically, I blame it on the government, it's the government's fault, you know, because they didn't provide us with everything that we needed at the time ... Either you go legit or either you go crooked, like, and the easiest way for us in the Lebanese community was to go the crooked way.

Here, Iash blames the Australian government and the community for his criminalisation and that of his family and local community by suggesting that the Australian government essentially enslaved his people to do 'bodgy' jobs that were interpreted as being 'beneath' mainstream Australians. Further to this, Iash claims that the Lebanese sections of the community were then ostensibly starved of the means by which to survive in more prosocial ways in mainstream Australian society. That is, their social capital was restricted. In offering this account, Iash is engaged in a rhetorical strategy designed to reduce his agency in the performance of an identity that he believes was prescribed to him by this country. Specifically, he claims that he was prevented from having access to the resources and opportunities that would have allowed him a different experience (see Collins et al., 2000). Although Iash's argument is a distortion of Australian immigration policy and practice, the rhetorical import of his words are clear and reinforce his chosen identity, in addition to justifying his illegal behaviour and that of his family and other Lebanese people in Australia.

Ethnic Identity is Complex

The accounts of offenders from non-dominant cultures demonstrated that ethnic identity is complex and has performative aspects that are often contradictory.

Genuine is a Vietnamese-born Australian, who identifies as Vietnamese–Australian. He chose his pseudonym specifically because he believes that being able to move between two cultures allows him to be inherently 'genuine', suggesting that there is some tangible value to being bicultural, at least in this country. However, this is difficult to identify in his account.

> **Genuine (Vietnamese):** Well ... [long pause] ... well I have to say the family ... I'm sorry, I sound like I'm discriminating, you know what I mean, about Australians and always generalising it, but that's what I find hard sort of raising up ... mostly in jail, in boys' homes, institutions, that I come to find this ... one particular occasion, where a visit at boys' home, where I witness an inmate, ah, an Australian, swear to his Mum and Dad. I thought 'fuck', you know, that's the baddest word, you know the filth that come out of the tip of his tongue, you know what I mean ... he's just spitting it out to his own Mum and Dad ... and even though he made a big [emphasised] scene ... to me, I say I never do that. I've done worse [emphasised], got in worse [emphasised] trouble, you know what I mean, than ... than a lot of people I can thought of ... got punished, like bad too, but never, I would never ...

Despite his apparent identification with, acceptance of, and affection for Australia, Genuine focuses on his mother culture and suggests that 'Australians' possess negative qualities that are inconsistent with his own (presumably Vietnamese) values. He apologises for being potentially 'discriminating' through the use of a disclaimer (Potter & Wetherell, 1987); however, Genuine is clearly articulating his position in relation to what he considers to be the inherent Australian culture, which is seen as negative and disrespectful.

Sammy, an Australian-born man, who identifies as Turkish–Australian due to his parents' heritage, also separates himself from 'Australians', despite his initial identification with the perceived ethnic culture of this country. Sammy refers to Australians with the term 'gavur', which is both a disparaging and derogatory term and means an 'infidel' or 'non-believer' in Turkish. The fact that Sammy identifies so strongly with Turks/Middle Easterners, as distinct from *gavurs*, is likely also a function of the greater social cohesion that is formed under conditions of stress or threat (Tajfel, 1978), such as that experienced in jail. In other words, stronger social cohesion (in this case, ethnic identity) achieves social aims in particular situations, which may be about increasing perceived safety within the group and this is particularly important in the jail system.

Ethnic identity may also be actively constructed in relation to anticipated social need and situational demand.

> **Kadr (Lebanese):** … like when I was young … I always like went to a school, where the whole relationship was all Lebanese, you know what I mean? My Dad owns a mechanic shop, all my customers, were all Lebanese … And I always see people you know, like he's doing this, he's doing that … and for me personally, I caught up to it straight away, you know what I mean? Fuck, I want to be like him, I want to be like that, I want to be like this bloke … the whole area, they're all Lebanese … Like there's a bloke getting bashed, this bloke's doing this, this bloke's doing that, and it just happened that I had to come out the same way …

This quote speaks to the subtlety and complexity of constructing identity for members of a minority group (Hall, 1996). In contrast, Kadr described making an active choice in ethnic cultural identity and affiliation on the basis of the perceived values and gains associated with the Lebanese culture for him 'Fuck, I want to be like him, I want to be like that'. In relation to the activities of Lebanese people that Kadr describes, he is referring to crime and the social standing and financial benefits associated with this behaviour and lifestyle within the subcultural community. However, on the other hand, Kadr accounts for the development in his ethnic identity as being shaped through the process of ostensibly 'soaking' in culture, not only through his family, but also his local community, such that 'it just happened that I had to come out the same way'. This serves to minimise Kadr's performed criminality and the idealisation of criminal values that his assumed identity implies.

Aligning oneself with a culture in this way can have particular social and political implications through the articulation of certain shared symbols and images that constitute 'sociocultural capital', which may then be drawn on in establishing identity and in negotiating relationships with others, both within and external to that community (Fisher & Sonn, 2002). Such capital refers to the material, social and psychological 'goods' that people may draw on in order to achieve particular interpersonal ends. This will be expanded on in subsequent sections of this chapter.

Identity has both public and private aspects and, at times, the public performance of identity may become particularly salient in the context of individual needs for identity, belonging and cultural affiliation. For example, T demonstrated a strong need to be publicly aligned with Samoan culture and values. T was born in New Zealand to Samoan parents and even though he has never been to Samoa, he has a strong need to be identified culturally as Samoan.

> **T (Samoan):** ... and I want to learn more because I'm starting to identify myself as a Samoan and I want to learn more about my [emphasised] culture. Where I'm from ... What I want to do ... as a Samoan ... like I don't want to be half-hearted, you know what I mean, like I want people to recognise me as Samoan, not as a Samoan that can't speak Samoan ... I want to be a proper Samoan so that people know I'm Samoan, plus the Samoan people will know me, not as a, like some people might call me a Fa'a Palangi, that means you want to be White ... and I don't want that sort of name.

T articulates the need to be publicly identified as Samoan, particularly with Samoans, as distinct from non-Samoans, who, in this case, are White people. To this end, he claims that he needs to perform as a 'proper Samoan', implying that there is a taken for granted standard within that culture, which embodies the epitome of Samoan values. This is rendered particularly powerful through T's choice in using the Samoan term 'Fa'a Palangi' to refer to someone who is White. This public recognition of 'Samoan-ness' provides T with an added sense of (cultural) identity, which, in the absence of such reinforcement, would be inherently fragile and nonconstitutive, given that he was born and raised in New Zealand and has lived in Australia for many years. This public aspect of identity and culture is likely to become particularly salient for those with 'obvious' ethnicity; in other words, in Australia, people who are non-White, and who may not have available to them other means of achieving identity within the dominant discourses of the community (Collins et al., 2000; Moreton-Robinson, 2000).

Lucky also speaks to this issue clearly in discussing the motivation for a tattoo on his arm. This tattoo says 'KVT' and reportedly symbolises an abbreviation of the word Fijian in the Fijian language.

> **Lucky (Fijian):** ... [pause] Because I'm half-blooded. Half European and half Fijian, you know what I mean, back home ... [pause] It's um ... it's pretty hard ... to be ... to try and be the same as everyone.

Interviewer: So you feel different?

Lucky: It is different, know what I mean? ... even in school or down the street ... [pause] because I've got two blood, you know what I mean, I'm not really pure Fijian, so everybody's ... they pick mostly pure Fijians on the footy team, so it's more like I, I have to ... what's the word? [clicking his fingers] ... I have to prove that, I'm there, you know what I mean ... I am [emphasised] Fijian ...

Just as T referred to a 'proper Samoan', Lucky identified the standard of a 'pure Fijian', and his account suggests that he does not have equal access to this standard when compared with other Fijians, who are of more 'pure' blood. This perceived sense of difference for Lucky is very powerful and appears to have shaped his identity for much of his life, such that he has had to 'try and be the same as everyone' else. Further to this, Lucky suggests that others in his cultural community are aware of his 'impurity' and this has impacted on his experience in many ways, such as not being chosen for a football team. As Lucky feels that he is not as 'pure' as 'real' Fijians, he has a strong need to prove his 'Fijian-ness' and to establish a valid cultural identity, not only to himself but to others and his tattoo goes some way to fulfilling this need. This is particularly powerful for him, given his statement that he is 'half-blooded' and, consequently, Lucky does not see himself as being inherently and legitimately Fijian but, rather, somehow different from other Fijians and less pure.

Lucky: This is ... a reminder ... always of what's in my background ... Not only for me but for people, you know what I mean ... like other, Fijian boys when they see it they know and they realise ...

Lucky uses his tattoo as a public claim to identity, such that others from his cultural community may see this tattoo and recognise his cultural affiliation as legitimate. As such, for Lucky, this tattoo has private and public meaning that enables him to obtain necessary social and cultural capital with which to establish identity, which without such capital is inherently fragile.

Migration Challenges Identity

Several of the offenders suggested that the experience of migration to Australia created specific challenges to identity, which were further exacerbated by virtue of being a member of a minority group in this community. Ngahau was born in Australia, but lived in Tonga for much of his life and he described the process of relocation to Australia as contributing to a loss of cultural connection and identity.

> Ngahau (Tongan): ... I've lived in the islands most of my life ... So I come here ... and you tend to forget who you are ... you know what I mean? Now all the things that were still good and you come to this country, even though I was born here, but yeah, you ain't got no money, you ain't got nothing, you know what I mean? ... And it tends to ... dig away at your roots ...

According to Ngahau, the dominant cultural values of this country are different to those of Tonga, which he experienced as contributing to an undermining of his Tongan values that are seen as being somehow more positive. This challenge to identity and cultural values is experienced negatively by Ngahau, causing him to 'forget' who he is (that is, his identity) to some degree. Such a dilution in identity is not uncommon within the complexities of modern western living (Lupton, 1999b) and has been suggested to contribute to a range of social ills, including crime (Staub, 2003; Wetherell & Potter, 1992).

Richarn was born in New Zealand, but identifies strongly with the Samoan culture. He came to Australia during his teenage years and described finding the adjustment to this country difficult.

> Interviewer: ... how did that make you feel ... ?
>
> Richarn (Samoan): Insecure. Um it's like ... I just gotta ... prove myself ... to other people. It's like ... look I'm at your same level so ... I didn't feel accepted by them . . .
>
> Interviewer: Was it more important to prove yourself and be accepted by White Aussies or was it more important for you to be ...
>
> Richarn: I didn't care about the White Aussies ... it was just other cultures.

The particular challenges associated with relocating to Australia meant that Richarn felt an increased pressure to demonstrate his (cultural) identity to others, such that he was seen as being legitimate and at the 'same level' as others. He described this as a need to 'prove' himself, interestingly, more to those from other minority groups, rather than the dominant Anglo–Australian majority. This may be reflective of the limited social capital that is available to those of minority status, as a result of which they must compete with each other for important social resources.

Cultural Reconnection in Jail

The preceding discussion has highlighted that cultural identity, according to ethnic status, is complex and variable and may be vulnerable to specific challenges associated with migration and membership of a minority group. An interesting finding is that for some offenders being incarcerated allowed them to reconnect with cultural identity in a way that was beneficial. This was predominantly for those from group-oriented or minority cultures who claimed to have had a positive experience of jail, as it allowed them to become more knowledgeable about and connected with their identified ethnic culture.

Sammy, Kadr and Iash, all Muslims, describe how their criminal behaviour occurred in the context of a loss of Islamic identity and connectedness. These offenders highlighted how the experience of jail allowed them to reconnect with their faith and to develop a more solid identity consistent with their religious and ethnic cultural values.

> **Sammy (Turkish):** I have discussed this with my Mum. I said, 'There's been good, there's been positives … and negatives to come out of this, what's happened'. You know what I mean? And mum said, 'What's the good that you've found?'. I said, 'The good that I've found is I've found my religion. I'm praying five times a day. I'm staying away from the drugs. It's a lot different to what I used to do'. And she goes 'It's true'. And the bad aspect of it is that I had to take someone's life and be in jail and steer away from everything that I should have been heading towards …

Through the experience of being incarcerated, Sammy has been able to reconnect with his faith, such that he is now engaging in a personal routine that prioritises the practices of his religion, including praying five times a day and maintaining abstinence of drugs. He claims that these values prescribe for him a more helpful and moral (noncriminal) way of living.

> **Ngahau (Tongan):** I lost my culture when I started living like this … I got to adapt to … this western world. You need money for this, you've got to have things, you got to work for things, you know what I mean? You ain't got no money, you got nothing … [pause] … like the last 18 months … I've been in jail … I just get it [cultural connection] back.

Ngahau was born in Australia, but identifies as Tongan and he accounts for his criminalisation as occurring with the context of conflicting values between his culture and that of the Australian community, suggesting that he engaged in crime because he was unable to meet his social and material needs through other means. A loss of cultural connection has been theoretically linked to criminal behaviour (Wetherell & Potter, 1992) and, therefore, in order for someone to 'find' themselves and establish a more stable and positive identity, presumably an antidote to crime, it is important to fully immerse oneself in culture and community. This has been referred to as the process of 'reculturalisation', which occurs when people from displaced groups in the community overemphasise their connection to cultural identity within a foreign setting (Hazelhurst, 1987), which for some may relate also to being members of minority groups within the community. The process of reculturalisation provides a strong sense of personal identity through connection with the wider cultural group (Ang et al., 2002; Negy, Shreve, Jensen, & Uddin, 2003) and appears to be experienced as a positive personal shift. However, whether this will produce any reduction in criminal behaviour for these men remains untested in the community, where there are other subcultural pressures that will contribute to crime.

In summary, discussion highlighted that, similarly to culture, identity is inherently dynamic, flexible (Lupton, 1999b; Rhee et al., 1995) and multiply constructed (Hall, 1996), and may be used in different ways depending on context (Collins et al., 2000; Poynting, Noble, & Tabar, 1999). This is in contrast to traditional and overly simplistic notions of identity that suggest identity is both singular and fixed, such that behaviour and relationships are shaped in defined ways with respect to identity.

Identity is dependent on ethnic culture, both in terms of the experience of culture and the internalised values of culture. Further to this, identity is responsible to situational demand, which may implicate culture through the effects of racism or as a function of the socialisation practices of the dominant majority (Moreton-Robinson, 2000). This may be particularly so for people whose ethnic identity is more vulnerable on the basis of their other social experiences and standing. For such people, ethnicity particularly might be a rich source of identity.

Ethnic identity is complex (Negy et al., 2003) and can relate to participation in community and connectedness to territory, over and above racial characteristics (Colombo & Senatore, 2005). This issue becomes more complex for those in migrant communities, who may have multiple allegiances to race, ethnic group and mother culture, and they will experience these multiple attachments differently depending on the social context (Ang et al, 2002, 2006; Poynting et al., 2004). These have been referred to as 'hybrid' cultural identities and may be used variously to meet particular sociopolitical ends (Poynting, Noble, & Tabar, 1998; 1999), especially in social situations in which other capital by which to achieve assumed standards of success is unavailable. This multiplicity has been associated with problems of identity, both socially and personally (Turner & Brown, 1978) and, in the present case, is suggested to also be related to the performance of interpersonal violence.

According to Staub (2003), experiences of perceived culture and community are essential in fulfilling the needs of identity. However, as the western world becomes more complex and society more urbanised, people are suggested to be losing touch with their extended social networks and experiencing a progressive loss in identity as traditional, cultural and social ties become more disconnected (Lupton, 1999b). If this is the case, we might expect the strain of this to be even more pronounced for those people who have been raised in collectivist cultures but who are living in individualist communities; such as the many migrants from group-oriented cultures, who are living in the multicultural societies of Australia and its modern democratic western counterparts.

Identity II — Crime and Identity

The migrant and disadvantaged sections of the community are often blamed for crime (Ferrell, 1999) and there are a number of theories that seek to explain why there may be an association between poverty and/or social disadvantage and criminal behaviour (e.g., strain theory — see Chapter 3). However, as reviewed earlier, the social constructionist position that includes reference to issues of culture and identity suggests that crime can occur in disadvantaged groups as a function of the relative lack of available means and opportunities for social success in relation to the dominant majority. This may be extended further by suggesting that engaging in criminal behaviour is one way in which people can 'do' identity (Mullins, 2006), particularly in situations where other means of achieving sociocultural 'capital' are not readily available. Specifically, criminal violence seems to occur when identity is challenged, such that a decisive response is required in order to reassert identity and this can occur both privately and publicly.

Challenges to Identity

Crime and violence can become a means by which people express their identity and make their voice heard in response to perceived challenges to identity (Mullins, 2006). Such challenges may come from a variety of sources that 'attack' people's sense of Self, cultural identity or physical safety. The presence of such threats to identity was salient in many of the offenders' stories of their criminal behaviour.

Eloqui, an Anglo–Australian man, was involved in the shooting of four people and he offered this account in relation to his offending.

> **Eloqui (Anglo):** I was in and out of depression for a long time and I was um, trying to find my own way … trying to find my place … and trying to find myself … I was placing all the significance on where I [emphasised] was at on the way other people were towards me. So I blamed them very invariably for the way I felt in myself. So I was envious, I was jealous … and ah … [long pause] drinking a lot … and working … in a job that probably wasn't suited for me. But I was … looking for … where I fitted into the scheme of things.

Eloqui identifies that his assumed identity was inherently vulnerable, such that he did not know where he 'fitted into the scheme of things' and this is a function of several significant experiences in his life. He describes a series of events that occurred in relation to the victims in the lead up to the offences and these are discussed in detail elsewhere, but were experienced by Eloqui as 'more like … an attack on me', thus complicating his effort to create some personal stability and 'find my place … find myself'.

Eloqui highlighted that he placed responsibility for his self-worth with others, which generally left him wanting. Specifically, with respect to the victims, Eloqui perceived that their interactions with him challenged his sense of identity (and masculinity), such that he felt both inadequate and unsure of himself, which he experienced as being destabilising both emotionally and socially. Eloqui's offending can be seen as being an attempt to regain control, of himself as much as the victims in the context of powerful challenges to identity (see Starzomski & Nussbaum, 2000 for a similar analysis in relation to cases of domestic homicide–suicide). He reasoned that shooting the victims would remove the source of the perceived threat to identity, which would then allow him to feel as if he had a greater sense of security in himself.

Eloqui also refers to the personal consequences of being the victim of sexual abuse by an older male when he was 14 years of age, and this had a profound impact on his emotional wellbeing, as well as contributing to his offending behaviour.

> **Eloqui:** It was like blowing myself away ... I was searching, I guess ... to do away with my own life. I remember thinking at the time when I was sitting in the car with a rifle in my mouth ... I was sitting there for some time ... and the thought that stopped me from doing that was 'No, I can't let Randall [his abuser] have the knowledge that I've done this' ... 'cause when I was driving along, I was like 'Fuck you, fuck you Randall, you've done this to me [emphasised]' ... 'You've created this monster that I am', blah, blah. But the monster that I was trying to keep in control, so I guess I disassociated myself from those actions by saying that that wasn't me [emphasised].

The experience of sexual abuse challenged Eloqui's identity and masculinity (Ben-David & Silfen, 1993; Stewart, 2001), the effect of which was further exacerbated by the fact that he did not disclose the abuse at the time and he was living in a rural town, where the lifestyle was insular. Eloqui blames his abuser and his victims for making him feel insecure and, therefore, for Eloqui, his criminal violence served the purpose of allowing him to reassert identity, such that he was able to feel more secure and negate the specific and deleterious effects on his identity of being the victim of sexual abuse and the recipient of perceived disrespect and social alienation.

Richarn was born in New Zealand to parents of Samoan heritage. He migrated to Australia as a teenager and, not long thereafter, was involved in the murder of a taxi driver who allegedly made racist comments about Pacific Islanders, suggesting that Islanders were 'too poor', 'stupid' and 'bad people'.

> **Richarn (Samoan):** Yeah I sort of remember look this is, you know the first time that someone's actually being racist ... the more I thought about it like I kept saying to myself ... this is my [emphasised] pride, this is my, my people ... you know, we didn't do anything wrong.

Richarn experienced the victim's comments in racist terms, whereby he perceived that his sense of identity as a Samoan was being challenged. His words highlight how Richarn's personal identity became somewhat conflated with that of his entire cultural group (Pacific Islanders), such that he responded to the alleged insults on behalf of his cultural group, who were seen as being innocent of any wrongdoing and thus undeserving of racist remarks. Such a challenge to identity was particularly significant for Richarn, given the inherent fragility of his ethnic cultural identity, which he described as follows.

> Richarn: ... being a Samoan and being a New Zealand-born Samoan ... it's sort of hard where your loyalties rely on ... as I grew up I didn't really ... think about Samoans ... I felt different to them ... It's like we just didn't ... my people and myself, we didn't just click on.

In the above quote, Richarn acknowledges how different he felt from other Samoans, who are seen as more legitimate given their birth in the Pacific Islands. Having been brought up in New Zealand, Richarn spent much of his life not thinking about Samoans and associating more with New Zealanders, even though he identified Samoans as his people. When Richarn migrated to Australia, he was able to develop a stronger connection with his ethnic cultural background, which to some extent was a function of the challenges to identity he experienced as a result of being a member of a minority group in this country (Fisher & Sonn, 2002). Perhaps in support of this newfound identity status and legitimacy, Richarn felt the need to respond with violence against the victim, as he was not prepared to 'let him get away with' making racist and derogatory comments about Pacific Islanders. In this sense, the challenge to identity and (ethnic) honour was perceived as intolerable by Richarn, requiring a decisive and violent response (Polk, 1994) on behalf of his entire cultural community.

Sammy also suggested that his offending was precipitated by a direct threat to identity. Sammy murdered another inmate in jail, who called him a 'dog', thus inferring he was an informant, which has very specific implications within the jail culture.

> Sammy (Turkish): Well they come up, they smashed my window, they called me a dog, and in jail, you get called a dog you can't walk away from that, you have to go and face them and usually it leads to a knife ... Well they called me a dog in front of the whole unit ... and the jail ... the way it's set up, you have to go out on the main walkway to go and get your buy-up. You can stay in your wing and hide out but you're not going to get your buy-up, you're not going to get your cigarettes and you may as well be in the bone yard on protection. Well, I weren't going to do that, you know what I mean?

Being called a dog in jail is a dire insult and makes one a target for retribution as one of the norms of the criminal subculture is that inmates don't cooperate with authorities and they also do not inform on other inmates. Further to this, there are certain consequences of being called a dog, which at a minimum limits one's ability to participate actively in jail culture, such as by receiving weekly 'buy-ups', which include food and cigarettes and, at worst, can result in death at the hands of other inmates. Sammy suggests that not being able to participate in the jail community is like being on protection, and these inmates are typically very limited in their routine and activities in jail. Moreover, protection inmates are not allowed to associate with other 'mainstream' inmates due to fears for their safety, thus implying that they are unable to protect themselves. Protection status often has very powerful effects on inmates' experience of jail that lasts many years, often across sentences. These issues contributed directly to Sammy's motivation for violence, which in many ways was a deliberate attempt to establish and maintain identity within the cultural community of jail (Sim, 1994). That is, in retaliation for being referred to as a dog, Sammy's violence had the effect of restoring his image in the jail as someone who was willing to participate in jail culture and who was aware of the social priorities in jail.

Maintenance of Identity

From an exploration of offenders' accounts of their criminal violence, it is suggested that one of the purposes of such violence is to maintain identity, either privately or publicly. That is, in response to specific threats to identity, offenders engage in violent behaviour designed to achieve the social aim of establishing credibility and status, both to themselves as well as to important Others.

Jim, an Anglo–Australian, is serving a custodial term for a series of sexual and physical assaults. Like other offenders, although this is his first time in jail, Jim has a long history of involvement in criminal behaviour, including acts of violence, and his identity is well established in terms of antisocial subcultural norms. Jim ostensibly denies the rapes by suggesting that the sex was consensual, and this is a common distancing technique used by many sex offenders to navigate responsibility and the challenges to identity associated with the perpetration of sexual abuse (Hudson, 2005). Jim is adamant that the sex was consenting because, even though he acknowledges being angry in the period leading up to the alleged rapes, he claims that he had 'ultimate … clarity' from this anger, which served to ostensibly sober him up, such that he regained control of himself, thereby preventing him from raping the victim as charged. However, it is noted that Jim uses the exact converse argument to this in relation to the physical violence, which he acknowledges and at times embraces.

> **Jim (Anglo):** The fighting brings the exhilaration ... not only am I 100% in control but ... [pause] ... everything is crystal clear ... Home court advantage. I lay the rules, do you know what I mean? And with the violence, it's you play by my rules or you get hurt ... As much as I didn't want the rules to be broken, I enjoyed that they were. Therefore, when it come time for the headmaster to come down with the cane and 'phw, phw, phw' [makes a sound as if the whipping of the cane], there was ... no hesitations ...
>
> **Interviewer:** ... this kind of in a way became almost being part of who you were, part of your identity?
>
> **Jim:** Yes severely ... Everybody knew me because of my capabilities ... I had friends because of my capabilities, you know? Women ... I'm not going to say they were attracted, but they were ...

Jim discusses his violence as bringing 'exhilaration', not only because of the physical adrenalin rush associated with violence, but because through the use of violence, Jim is able to exercise control and set the social agenda with others. Further to this, Jim suggests that this contributes to his perceived identity with others, in that people were attracted to him, both sexually and socially, because of his violent practices.

Jim uses his violence as a deliberate means of constructing identity, both personally and publicly. He identifies that, as a result of his specific capabilities, he has exposure to a certain 'power', which although he experiences as 'corruptive', enables him to establish identity by gaining social capital and becoming 'something' when 'you're nothing'. This suggests that without violence, Jim's sense of identity is fragile and lacking in the capital required to achieve social aims. Therefore, according to the values that Jim has internalised, acknowledging violence serves to confirm his status, both publicly and privately. However, admitting to rape would challenge particular aspects of his identity, relating to him being caring, nurturing and loving, which has both personally and socially unacceptable ramifications for Jim.

There is also a degree of impression management at work in Jim's accounting for his criminal violence, as for other offenders who were interviewed. Goffman (1959) suggested that whenever two people interact, certain social actions are engaged with a view to controlling impression and the sharing of information. As such, individuals are motivated to embellish positive impression, while at the same time minimising any potential negative impression. In particular, Goffman (1959) stated that the need to engage in impression management is particularly high when the parties are unknown to one another or when the potential consequences of action for one party are significant.

According to van Dijk (1987), efforts at impression management are more likely to occur in situations where 'delicate' topics are being discussed and where there is the potential for negative impressions to be formed of the speaker. In other words, people present a positive face in order to avoid any negativity from the person with whom they are interacting. This is particularly salient in discussions of criminal behaviour, where offenders will be acutely aware of the potential for judgment, criticism or disfavour (Hudson, 2005), especially with an interviewer who is female and unknown to them.

At times, the performance of identity through criminal violence may have specific public effects, particularly for those from cultures that prioritise a sense of collectivism. Lucky is a Fijian man who came to Australia as a teenager and he is currently serving a sentence for the murder for a taxi driver. In this quote, Lucky is discussing the motivations for his offending, which occurred in the presence of other Fijian youths, who were also members of his extended family.

> Lucky (Fijian): ... I was the oldest ... and the thing was ... it wasn't all about power ... it was all about losing face, know what I mean? ... In front of, of the boys ... I was never [emphasised] gonna go and let them, let him go down and ... let him put it over me ... I was never going to, you know what I mean ... I was never gonna let my knee buckle ...

Through his words, Lucky creates the powerful image of strength in the face of others, such that he felt as if he were unable to show any sign of weakness by failing to act in this situation. He refers to this as not wanting to 'lose face' and this can be a strong challenge for many men, associated with acts of violence (Polk, 1994; Sanko, 1994). Like Eloqui, Richarn and Sammy, Lucky perceived the actions of the victim as creating a particular challenge to identity, which, specifically, related to his status as a Fijian, an older male family member and as a man. It is clear that Lucky is identifying personally salient aspects of identity

here; however, he is defining these aspects of identity largely in relation to important Others to which he is connected, including both
family and Fijians. Although he doesn't articulate this clearly in his
account, Lucky is aware that there will be social ramifications of any
choice he might make in response to this perceived challenge to identity and this has strong cultural, emotional and social connections for
him, which were especially salient in the presence of his co-offenders,
who were also Fijian, thus privileging certain discourses about culture,
identity and masculinity.

Markus & Kitayama (1991) suggested that the means by which one
seeks to maintain or assert identity will be dependent on the culturally
mediated model of Self one is operating on. As such, for those with interdependent selves (towards the collectivist end of the cultural continuum),
they are more likely to seek public means of performing identity, when
compared with those from more individualist cultures. This is due to the
particular salience Others have in discourses of collectivism.

The above analysis of offenders' accounts for their crimes suggests
that the performance of criminal violence can achieve the establishment and/or maintenance of identity within the social environment
and this might fulfil both private and public needs.

Tedeschi and Bond (2001) proposed the social interactionist
theory of coercive actions, which argues that there are three main
motivations for engaging in coercive behaviours and these relate to
social control, justice and identity. According to these authors, individuals may be motivated to engage in coercive or aggressive behaviours in order to either establish identity or to maintain identity in the
face of a perceived threat to the Self, which if unanswered may result
in personal or social instability and vulnerability. This is particularly
the case in 'street culture', where respect is an interpersonal currency
associated with status and protection (Mullins, 2006).

In other words, engaging in violent crime facilitates social capital,
which refers to the particular material, social and personal attributes
that allow for the achievement of specific sociocultural actions, including the establishment of identity. This might be particularly salient for
those from socially disadvantaged backgrounds, who generally lack the
material and social resources deemed necessary to establish identity in
other more prosocial ways (Collins et al., 2000; Presdee, 2000).
Individuals from minority cultures are likely to experience particular

challenges to identity that promote criminal violence and, to some extent, this is a function of the degree to which their (ethnic) cultural identity is experienced as vulnerable. For these people, drawing on ethnic culture or identity may be an added avenue for social capital in the establishment of identity and status necessary for social interaction in community.

Identity III — Group Identity and Crime
Presence of the Group

All of the offenders from group-oriented cultures involved co-offenders in their criminal behaviour, whereas only one of the offenders from an individualist culture committed a crime in the presence of co-offenders. This discrepancy makes sense in the dynamics of identity within cultural values and is worth exploring.

Criminal behaviour can occur within stylised subcultures that have their foundations in socially disadvantaged and often immigrant sections of the community (Ferrell, 1998a; Presdee, 2000) and this relates to the social capital available to such groups within the community. In addition to many of the other challenges such people face, the pressure of cultural and community dislocation cannot be ignored. As discussed above, several offenders identified that coming to Australia and participating in a multicultural society as a member of a minority group caused them to feel disconnected from their cultural heritage and as if they had to conform to 'western' ways of being, and this was experienced as a challenge, often specifically relating to identity. For some, therefore, bonding with a group of others who share the same cultural heritage can be about reconnecting with and showing solidarity to the group, as well as establishing a bond that allows one to realise the tasks of being a member of a culture, which is intimately associated with the performance of identity (Brewer & Gardner, 1996; Ferrell, 1995; 1999).

Richarn discusses how the presence of his co-offenders, also of Samoan heritage, allowed him to feel accepted and as if he were part of their friendship network, which ultimately contributed to his decision to offend.

> **Richarn (Samoan):** And it's also like a sense of belonging, I wanted to belong … [sigh] to a group … I just wanted to be accepted.

Richarn's ethnic identity was particularly fragile given that he has Samoan parents, was born and raised in New Zealand, and then relocated to Australia as a teenager several years before the offence. In response to the specific challenges to cultural identity he faced in coming to Australia and being a member of a minority group, Richarn also began the process of connecting with his Samoan cultural heritage in the period leading up to his offending. As such, he perceived a strong need to belong and feel accepted, particularly by others from his own cultural group, who would have allowed him to establish greater credibility both socially and culturally, thus reinforcing his ethnic identity. This desire to belong contributed to escalating the violence against his victim, seemingly in an attempt to be accepted by his co-offenders and show his cultural allegiance.

Genuine, a young Vietnamese–Australian man, was an active member of a gang that involved other Asian youth from his local area.

> Interviewer: What did you find that you gained from being part of that kind of group or gang culture? How was that helpful to you?
>
> Genuine (Vietnamese): … [long pause] … well it's not helping, as you can see, I'm here [in jail]. But in the past … I think it helped me … have an identity, you know what I mean? It help me feel belong to something …

Although he is willing to acknowledge that participating in a gang has been unhelpful, specifically in relation to encouraging his involvement in criminal behaviour, Genuine identifies that being a part of such a group enabled him to feel as if he belonged to something that gave him a sense of worth and 'identity' that was reinforcing enough to continue his involvement in gang activity.

The majority of co-offenders chosen by offenders were of the same or similar ethnic background. This appears to be related to issues of trust and solidarity, which offenders suggest is a taken for granted with others who share the same cultural heritage and, thereby, who also presumably share similar understandings and worldviews and perform identity in similar ways.

Iash committed the crimes for which he was sentenced with other Lebanese men and, although initially he denies that this was important, he then goes on to discuss the particular reasons why having co-offenders from the same ethnic community was, in fact, very important to him.

Interviewer: Was that important to you to have Lebanese guys in there with you?

Iash (Lebanese): Oh not really, not really. To the way I look at it is they're the people I trust the most because they're people that know me and know what I'm about ... and know what kind of person I am ... and so I wouldn't expect them to step up and say, oh in a court of law, 'Yeah that Iash did that' — you know what I mean? So I thought I was safe with them ...

Interviewer: Like safer than you would be with an Aussie bloke, for example?

Iash: Yeah, because you can't trust him, you know? Like maybe if I, if I knew him for the amount of time as I knew these people, yeah I would probably trust him, you know? But I didn't know ... any Australian people out there. I didn't associate with any ... I just stick with my own kind, my own people. People that I can trust and that I grew up with ...

Iash refers to other Lebanese people as his 'own kind'. Being of the same 'kind' generally invokes a shared history, as well as a shared understanding, that allows him to feel a greater trust in Lebanese people. This is particularly important within the criminal subculture, as trust relates to safety, such that there is a sense of security that one's co-offenders or associates will not 'give you up' to police.

Sammy, a Turkish–Australian man, jailed for a series of offences, including murder, expressed a similar sentiment to Iash.

Sammy (Turkish): Like, I had a lot of Lebanese mates there, back then, and over the years, they've come back to jail and that and they said, 'Mate, we were there, why didn't you call us, why didn't you tell us to come and let us know what was going on? We would have backed you up', and I said, 'Mate I didn't want to get youse involved', and that wasn't the truth. I didn't trust them, you know, because to me [emphasised] they were all outsiders ... and the only ones that were on the inside with me were my countrymen and that's the way I looked at it.

Sammy describes his 'countrymen' as 'insiders', suggesting that such people are privileged with a level of trust that 'outsiders' are not. Within conventional social practice, outsiders are imbued with negative characteristics, are likely to have their feelings disregarded and to be the victim of harsh practices (e.g., Collins et al., 2000). In comparison, those who are deemed 'inside' and thereby similar to the Self, are seen as being inherently positive and desirable and worthy of protection (Reynolds & Turner, 2001) and this is consistent with the accounts of both Iash and Sammy.

Norm was the only one of the Anglo–Australian offenders to have offended in the presence of other people, who were also friends and criminal associates of his. Norm identified the presence of these people as being important in his decision to offend, which he couched in discourses of loyalty and mateship.

> **Norm (Anglo):** It's just that ... you don't want to let your friends down, they're all going and they're saying 'Come on' ... and um, when you believe that ah, well in yourself — you, you think it's justified that it does [emphasised] happen, well, it made it easier for me to go.

To some degree, Norm acknowledges the social expectation that was operating on him, in that he did not want to disappoint his friends. However, unlike those offenders with collectivist cultural experience, Norm was quick to account for his behaviour as being primarily motivated by a desire to defend his personal principles, which he claimed 'justified' the offending. In this way, even though the presence of the group is important in facilitating Norm's offending, he accounts for his violence as being about the act of demonstrating the inappropriateness of the victim's behaviour. Norm minimises the group nature of the offence, although both group and individual motives are at work in his offending.

Over and above issues of cultural and ethnic identity in group, it has been reliably shown that group decision-making processes can be notoriously poor and swing collective action towards the extreme, including deviance and criminal behaviour (Forsyth, 1999; Street, 1997). T, a New Zealand-born Samoan, was involved in the violent sexual assault of a woman during a break and enter, with four co-offenders present. He claims that one of his co-offenders initiated the sexual assault and suggested that his own behaviour was a function of group influence.

> **Interviewer:** Do you think you would have sexually assaulted the victim if you were on your own?
>
> **T (Samoan):** No ... I guess just the influence that was there ... Just like I said when it just happened ... it was all of us, you know what I mean? It was ... it was all of us, so I just ... so I jumped in ...

Referring to himself as having simply 'jumped in' implies a degree of passivity and thereby also minimises criminal intent. Therefore, the presence of others allowed T to engage in necessarily violent and abusive behaviour, which he believes he would have otherwise not been capable of (Blanchard, 1959; Winlow, 2001). This is highlighted by his repeated reference to 'it was all of us'.

It appears that there is a link between criminal behaviour and the presence of group, particularly for those from cultures that prioritise collectivism, such that they define their identity and experience directly through connections with others. It is not the cultural values per se that are suggested to contribute to crime but rather the particular position that culture engenders that allows people to experience events in certain ways.

The importance of group highlighted above has obvious connections with criminal gangs (Aumair & Warren, 1994; Staub, 2003), which may be even more salient for young men negotiating the complexities of hegemonic and dominant masculinity from a position of disadvantage (Messerschmidt, 1993). Often for members of marginalised communities, relationships with others from similar positions are prioritised and can be experienced as resistance to the dominant practices of racism operating within the community (Poynting, Noble, & Tabar, 1998). As such, criminal behaviour may be shaped by the presence of important Others and by social practices that construct relationships between people in particular ways and this is often related to the performance of culture.

Promotion of Group Identity

It was argued earlier that criminal violence can be a means of establishing or maintaining personal identity in response to perceived threats to the same. For those offenders from collectivist cultures, it appears that criminal violence served a similar purpose with respect to the promotion of group identity. For example, the following quote pertains to Iash's accounting for offences relating to violence in retaliation for being refused payment by a man who owed him for (antisocial) services rendered.

> Iash (Lebanese): Like, I've had a reputation growing up, when me and my family — where, you know, nobody mucks around with us, nobody rorts us, nobody talks shit about us, you know, and if people ever tried to, they know what will happen to them … and the way I was doing things, I had [emphasised] to do something to this person when I eventually caught up with him. So then the word gets out that, you know, don't do that to him, did you see what he done to him? …

> And people start to think twice if they ever tried to rob me or rob my family or, you know, tried to rort me or my family members ...
>
> **Interviewer:** So whose reputation were you thinking of? Was it just your own or your own and your family?
>
> **Iash:** Oh it was mine, my cousin's, was my uncle's ... was my brother's, you know? ... because I come from a real large background Lebanese family ... with uncles and cousins and all that. A lot of them are in jail as well, so I was also thinking about them too. Because ... for them to hear that 'Oh yeah, [Iash's last name suppressed] got ripped' ... and it rubs off in a bad way on them too ... So I wasn't just thinking about me, I was thinking about them as well at the time ...

Iash begins by referring to his 'reputation', which is clearly important to him and Self-focused. However, Iash accounts for his reputation in collectivist language, claiming that 'Nobody mucks around with us, nobody rorts us, nobody talks shit about us'. This suggests that, for Iash, identity is more conflated than simply referring to the Self or the Other.

With respect to his criminal behaviour, Iash focuses more on the reputation of his significant group, including his immediate and extended family, to which he felt a sense of obligation, particularly due to the belief that these people would be publicly tainted by any demonstrated weakness on his behalf. Hence, Iash suggests that he felt almost compelled to engage in criminal violence as a means of maintaining that identity, such that his reputation as well as that of his family remained intact.

The cultural connections in Iash's account of his criminal behaviour are obvious within collectivist cultural values that privilege certain discourses about appropriate behaviour, responsibility and community. However, he utilises these values and relationships in the service of an individualist identity, which also contributes to his offending. Further to this, it is noted that Iash's wider social group, as well as his extended family, are actively engaged in an antisocial subculture and this also contributed to his decision to offend and to his beliefs in this regard. Therefore, while Iash prizes values consistent with collectivist ideals, he utilises these within an individualist framework, somewhat confusing notions of ethnicity, culture and criminality.

Genuine, too, suggests that his offending was motivated by the desire to maintain reputation and identity among his group, although in a different way to Iash. Genuine is a Vietnamese-born man who was involved in a series of violent assaults, which were perpetrated in retribution for an attack on a friend and fellow gang member. For Genuine then, the relevant group is his gang, the presence of which provides him with identity and the means by which to achieve this socially.

> **Genuine (Vietnamese):** And the other guys who fight just to see a bit of action ... Go to another school, meet up and all just go another school ... put a student on the spot and get their uniform so I can mingle in, you know, mix in with the school in other ways and ... we would trash their school sort of thing ... going to parties at a young age with the old boys ... it does ... um feel a lot of respect, you know? ... people were always talking about he knows all these people and all that people ... they always talk about people ... and money and ... I, or maybe because I was with the older boys, you know, so I didn't go to school, I might have picked up a ... bit too fast but ah ... we used to go somewhere where they have a good time, you know, and there's one would go and you know look for the girls, and one would go look for, you know what I mean, just looking for to fight [laughs], you know that was like me, I always like looking to fight and I would just sit there at a party, give me an excuse to hit you, you know, give me an excuse, look at me once, look at me twice, you know what I mean ... and at the end of the night there will [emphasised] be fights, that's what we've came looking for ...

Genuine suggests that gang participation and the performance of violence allowed him to achieve a level of respect and reputation that was not available to him through other means, not only as a result of his minority group membership, but also because he wasn't achieving in more conventional avenues of success, such as through academic attainment 'I wasn't going good at school'. As such, he developed ways of being in the context of this group, which prioritised violence, as a means of public identity. This identity also reflected on the group and the group's status within the (subcultural) community.

Pride

Maintaining a positive self-image is important and this is achieved differently for people with varying cultural experience, along the dimension from individualism to collectivism. Markus and Kitayama (1991) suggested that for people with an independent self-construal, that is, who are members of individualist cultures, positive self-esteem is associated with fulfilling the tasks generally associated with independence, including being autonomous, unique, assertive and able to care for oneself adequately. However, for those with interdependent self-construals — that is, from cultures valuing collectivism — positive self-image is achieved by fulfilling tasks associated with protecting and nurturing important connections with salient Others. These might include maintaining harmony, engaging in socially appropriate behaviours, or fitting in comfortably with the group. One of the ways in which this may also be achieved is by promoting the values or goals of the larger collective or group, that is, by maintaining pride. In this context, pride refers to the sense of worth that comes from performing in ways that are consistent with the internalised group, which, for some, also relates to the value that comes from prioritising ethnic culture (Hazelhurst, 1987). As such, it is larger than individual pride, to the extent that the individual becomes somewhat lost and the group is prioritised in constructing identity. This may be particularly important for those offenders whose assumed ethnic or cultural identity was more fragile, given their other life experiences, such as being raised outside of their identified mother culture or perceiving an illegitimacy to cultural claim (Wetherell & Potter, 1992).

> **Richarn (Samoan):** … I guess it's more of my learning of my culture … that gave me a sense of pride. Where someone was making … negative comments about it. Then … I sort of just lost it a bit.

Richarn suggests that his involvement in the murder of a taxi driver was directly related to his sense of cultural pride, which was challenged by the victim's alleged 'negative comments' about Richarn's culture. He perceived that this attacked his 'sense of pride', which Richarn gained through learning about and connecting with his Samoan heritage.

> **Richarn:** Yeah, I sort of remember — look, this is, you know, the first time that someone's actually being racist … but the more I thought about it, like I kept saying to myself … this is my [emphasised] pride, this is my, my people … by the time we got out [of the taxi], the only thing that was in my mind, this is for my people … It's something that I don't [emphasised] wanna do, but it's something that … I'm not gonna let him get away with.

Richarn thus accounts for his criminal behaviour as being an almost social obligation, given that he claims he did not want to offend, but was not prepared to let the victim 'get away with' making allegedly racist slurs against Pacific Islanders. Richarn's extreme reaction to the perceived cultural insults of the victim was likely a function of the inherent fragility of his cultural identity. In particular, he perceived the behaviour of the victim as being an affront to not only his sense of cultural pride, but that of his entire cultural community, which took precedence over any individual need. He therefore felt as if he needed to retaliate against the victim as a means of reasserting that pride and cementing the status of his people culturally. The emphasis on the word 'my' for Richarn highlights the importance that this had for him.

Lucky's sense of cultural pride was also strong and contributed to his offending behaviour. Lucky was born in Fiji and relocated to Australia as a teenager. Several years after coming to this country, he was charged with the murder of a taxi driver, which he committed with several co-offenders who were either members of his extended family or other Fijian youth.

> **Lucky (Fijian):** ... I know this sounds bad but I mean I'll be straight up with you — you may not know, things that happen back home in Fiji... not only once, twice, a couple of times, Indians just try to take over Fiji, know what I mean? ... 'cause I knew he was Indian ... and I knew I was Fiji, no way, they didn't take my land and no way he wouldn't take my pride ...

Lucky identifies the victim as having been Indian early in the interview and even though Lucky suggests that the culture of the victim was not important, it is clear from his account of the offence that cultural pride was actually highly significant for him. Lucky acknowledges an awareness of the history of conflict between Fijians and Indians, which he perceives culminated in Indians attempting to take control of Fiji on several occasions. As such, in perpetrating violence against the victim, Lucky saw himself as ostensibly standing up for all Fijians, such that another Indian would not be able to take advantage of another Fijian. He suggests that his offending behaviour allowed him to maintain pride, which is intimately connected with his ethnic identity and cultural status. Like Richarn, Lucky's sense of ethnic pride is fragile, although for him this is a function of his being 'half-blooded', which he believes renders him less legitimate than a 'pure Fijian'. In offending, it can be argued that Lucky's sense of individual pride was conflated with that of his entire cultural community, which is highlighted by his powerful statement 'I was Fiji'. As such, for Lucky, the individual is rendered irrelevant, with the focus being on the group, consistent with values of collectivism.

Genuine, a Vietnamese–Australian man, identifies the pride of his 'gang' as being the driving force behind much of his criminal behaviour. In the following quote, Genuine is accounting for the 'principle' behind his offending behaviour, which involved engaging in violence against members of a rival gang for the alleged assault of a friend and fellow gang member.

> **Genuine (Vietnamese):** ... Sort of pride ... It's pride because ... words get around, you know what I mean? And ah ... you don't want to ... put a bad impression on ... [pause]
>
> **Interviewer:** On your group?
>
> **Genuine:** Yeah because ... 'cause ... if something happened to someone, you know, you don't often hear the good thing that happened to them ... you only hear the bad thing. If someone got shot, if someone got stabbed, you will hear who and why, and you know, they'll have their ... ideas of who did it, you know what I mean? More action than ... words gets around, that's all.

Genuine suggests that his criminal behaviour is motivated by the desire to maintain the pride of his group, both privately and publicly, with respect to their interactions with others, including members of other gangs. The reputation of the gang is very important within anti-social cultures and Genuine speaks to this as if the group must maintain a sense of pride in itself and in its values in order to maintain status within the subcultural community.

Ngahau, who was born in Australia, but identifies as Tongan, also invokes notions of pride.

> **Ngahau (Tongan):** ... Back then it was ah ... I guess keep my reputation ... I've got too much pride ... You know what I mean ... out there ... in my area, everybody knows me. I used to love to see people fear me ... that was the power I had ... to see people's fears in their eyes. People ... would see me (emphasised) and they would run. People wouldn't walk down the same side of the street with me, they would just cross the road, even getting hit by a car, they wouldn't care, because they saw me. You know what I mean, to me that's ... that would feel good ... that's my reputation.

Unlike other offenders with experience of collectivist cultures, pride for Ngahau is very much self-focused. He defines his sense of pride in relation to how others see him and, specifically, with respect to the extent that he is feared by others, consistent with his performed criminal identity (Winlow, 2001). This pride has subcultural capital for

Ngahau in allowing him to both establish and maintain identity within his community. This does not implicate ethnic culture specifically, unlike the accounts of other offenders and, again, highlights the complexities in identity, particularly for those offenders with competing ethnic and cultural allegiances.

Notions of pride were present in the accounts of some offenders with collectivist cultural experience, as discussed earlier. However, pride was absent in the accounts of offenders from individualist cultures. These offenders highlighted status, reputation and feelings of satisfaction tied to individual accomplishments, which also related to the control exercised over Others, at times, although this did not have the same flavour as pride for offenders from cultures that are considered more collectivist. Specifically, pride, as discussed here, uses discourses of cultural allegiance and ethnic identity, whereas for offenders from individualist cultures, that is, Anglo–Australians, positive feelings were more related to individual accomplishments and personal power.

In sum, for those offenders from cultures that prioritise collectivism, crime appears to have served specific purposes in identity that are consistent with cultural values. It is not culture per se that is considered to have caused crime for these men but, rather, cultural values provide the frame of reference from which to interpret experience and this prioritises certain ways of being that for some offenders may be understood to contribute to criminal violence. Specifically, offenders from more collectivist cultures offended in the presence of others, often from their own ethnic group, which facilitated a particular form of identity associated with belonging and connectedness (Markus & Kitayama, 1991; Triandis et al., 1988). Further, these offenders also engaged in criminal violence as a means of promoting group identity or facilitating cultural pride. For some, this was particularly salient in the context of otherwise inherently fragile cultural and ethnic identity, such that performing violence affirmed the identity and self-worth of the offender as a valuable member of the collective. This vulnerability in cultural identity appears to be important in understanding the accounts of offenders from nondominant cultural groups, in that such fragility in identity may have certain effects over and above culture in defining experience and contributing to choices in violence.

Identity IV — Criminal Identity
Criminal Subculture

A criminal subculture is a complex weave of relationships, experiences, meanings and symbols framed within antisocial values that create a collective way of life for those who participate in it (Ferrell, 1999). This subculture tends to develop in the economically and socially disadvantaged sections of a community as a means of attaining social capital and is defined in relation to antisocial behaviours, which are often perpetrated in retaliation to the social forces that shape the inequalities in the first place (Ferrell, 1998b; Presdee, 2000). As such, crime becomes a social exercise, with often political effects. The behaviour of members of criminal subcultures tends to be defined as deviant simply by virtue of being associated with the culture of the group, and Adler and Alder (1994) suggested that members of such subcultures often take on the identity of deviance or criminality as a symbol of membership to the group. In this way, criminal identity can become powerfully associated with the development and maintenance of a functional social and personal identity according to salient subcultural norms (Mullins, 2006). The performance of this identity then becomes a mechanism for achieving social capital in interaction. Therefore, criminal identity, like other aspects of identity, is a function of cultural experience and is constructed in relation to social expectation and values that contribute to certain ways of being.

Criminal Violence Maintains Criminal Identity

It has been suggested that engaging in criminal violence can serve to establish or maintain identity, including that related to cultural identity. Criminal violence can also become a means of performing and reinforcing criminal identity, which is highly prized within actively antisocial sections of the community (Winlow, 2001). Further to this, the active construction of identity through identifying with criminal values may be particularly salient for minority groups, who do not have other means of 'doing' identity readily available (Taylor Gibbs & Merighi, 1994). This is likely to be exaggerated for men in prisons, which are environments inherently constructed in relation to criminality, where identity is reliably challenged and negotiated between inmates and officers (Sim, 1994).

Sammy refers to a 'proper crim' at interview and this proper crim informs the standard taken for granted according to which people who participate in this subculture are judged, invoking particular characteristics and values that such a person should have and uphold. Iash describes well this essential set of criminal ethics in accounting for how important Others in his life see him.

> **Iash (Lebanese):** They know I'm fair but ruthless, they know … I don't lie. I don't talk shit to anybody. I do what I have to do, when I have to do it, you know? I don't go out of my way to start trouble and they're the people that do the exactly the same thing as me … and I think that being raised up to, not to give up people, not to snitch on people, not to dog (inform on) people …

Despite being in jail for the first time, Jim has a long history of involvement in antisocial and violent practices, in relation to which he has positioned himself as criminal.

> **Jim (Anglo):** … like with what I'm in [jail] for now, it's not just something that's 'boom [emphasised — sound like an explosion] oh fuck, what happened?'. This is something that I was bred [emphasised] for … if you can understand what I mean? I had the whole world against me, you know? Me Dad was a cop, he's supposed to be trusted … I was getting my head kicked in by cops, they're supposed to be trusted. So I turned into what they didn't want me to turn into.

In suggesting that he was 'bred' for violence and crime, Jim understands that his identity was shaped for him by those important people in his early life. He describes this development as occurring in the context of being the victim of physical violence by trusted Others, such that he developed this identity in reaction to these people and their assumed values. In claiming that he was 'made' into a criminal, Jim minimises responsibility for his criminal behaviour and antisocial lifestyle through the removal of any assumed agency.

The criminal identity, as with any other cultural archetype, has a well-defined set of values and characteristics that are assumed to contribute to performing this identity and this is the yardstick of the proper crim referred to above. Many of the qualities of this essentialised criminality are also consistent with dominant discourses of masculinity and this will be discussed in more detail subsequently.

Adhering to this identity, including the public performance of criminality, affords one certain (emotional and social) privileges; that is, it allows for the accumulation of social capital. Adhering to these cultural values may also enable offenders to focus on material pursuits and, in this way, performing the criminal identity becomes a lifestyle choice that is actively reinforced and reconstructed through criminal behaviour. Norm describes this as being a 'daily thing', much like others in the community would 'go to work'.

Criminal Identity is Restrictive

Despite the apparent gains of criminal identity, this identity may also be experienced as a constraint, stipulating various ways of being that cause one to feel 'contaminated' (Genuine) as a result of cultural expectation. In other words, there is an inherent power associated with this identity that influences ways of being that can be experienced as prescriptive and limiting.

> **Sammy (Turkish):** A lot of blokes that are pinched inside, they don't follow their ... culture's ways from, you know what I mean, whether they're Turkish or Lebanese or whatever they are ... it's the culture of the jail, they have to follow the rules of jail, is what you have to abide by ... and the rules of the Corrective Services Officers is totally different from our [inmates] rules and our conduct, you know what I mean? We've been brought up to not snitch and tell on people and ... not be buddy buddies with the screws [officers] and ... not call each other a dog because it's going to raise major conflicts ...

In this quote, Sammy, who has spent a great deal of time in jail being exposed to this subculture, describes the influence of criminal identity in shaping behaviour within the jail context. He describes some of the qualities of the criminal subculture that are important and jail is a place where this is obviously emphasised (Sim, 1994). This relationship is reciprocal in that criminal behaviour may also be motivated, at times, by the desire to perform or maintain certain identities, including that of a proper crim, which has particular subcultural effects.

> **Iash (Lebanese):** I wasn't proud of what I was doing but I had to do it to survive. That's the way I looked at it ... and the way I was doing things, I had [emphasised] to do something to this person when I eventually caught up with him. So then the word gets out that, you know, don't do that to him, did you see what he done to him? ... And people start to think twice if they ever tried to rob me or rob my family or, you know, tried to rort me or my family members and that.

This quote highlights a number of motivations relevant to an under-standing of Iash's criminal behaviour. In general, he suggests that he needed to engage in antisocial enterprise in order to make money and 'survive' within a community that he believed was not supportive of either himself, his family or his cultural community. However, in rela-tion to this particular charge, Iash suggests that his criminal violence was motivated by the desire to maintain his antisocial reputation and, thereby, secure the future of his antisocial business. In this case, Iash kidnapped and physically assaulted a man who had refused to pay him money that he was owed. After he and his co-offenders assaulted the man they let him go, although Iash stole the man's car, which he sub-sequently drove around in with the hope that other members of the criminal community would witness this and know that Iash had retal-iated against the victim for seeking to take advantage of him. In behaving this way, Iash is demonstrating the need for his identity as a capable and dominant criminal to be reliably established within his (antisocial) subculture, such that it is publicly witnessed by Others. In this way, Iash highlights the process whereby offenders might feel compelled to act in ways that are consistent with the norms of this criminal 'culture', including engaging in violence. Such behaviour reinforces criminal identity, both publicly in the eyes of relevant Others, but also privately, with respect to the internalised values according to one's lived experience of the social world.

Identity V — Masculine Identity
The Dominant Discourse on Masculinity
A relationship between the performance of stereotypical masculinity and criminal behaviour has been well established in the literature (Goodey, 1997; Messerschmidt, 1993; Mullins, 2006). The concept of masculinity is a sociocultural one (Smith, 1992), which seeks to extend the boundaries of sex typically attributed by gender. It is shaped by history and experience, and implicates particular discourses not only about masculinity, but also about femininity, to which masculinity is inherently related (Connell, 1987). Masculinity has been shown to be fluid, multiply defined and situationally relevant, according to the demands of interpersonal interaction (Goodey, 1997; Winlow, 2001) and is thereby performative in nature and cultural in both its con-struction and expression. As such, although masculinity is experienced

by many men as a 'right' by birth (Smith, 1992), it is, in fact, 'accomplished' by men in their interactions both with other men and with women (Connell, 1987; 1995), in reference to existing social structures and discourses, and may be different across situations even for the same person.

Messerschmidt (1993) refers to masculinity as a form of 'structured action' by which men perform certain ways of being, which are prescribed for them by the subcultures within which they participate. For example, there will be different opportunities for men to be men for those who are educated and in positions of prestige compared with those who are exposed to relative social disadvantage and in poverty.

Recognising the complexities in the concept of masculinity, Connell (1995) has offered the following definition, which allows for the flexible nature of masculinity, in addition to its social construction and relationship to other social variables, such as class and culture: masculinity is 'simultaneously a place in gender relations, the practices through which men and women engage that place in gender, and the effects of those practices in bodily experience, personality and culture' (p. 71).

Western individualistic cultures have a particular discourse on hegemonic masculinity that dictates the means by which dominant masculinity is performed and achieved. This stipulates that men should be independent of others, autonomous, in control, competitive and dominant, successful and financially stable (Messerschmidt, 1993; O'Sullivan, 1993), which, it is noted, tend to also be the primary qualities of individualism. This masculinity also encourages men to be unemotional, as emotions are inconsistent with discourses of rationality, which has long been seen as traditionally masculine (Smith, 1992). Ostensibly, men are socialised to be emotionally incompetent (Goodey, 1997; Jakupcak, Tull, & Roemer, 2005) and strategic in their relationships with others (Jenkins, 1990), particularly women, who are seen as the vehicle by which a man can prove his sexual prowess (O'Sullivan, 1993), which is also important in achieving dominant ideals of masculinity.

The stereotypical man who performs this masculinity is also expected to provide for his family, often at the expense of his own personal wellbeing (Starzomski & Nussbaum, 2000). This is understood in reference to material and financial wealth, traditionally as a consequence of employment (Winlow, 2001). These are aspects of masculinity that are not readily available to certain sections of the community, thereby theoretically compromising their ability to achieve masculinity.

Hegemonic masculinity draws on notions of the warrior (Smith, 1992) who is embodied in the hero archetype; for example, the image of the 'Marlboro Man'. According to Connell (1987), such archetypes represent fantasy figures that embody dominant masculine values and they are powerful for both men and for women. Despite their basis in fantasy, the dominant socialisation practices in this country provide men with this standard, according to which they should compare themselves, creating expectations that inevitably leave men wanting.

Subscribing to hegemonic notions of masculinity has not only been linked to crime in general, but also to aggression (Kinney, Smith, & Donzella, 2001; Moore & Stuart, 2004), violence (Copenhaver, Lash, & Eisler, 2000; Messerschmidt, 1993), domestic violence (Hanser, 2001), and sexual assault (Doherty & Anderson, 2004; Jenkins, 2000). Ostensibly, violence is naturalised within dominant discourses of masculinity and can become a specific asset designed to achieve status associated with hegemonic masculinity, particularly for those men who do not have access to conventional means of masculine 'success' based on their sociocultural position.

Masculine Capital

The dominant practices of masculinity prioritise occupational success, financial stability, social power and independence. For most men, this is achieved through their professional experience, in addition to associated financial wealth and standing within the community. That is, these factors give men masculine 'capital' to use in the accrual and performance of masculinity, both publicly and privately. However, for certain sections of the community, such as the working class, ill-educated or marginalised (e.g., by ethnicity or sexuality), these achievements may be outside of their reach due to the particular socialisation experiences to which they are subject and the social constructions that prevent their participation. Winlow (2001) refers to the psychological impact of such experiences as being equivalent to a 'removal of identity' (p. 37), which, based on earlier discussions, can be particularly threatening and confronting, and contribute to criminal violence.

For those men who fall outside the realm of dominant masculinity, there is still a strong need to contribute to sustaining hegemonic masculine practices that privilege certain ways of being to which men perceive they are entitled (Connell, 1987). Other means of attaining masculine capital must therefore be used and this tends to include the utilisation of violent practices, which have particular power in demonstrating masculinity in the presence of other men and in response to challenges to masculine honour and reputation (Polk, 1994; Sanko, 1994). For some, this may also involve the development of an anti-authority attitude, which can facilitate criminal identity (Winlow, 2001).

The Relationship Between Violence and Masculinity: An Exploration of Offenders' Stories

Achieving Status and Reputation

Masculinity is something that needs not only be established in terms of personal identity, but masculinity also needs to be publicly accomplished so that one may be judged as *essentially* masculine. As such, there is a burden of proof on men to establish their masculinity in front of others (Smith, 1992), generally through the performance of masculine behaviours and interactions (Messerschmidt, 1993). For men with limited access to other more conventional means by which to prove masculinity, crime and violence can become meaningful ways to establish, communicate and maintain masculinity by achieving status and reputation (Goodey, 1997; Taylor Gibbs & Merighi, 1994). Often this occurs in response to a perceived challenge to masculinity (Mullins, 2006) or honour (Polk, 1994), similarly to violence being enacted in response to challenges to other forms of identity as discussed earlier.

Ngahau, a Tongan man, was incarcerated for two separates offences, both of which involved the commission of significant violence. He perpetrated one of the offences in response to becoming angry when a friend told him that another man was disparaging him in front of his then girlfriend.

> Ngahau (Tongan): So ... he took me home ... and later um ... one of the boys come round ... they were at some bloke's house ... the girl that I was going out with at the time, she was there too. And um ... he went there, like to do something there, some business, he come over and told me there's a bloke backstabbing me ... he doesn't even know who I am. But because he knows the girl I was going out with at

> the time he started talking to me, it's ... if you wanna play the game
> ... there's always people that's going to suffer. It's like, if you want to
> backstab people — you know what I mean, be a man and say it to
> their face ... like, if you wanna backstab me ... you want to take this
> through your life, I might not catch ya tomorrow but I will
> [emphasised] catch ya.

In Ngahau's account of this incident, there is an implicit threat to his masculinity in the victim's behaviour through social reputation due to the presence of other people at this event. However, this perceived threat appears to have been magnified for Ngahau by the presence of the woman he was dating at the time, which exaggerated his felt need to establish masculinity (Mullins, 2006).

Ngahau describes the victim's behaviour, in disparaging him to his girlfriend, as initiating a 'game' in relation to which there are presumably a taken-for-granted set of rules that draw on understandings of how 'a man' should behave. As such, this game relates in part to the performance of stereotyped masculinity. Ngahau suggests that the actions of the victim were inconsistent with the 'rules' of this game (read 'proper' masculine behaviour), so that he felt the need to respond in stylised masculine terms, exaggerating his physical capability and dominance in order to reassert his masculinity in the presence of both his girlfriend and the victim, as well as others who were present at the time. He performed this through engaging in exaggerated violence.

> Ngahau: So I went to this bloke's house and just busted his door in
> and just went in and ... I think about five blokes were there ... I just
> bashed them ... I just grabbed a dumbbell and bashed him across
> the head ... I went to cut his throat and then I walked out going, 'I'm
> going back, I don't want to shoot ya'.

Ngahau describes his significant violence using extreme language, which is also lacking in emotional content. Further to this, he makes reference to five other males being present at the time of the offence, intimating that he was able to commit his offence without the intervention or challenge of these other men whom he allegedly also 'bashed'. Accounting for his violence in this way paints Ngahau as a strong and capable man who is invulnerable to threat from other males. Ngahau also ends this quote by making reference to his desire not to shoot the victim. This implies that not only is he capable of such extreme behaviour, but that he is 'man enough' not to act on his emotions by behaving in such a clearly exaggerated manner, drawing on discourses of rationality (see Smith, 1992).

Iash, a young Lebanese–Australian man, was serving a custodial sentence for two series of offences, one involving the kidnap and assault of a man who owed him money and another for orchestrating, while in jail, the violent assault of several men who had threatened his wife and family. In accounting for the first offences, Iash suggests that public notions of reputation and masculinity are at stake and this directly motivated his engagement in violence against the victim.

> Iash (Lebanese): Yeah, I think that maybe what they would see ... they'd probably see his face all busted up and bruised and all this sort of stuff and, you know, like um and his car was also taken off him, so he probably would have, they would have seen me [emphasised] driving his car, you know, all that sort of stuff.

In this quote, Iash is suggesting that, in thinking about his offending, he believed the consequences of his behaviour would be observed by others, which would then serve to establish his reputation in the eyes of criminal associates. Further to this, he discusses how others would have seen him driving the victim's car, thus implying that he was able to take the material possessions of another man, reinforcing his status in relation to this other man — the victim. The public demonstration of wealth and the attainment of material possessions is a powerful way to perform masculinity publicly and Mullins (2006) refers to this as 'flossing'.

The following relates to Iash's accounting for the second set of offences, which occurred when he was already in jail and in the context of threats being made against his wife and children.

> Iash: I'm incarcerated and somebody's doing that to my family and if I just turn around and put my hands up and say, 'Yeah, don't worry about it', people are going to start running though their head, you know, 'Look what happens to Iash's wife and that, and he didn't do anything about it' ... So then they're going to want to take things, they want to come and, you know ... it's hard for me too, like they're going to come and try to take a little bit of my business, a little bit of this, a little bit of that ... because they know I'm getting soft in jail, you know, so it was also about reputation as well.

Iash's accounting for these offences also draws on notions of reputation and status. However, unlike the first offence, Iash was already incarcerated at this time and therefore his status in the (criminal) community was more vulnerable as a result of his absence. Of particular distaste for Iash was that he had been kind to the victims and provided for them in times of need, implying that he was able to provide for members of his extended family and those perhaps less fortunate, which again highlights dominant masculine values. In threatening his family, Iash perceives that the victims 'took my kindness for weakness', which is experienced as a direct challenge to Iash's masculinity and honour, thereby requiring a swift and violent response (see Polk, 1994). This was particularly salient in relation to being perceived by not only the victims, but others in the community, as weak and inadequate, which are qualities inconsistent with dominant male practices. It appears, from Iash's statements that the threat of being perceived as weak was perhaps even more significant to him than the threat to his family's safety.

Further to this, the previous quote highlights that Iash's concern in this situation extends to the success of his criminal business, which is also vulnerable in his absence. At other times, Iash talks at some length about the financial security he has from his business, which has allowed him to purchase property and have 'a lot of nice things' in his home, also contributing to his achievement of masculine capital within the community. Such values also have their foundation in individualist notions of status and the importance of material possessions. This highlights the multiple layers of culture (ethnic/masculine/criminal) that impact on identity and behaviour.

Iash believes that if he does not demonstrate and exaggerate his status in the community, his business will be taken over by others. Therefore, he experiences a pressure to continue to demonstrate his capability, even from inside prison.

> Iash: That's just the kind of thing you've got to always [emphasised] maintain, you know? ... You can't slack off for 30 seconds, or a minute ... you just can't, because as soon as they see you starting to show weakness or even if you show a bit of kindness to someone, they take it for weakness too, you know?

Iash suggests that the establishment of masculinity comes through violence and aggression, rather than any words that he might use. This violence then creates reputation, which does the work of promoting status and thereby masculinity, with others.

> Iash: ... like was I saying stuff like this is what happens if you fuck around with me and all that? Nah, nah, nah, you don't have to say

things like that … You know, like, where I've grown up and all that sort of stuff, people see with their own eyes … and one thing I've learnt in my life and like I've been taught is, you know, you don't have to open your mouth, you do everything with your fist. You don't have to brag and carry on …

Lucky, a young Fijian man, also invokes masculinity in accounting for his offending behaviour, which involved physically assaulting and killing a taxi driver, whom he claimed took he and his co-offenders 'the long way' home, in addition to demanding additional money for the fare and threatening his younger cousin when they refused to pay the excess.

> **Lucky (Fijian):** …I didn't want him to walk off with my cousin, you know what I mean, it's more … I think, I know it sounds harsh … but it's, for me, you know, a man has to stand up for himself … He can't just stand there.

Like Iash, Lucky refers to the notion of 'a man', implying that there is a standard version of 'manliness', which men have access to and that shapes behaviour in particular ways. This discourse of masculinity, for Lucky, means that he has to 'stand up for himself' in response to the taxi driver's alleged attempt to cheat him and his co-offenders, and this speaks to Lucky's perceived sense of Self. However, Lucky felt this responsibility particularly keenly as his cousin was apparently threatened by the victim, as well as the fact that he was the oldest in the group, implicating the role of important others (such as family) in his behaviour. This highlights that offenders may draw on issues of culture, identity and relationship variously, depending on social and personal need in interaction. Lucky claims that were he to 'just stand there' and do nothing, he would have been behaving in a manner inconsistent with his understanding of dominant masculinity (i.e., 'a man'). This would have resulted in his 'losing face' in front of these people, thus creating a direct challenge to his status and reputation (Polk, 1994; Sanko, 1994).

In accounting for his violence in this way, Lucky ostensibly blames the victim for creating a situation in which he felt he had to respond with violence and aggression in order to assert his masculinity and status in the group. As indicated earlier, this perceived threat to status was particularly salient for Lucky in the presence of his co-offenders, who were also members of his cultural community, as his own sense of

'Fijian-ness' was rendered vulnerable by his being 'half-blooded'. Therefore, for Lucky, masculinity can be seen as being inherently tied to issues of ethnicity, which, within his cultural framework prioritised 'saving face'.

Jim, an Anglo–Australian man, has a history of violence and aggression, which he suggests has allowed him to build a particular reputation that has its foundation in his physical capabilities.

> Jim (Anglo): I was copping it from home in blue [police], I was copping it outside from blue, it got to a point where I learnt to fight … and then it got to a point where I learnt to … not professionally fight but … relatively handle myself. So then it got to a point where … 'You're supposed to be better than me but you're not' … and it become exhilaration. 'I'm better, I know it, come and get it' … Then it got to a point 'I am [emphasised] the best, bring it on'.

In this quote, Jim describes the development of his physical capabilities, which he claims occurred in response to the violence he was subject to at the hands of police, including his father. Jim suggests that as his fighting prowess developed, he achieved a sense of 'exhilaration' from its use, in addition to a sense of self-esteem and identity, as he perceived his skills were better than those of others. This enabled him to live a competitive existence whereby he sought to maintain his reputation through carrying out violence on others, particularly men. As such, he tended to see himself in stereotypically masculine ways that prioritised violence and aggression (James et al., 2002; Winlow, 2001) and this had implications for his relationships with others.

> Jim: Anger, little feelings turn into big feelings, so frustration and more blah, blah, turns into anger and anger turns into rage, rage turns into hate. All of these turn into power and when unleashed physically … on others, it becomes fear. Fear brings a desired response … I'm the one leading, with whatever I was feeling at the time … and I'm the one using the violence to control the situation.

Jim does not like being told what to do by others, or perceiving that he is not in control and this relates directly to his criminal violence, which is used as a means by which to control others and get his needs met. Often, this occurs in response to feelings, which are experienced as uncomfortable for Jim, and which may, in part, relate to his sense of inadequacy in managing feelings without violence (e.g., Jakupcak, Tull & Roemer, 2005). This is consistent with sociocultural theories of violence that suggest men are socialised to use violence as a problem solving technique in order to maintain hegemonic power associated with essentialised masculinity (Jenkins, 1990).

Associated with the performance of masculinity for Jim is the assertion that violence is often a response to a perceived threat to masculinity that involves the suggestion of subordinate masculine status, which, for Jim, relates to his small stature.

> Jim: 'Fuck it!' [said quite harshly] … That's where the 'fuck it' came in [chuckles].
>
> Interviewer: Yeah? 'Fuck it' — finish the sentence for me.
>
> Jim: 'Let's go, let's rumble, let's bring it on.' Oh, I don't know — 'You better watch yourself' … Now if you can picture this, my mate is 6'6" and built like a Sherman tank, so he's not a little boy, OK? And he got up in court and testified that he was in fear for his life … They looked at him, they looked at me and half the jury laughed.

In this context, Jim discusses his violence as bringing about a moral victory for 'the little guy', which relates to the fact that as a physically smaller man, he is able to overpower and instil fear in men who are far bigger and overtly stronger than he. This discourse draws on cultural archetypes of the 'little Aussie battler' and of 'David and Goliath', with Jim asserting that he refuses to be 'stepped on' (i.e., overpowered) by others. To further highlight this point, Jim draws on a popular advertising campaign in identifying himself with a cockroach, which is a very powerful metaphor for Jim and has associations with identity.

> Interviewer: So the fact that a smaller guy like you can instil that kind of fear in a bigger bloke like that, what does that mean for you?
>
> Jim: Who-oo! [makes an excited sound, laughs], you know, go the little man. Um have you seen the ad with cockroach doing the push-ups with the dude's boot?
>
> Interviewer: No.
>
> Jim: Yeah, they have some guarana [energy drink] … and the cockroach is doing the little push-ups, the dude's trying to squash him … and he's going '1, 2, 3, who-oo [makes an excited sound], go the little bloke!'. I think back now and think 'Well, you idiot', but … he was trying to step on me. You know, trying to step on a situation that he [emphasised] couldn't control and I wasn't going to let [emphasised] him control.

Jim's description of this incident constructs a powerful image of a conflict around masculinity between two men, both of whom were attempting to assert their control and dominance. Given his history,

Jim used violence with respect to which he has some confidence as a means of responding to this conflict, despite the larger stature of his opponent. The fact that this man was previously Jim's friend is negated by the challenge initiated by this person, thus prioritising masculinity for Jim over other potential social obligations.

Like Jim, Sammy also perceived a challenge to his masculinity based on reference to his physical stature, and this impacted on his choices in violence. Sammy, an Australian-born man of Turkish descent, was involved in the jail murder of another inmate who threatened him both physically and socially, by referring to him as a 'dog' (informer) in the jail, which as described earlier, is a particularly powerful threat within the jail environment.

> Sammy (Turkish): ... he pulled a knife on them and this was over heroin as well, they didn't pay the money and he said, 'Mate, where's the money, how come you haven't you done it?' They said, 'It's been done'. He said, 'Mate, I've checked, it hasn't been done'. They said, 'What, are you calling my family a liar?' They king hit my friend, my friend ended up pulling a blade out, they smashed a milk crate over his head, split his head open and he ran, and he's a big boy, he's not a little boy, and I think that's what give them the courage and the determination to go ahead with what he they did with me ... because they thought, their understanding, to me, was the bloke that was bigger, that pulled out the blade, shit himself and ran. What is the littlest one going to do?

Sammy suggests that the victims decided to target him because he believes that they felt he would not be a sufficient enough threat due to his small stature.

> Sammy: I thought, well, silly mistake, I don't know you and you don't know nothing about me, you underestimate me and if you want to walk away, you'll have the opportunity, and that was basically my feeling for him.

Sammy interprets the victim's behaviour as underestimating him, which he describes as a 'silly mistake'. This issue is twofold for Sammy. First, it implies that he is perceived as being weaker by others because of his small size and second, it relates to Sammy's perhaps exaggerated sense of his own masculinity and capability, which may have developed in order to compensate for his small stature. Thus, in response to the victim's behaviour, Sammy perceived a need to retaliate with violence as a means of re-establishing his reputation in the eyes of others in the jail. This was particularly important in light of his being referred to as a dog, which occurred in a public setting, thereby directly challenging his status in the jail. In accounting for his decision to offend, Sammy directly implicates this potential for public weakness.

> **Sammy:** I thought, my best mate's locked up, I have to still go out and face it, you know what I mean? I have to be counted as a man. If I stay inside, I'm going to be labelled as a weak cunt ... and apart from that, you know what I mean, that leads from one thing to another and ... I ... really didn't fancy being someone's bitch basically.

Like others, Sammy refers to this taken-for-granted 'man', against whom his behaviour is judged, both publicly and privately. This man likely has particular significance within the jail environment, which is an inherently masculine setting (Sim, 1994). Sammy suggests that, if he does not retaliate, he will be 'labelled' by others as a 'weak cunt', such that he would be rendered 'someone's bitch'. Sammy uses words that are aligned with femininity in common slang parlance to highlight the threat to his masculinity, which would position him in a subordinate male position, equivalent to femininity (Connell, 1987). This is obviously derogatory to women, but has particular effects when used in reference to men and masculinity. Sammy's offending, like others, thus appears to be related to the desire to establish reputation and reinforce masculinity in response to a perceived threat to the same.

Eloqui's accounting for his criminal violence also draws on issues of masculinity and identity. Eloqui was born and raised in rural Victoria, and several events occurred in his life that served to challenge his sense of masculinity, which was particularly fragile. Namely, he believes he was supposed to have been born a female and he was also the victim of sexual assault at the hands of an older male when he was 14 years of age.

> **Eloqui (Anglo):** ...I was a little bit more sensitive that most [chuckles] ... so I was um, trying to do that masculine thing too ... well, I guess there was a feeling that there was something severely wrong with me ... and perhaps I might have been a homosexual although I didn't really know what that was ... because of the abuse ...

Eloqui's reference to being 'sensitive' draws on stereotypical notions of femininity, whereby women are seen as being inherently emotional, more so than men (Smith, 1992). In response to this, Eloqui chooses to engage in 'that masculine thing', which like the stereotype of a 'man', draws on established discourses of masculinity, implying that there are certain behaviours that establish masculinity by their very nature. In addition, Eloqui suggests that he was unsure of his sexuality, as a result of being the victim of sexual abuse some years earlier. Homosexuality is clearly associated with subordinate masculinity for Eloqui, and he equates this to there being 'something severely wrong' with him. This belief has as its foundation concern that hegemonic discourses on masculinity have with homosexuality as potentially undermining the practices of dominant masculinity (Connell, 1987, 1995). As a result of this sexual confusion and fragility in masculine identity, sex and intimacy with women were particularly salient for Eloqui and a means by which he sought to establish masculine capital.

> Eloqui: It was like the whole, the ideal [emphasised] thing … I was very unskilled and out of touch, it was more, how is she [emphasised] feeling. How does she feel? And ah as — as soon as there was some … just slight change in her behaviour it was like, oh, what have I done, you know? Over that time, she'd start saying things, like … 'You're acting strange, you're acting weird'. And the more of course she said that, it reinforced how I was … and that … wasn't once … that happened with virtually every relationship that I ever had … up until that point and ah, I was never really able to sit back and ask myself where are, you know … there is me [emphasised] here. I've, ah actually got something to offer here … I invariably became very frustrated [emphasised] … and pissed off and started drinking more and fighting more and …
>
> Interviewer: How did the fighting and the violence fit in?
>
> Eloqui: Um … [long pause] that manly quality I guess. Um and it was even reinforced by a number of people and women in particular on a number of occasions you know, like you know, be a man, stand up to them.

With each additional perceived failure at masculinity, Eloqui became increasingly angry and he coped with this by drinking more alcohol and engaging in more violence, which he referred to as 'that manly quality'. This suggests that Eloqui attempted to counteract his inadequate and fragile masculinity with overt performances of masculinity, which included acts of violence. This unfortunate situation culminated in Eloqui fatally shooting two people and seriously injuring two others, in an attempt to redress the injustices he perceived had been done to him by the victims and by others, and in order to establish some sense of identity and masculinity (Mullins, 2006), which to some extent was reinforced and supported by the women in his life.

The aforementioned discussion is consistent with the growing consensus in the literature that adherence to stereotyped notions of masculinity promote violence and aggression (Copenhaver, Lash, & Eisler, 2000; Goodey, 1997; Moore & Stuart, 2004). Recently, Mullins (2006) has extended an understanding of the relationship between masculinity and crime, especially violence, in suggesting that crime and violence are the primary means by which men, who do not have access to other means of masculine capital, achieve gender. As such, many men in positions of social disadvantage find it difficult to achieve masculine status through the commonly accepted means of wealth, power, resource accumulation and occupational success. For these men, engaging in practices of violence may serve the same ends, in establishing and cementing masculinity.

Violence, in particular, is associated with masculinity and reputation, given its association with the inherently masculine qualities of independence, toughness, competition, dominance and invulnerability (Smith, 1992). As such, crime in general, and violent crime in particular, represent strategies by which men respond to challenges to honour and status, and the means by which men may re-establish or confirm masculinity (Messerschmidt, 1994; Mullins, 2006; Polk, 1994). Moreover, crime and violence would be considered especially likely in subcultures where traditional means of achieving masculinity are less available, due to social disadvantage, for example, poverty or ethnic status (Collins et al., 2000). For this last group, in particular, this is likely to involve the presence of others, including other men.

Group Violence

Messerschmidt (1993, 1994) suggested that the need to prove masculinity may be particularly salient in contexts involving other men. Masculinity is performative and needs to be 'accomplished' by men in front of others if it is to have any significance (Mullins, 2006). This is likely to be even more important for offenders who prioritise collectivist values, which dictate that identity should be established in reference to Others; that is, within group contexts.

As discussed earlier, the offenders with migrant experience and a heritage of a greater value in collectivism all offended in the presence of co-offenders and this was contextualised in reference to the particular constructions of identity that are relevant to people with such cultural backgrounds. However, notions of masculinity were also relevant for several of these offenders in that the presence of other men shaped their choices in criminal violence.

For example, in accounting for his motivations for violence, Lucky suggests that he did not want to 'lose face' in front of the other males present.

> Lucky (Fijian): It wasn't all about power ... it was all about losing face ... in front of, of the boys, you know what I mean?

By referring to notions of power in violence, Lucky is invoking commonly understood motivations for violence, which include the assertion of dominance and power over victims (Ressler et al., 1993). However, Lucky states that this was not his primary motive for violence, which was, rather, driven by his sense of what 'the boys' would think were he not to react. This statement about 'the boys' implies a shared sense of masculinity that comes from participating in a group of males, which serves to dictate certain ways of being that prioritise stereotypical masculinity, in this case, promoting violence (see Polk, 1994).

Genuine also discusses how the presence of other males facilitated his involvement in criminal behaviour, including acts of violence.

> Genuine (Vietnamese): I mean, growing up, it's was always fight, meeting up after school, fight, go to another school, fight, and that was me, you know. In public school I was always in the principal's office, fighting, yeah, and um just rough playing even got me in trouble ... like ... and moving on to high school ... like I said, meeting up after school in parks having a fight. Me psyching other people up to fight, you know what I mean? And the other guys who fight just to see a bit of action ... Get to have [emphasised] a bit of the action, you know what I mean? Go to another school, meet up and all just go another school ... and um ... going to parties at a young age with the old boys ... it does ... feel a lot of respect, you know?

Here, Genuine describes the development of his tendency to aggression, which was reinforced by fighting from a young age with other youths with whom he went to school. He accounts for this as being 'a bit of action' that serves to establish one's credibility and capability to others with whom one is engaged. Further to this, for Genuine, the fact that he could engage in violence and criminal behaviour with these other young men, gave him a sense of reputation and status that allowed him to feel respected within his antisocial community. This was embellished by the presence of older males with whom he associated. Men tend to look to other men as role models of masculinity and older males may provide particularly salient examples of this, as they also have the subcultural or social capital to legitimise the masculinity of younger males (Mullins, 2006).

Offenders in the collectivist cultural group were more likely to engage in criminal violence in the presence of others than their Anglo–Australian counterparts. This is suggested to be related to aspects of identity, as discussed earlier, but may also implicate masculinity and there is some theoretical and empirical support for this notion. Specifically, it has been suggested that particular forms of masculinity, often subordinated, are available to men from nondominant or immigrant cultures (Collins et al, 2004; Poynting et al., 2004) and these may be related to exaggerated practices of violence, particularly in front of other males.

Poynting et al. (1998) draw on the notion of 'protest masculinities' (see Connell, 1995) in suggesting that young men from migrant communities are likely to respond with violence to the perceived injustices of racism and social marginalisation, which they may interpret as an attack on their inherent masculinity. Connell (1995) argued that protest masculinity is a marginalised masculinity, which exaggerates dominant themes of masculinity within subcultural restraints, such as poverty or racism. Engaging in the exaggerated performance of masculinity is, not surprisingly, also associated with exaggerated violence (Taylor Gibbs & Merighi, 1994).

Norm was the only of the offenders from the individualist group who offended in the presence of others. He was involved in a home invasion, where a man was physically assaulted, seemingly in retaliation for the alleged assault on a young female. He provides the following in response to being asked why he committed the offence.

> Norm (Anglo): Um ... maybe ... [long pause] ... I don't know, just to be one of the boys, the boys were going so I was going. So, not, not, not peer pressure or nothing it was my [emphasised] choice ... I think he deserved it and that. My mates were going so I was going.

Interviewer: So you wouldn't have done it if you were on your own?

Norm: No ... I didn't bring the idea up to go there, someone else did ... Like, if I had've run into the bloke in the street somewhere um, I might have, would've had a go at him there by myself ... it's like you don't want to let your friends down, they're all going and they're saying come on ... and um, when you believe that ah, well in yourself you, you think it's justified that it does [emphasised] happen, well it made it easier for me to go.

Norm's account of his offending shifts and, although he is clear to assert that he was motivated by the individual desire to defend a principle that he believed in strongly, it is also apparent that the presence of his co-offenders, some of whom were friends of his, was important in contributing to the form that his retribution took. An analysis of Norm's offending within the group context was discussed earlier; however, it is also worth commenting on the way in which Norm's offending, as well as the presence of co-offenders, drew on notions of masculinity. Like Lucky, Norm refers to 'the boys', who comprised an audience by which he is judged in relation to his masculinity. As such, Norm suggests that he felt as if he should behave similarly to the other males who were present by offending. Furthermore, in accounting for his criminal behaviour in this way, Norm draws on discourses of loyalty and mateship, which are both important masculine values. However, they are also values that are prized within the dominant Anglo–Australian culture to which Norm subscribes, again reinforcing the blurred boundaries between different notions of (cultural) identity on which offenders may draw.

Norm was quick to separate himself from notions of 'peer pressure', which are suggested to imply a level of weakness in will that is inconsistent with dominant discourses on masculinity. In this way, Norm's relationship to masculinity is complex, such that he is prioritising independence, but at the same time recognising the importance of mateship, while also implying that there is a taken for granted 'gaze' of masculinity that is enacted by the presence of men and which can shape behaviour in particular, and often unhelpful, ways contributing to criminal violence.

Silencing the Masculinity of Others

It has been argued that engaging in criminal violence is a means by which men can establish or cement their claim to masculinity, both publicly and privately. This is generally in relation to dominant discourses on masculinity, which prioritise independence, physical and sexual prowess, and control or dominance. However, according to Mullins (2006), hegemonic masculinity is only made legitimate through the performance of dominant masculinities in concert with the dismissal of subordinate masculinities. Subordinate masculinities are those that are seen as weaker or less acceptable due to their allegiance with values that do not constitute the commonly preferred masculine discourse according to a hierarchy of relationships between masculinities (Connell, 1987). Society is conventionally unsympathetic to men who violate norms of masculinity (Doherty & Anderson, 2004) and, moreover, there are often negative consequences for men who are identified as failing in masculinity, including being targets for violence by other men (Messerschmidt, 1994; Mullins, 2006).

As such, consistent with other identities, masculinity is inherently fragile and vulnerable, and needs to be constantly re-established and negotiated in action in order to maintain masculine capital in the community. One of the ways this may be achieved is through the dismissal of another's masculinity (Winlow, 2001). However, it is important to note that these subordinate masculinities are silenced through this process rather than eliminated altogether, as hegemonic masculinity may only be defined in relation to that which it is not; that is, subordinate masculinities and femininities.

As stated earlier, Norm was involved in a home invasion with several other men, which was perpetrated in response to the victim allegedly physically assaulting a young woman. He provides the following in response to being asked what he felt and thought about the victim.

> Norm (Anglo): ... [long pause] ... hatred I think ... well the bloke's a junkie — ah, well he uses heroin and that ... 'till today, he's still running around, um, stealing cars, breaking into houses and so, on top of what he'd done ... ah, I just thought, you know, she don't charge you or nothing, then he thinks he can just do it and get away with it ... and today, now he's a registered informant for Surry Hills police ... [long pause] that topped it off again [emphasised] ... I just thought, you're a bad swine, like ... you want to run around doing crime and everything but then soon as something happens to you [emphasised], like you can dish it out but you can't take it back. Oh, just ah ... basically just a low human being ... I didn't think I owed him any type of respect, any type

> of justification ... I could do what I want to him, 'cause like I just thought
> ... he doesn't count ... he deserves it.

In describing the victim in this way, Norm is relegating him to a position of subordinate masculinity, which not only serves to justify his offending against the victim, but also to embellish his own masculinity in comparison. Norm refers to the victim as being a 'junkie' who is addicted to heroin. This implies that the victim is not in control of his own life, which is instead directed by his need for drugs. This contradicts dominant discourses of masculinity that prioritise independence and agency, in addition to strength (e.g., Smith, 1992), which is compromised by addiction.

Norm also suggests that the victim is a hypocrite, who is himself engaged in criminal behaviour, but who has been cooperating with the police as an informant, thus breaching conventional standards of criminality and antisocial subcultural values. This is further exacerbated by the victim's use of the police for support in this matter, which implies that he perceived he could not manage the situation himself. Dependence on others, particularly police, is inconsistent with masculine, as well as antisocial, values (Winlow, 2001).

Above, Norm provides a veritable list of the victim's offences against masculinity, which one after the other 'topped it off again', adding insult to injury, and forcing Norm's hand. As such, Norm suggests that he does not owe the victim any form of respect, because he 'doesn't count' and is seen as deserving of the violence perpetrated against him.

Jim also described an occasion of violence when his behaviour was motivated by the desire to respond to another man's inadequate masculinity. The following quote relates to an interaction he allegedly had with a man who was claiming to be the boyfriend of a woman he was sleeping with.

> Jim (Anglo): He said 'I'm her boyfriend, if you've hurt her, I'll kill
> you!'. I said, 'What are you going to do?' ... Um he pulled out this
> little Victorinox knife and said 'I'll gut you alive'. So I've opened the
> door and I've got a machete in my hand, I said 'I don't think so'. He
> turned white and run and I went 'Boo' to his face [laughing] and he
> went running after him.

This is a particularly vivid example that Jim uses to demonstrate his inherent masculinity, which is exaggerated in the face of another's inadequate masculinity. This conflict of masculinity is symbolised by the comparison of knives held by Jim and the other man; namely, a 'little Victorinox knife' as opposed to a 'machete'. Jim suggests that the man was frightened of him, such that he ran away, even in response to such a childish comment as 'boo'. The ludicrous nature of this situation is further highlighted by Jim's laughter at interview. The effect of this interaction is to cement Jim's masculinity by demonstrating the vulnerability in the other man's weakness and fear, both of which are qualities that undermine masculinity.

Providing Sexual Access to Women

Masculinity is defined not only in reference to other masculinities, but also with respect to extant femininities (Connell, 1995; Mullins, 2006), which provide a set reference point with which to understand masculinity. Men who engage in violent practices tend to hold stereotypical views on gender (Jenkins, 1990) and they may experience threats to the accomplishment of gender from women. This can lead to men perpetrating violence on women (James et al., 2002).

Hegemonic discourses on masculinity thereby dictate certain ways of interacting between men, but also between men and women, in addition to providing men with particular ways of understanding and relating to women. Subscribing to stereotypical masculinity encourages the sexualisation (and objectification) of women, who are seen as vehicles through which men can achieve masculinity via sexual conquest and prowess (Kimmel, 1993; Miedzian, 1993; O'Sullivan, 1993). In other words, the sociocultural meanings of sexuality that are constructed within the dominant culture in this country (and other such individualist cultures) contribute to the performance of masculinity associated with sexual aggression and sexual violence.

Iash draws on these discourses of women in discussion of his attitude towards the Skaf gang rapes. These rapes are those that were perpetrated in the year 2000 by Bilal Skaf, several of his brothers and also other youths from their local community. Skaf is a Middle-Eastern Muslim and these rapes created public angst about the suggested inherent criminality and abusive nature of Middle-Eastern and Muslim men.

> Iash (Lebanese): The biggest stuff up in the Lebanese community in the last 5 years was these Bil Skaf people, you know what I mean?

Like don't get me wrong, like when I was younger, of course, I had plenty [emphasised] of girls ... where yeah they'll come and want to do things ... with me and my friend — you know, at the same time sometimes, this and that and they'd walk away and be happy, you know what I mean? But it's all about the way you treat them after you've finished ... that's what it's all about, the way you treat them kind of girls after [emphasised] you've finished. You can't treat them like ... what they did, they took her out to the Bankstown Sports Club and washed her down with a hose and that, that stuff's disgusting mate, you know? Like that's someone's daughter you're talking about there ... Like when I was younger ... my father always [emphasised] taught me to show respect for women ... because of my daughters, because of my sisters and my mother, because it's someone's mother and sister, mate ... and he always taught me, always sit and make sure you show respect for them, 'cause he knew, you know, he knew we were going to have girls, he didn't like it but he knew they were going to be there because of what we were doing.

Even though the superficial rhetorical impact of Iash's comments serve to distance himself from the rapists and eschew their criminal behaviour, Iash, in fact, aligns himself with stereotypical and misogynist views of women, which can be seen as consistent with attitudes supportive of rape (Burt, 1980; Ward, Hudson, Johnston, & Marshall, 1997; Yourell & McCabe, 1988). By referring to 'them kind of girls', Iash invokes images of stereotyped 'whores' who make themselves sexually available to men. These women are seen in a negative light, casting doubt about their character and implying that they cannot be harmed sexually, as they are experienced and available sexually, often also acting in sexually provocative ways that are assumed to have an arousing effect on men. This image is further cemented by Iash's reference to women being available sexually to both he and his friends. There are also religious and cultural supports for Iash's view, whereby within conservative Islamic and Lebanese values, the sexuality of women is painted as being all but nonexistent, certainly before marriage. As such, there are assumed behaviours that morally astute women engage in compared with those of more dubious character.

In addition to espousing such distorted and problematic attitudes about women, Iash's comments are also steeped in masculinity, prioritising the sexuality and dominance of men, and relegating women to a subordinate and powerless position. Iash refers to having engaged in sexual behaviour with 'plenty' of 'girls'. This comment both embellishes his own sexual desirability by suggesting that many females are attracted to him, but it also implies that women are inferior through using the term 'girls'. This has the effect of positioning females below men in terms of maturity, understanding and social experience. Further to this, Iash suggests that, after he and his friends have engaged in sexual behaviour with these females, the girls 'walk away happy', implying that he is a proficient lover, who is knowledgeable about the ways to please a woman, thus reinforcing his own masculinity.

With respect to the crimes of Bilal Skaf and his co-offenders, which Iash describes as being 'disgusting', he claims that it is 'all about the way you treat them [girls] after you've finished'. This suggests that the sexual experience is dominated by the male's need to 'finish', such that women do not have an agenda in sex. Moreover, Iash's comments also imply that a 'real' man should treat women in a particular way after any sexual encounter. Iash, clearly, has some insight into this and, therefore portrays himself as sexually skilled and a veritable gentleman. Further, it is suggested that describing sex in this way maintains women in a subordinate position, such that they should be placated in order to continue to be available for men sexually.

Despite his protestations to the contrary, therefore, Iash is, in fact, performing dominant forms of masculinity that seek to diminish women and relegate femininity to a subordinate position, thus reinforcing his own masculinity and maintaining male hegemonic power. This is not inconsistent with forms of dominant masculinity, as well as acts of rape. Further to this, it is noted that Iash has particularly strong views about these offences because he blames Bilal Skaf and his co-offenders for the negative and racist treatment of Muslims and Lebanese people in this country, in addition to the subsequent media reporting of these offences and other similar criminal acts perpetrated by Islamic extremists. This blame forms the foundation of much of his account at interview. Through Iash's accounting of feminine sexuality, he is able to construct his own masculine position, which draws on notions of power and sexual skill, thus prioritising the values of masculinity that he adheres to.

Jim, an Anglo–Australian man, also identifies misogynist views about women in discussion of his relationships with others, which are seen to be generally strategic and tactical, ignoring obvious emotionality and interpersonal connectedness.

Jim (Anglo): There were four women involved, I was sleeping with all four. OK? Now it was on, they all knew that I was sleeping with all four. It was on the basis that there was nothing more than ... Just sex yes. Um I was working at the time, OK? Um so I'd go away, I'd come home, there'd be one waiting there for me. If I was home for a couple of days, she'd leave and another one would turn up ... it was never meant to be anything serious.

Jim's beliefs allow him to have structured and stereotypical ideas of both men and women and these beliefs clearly operate on him, influencing his relationships and behaviour, including his offending. In claiming that he was 'trying to handle' four women at the same time, Jim constructs himself as someone who is desirable, who is a good lover, who is attractive and with whom women fall in love, almost despite their common sense. He states that he was clear in the arrangement with these four women; however, they did not play by his 'rules', changing the dynamics of the 'relationship' when they fell in love with him and became more demanding with his time.

Furthermore, Jim uses the term 'one' to refer to these women with whom he was engaged in a sexual relationship. This is a term that objectifies the women and removes any emotional connection. Referring to these women in this way allows Jim to maintain a superficial and strategic attachment to these women, which was 'just' about sex. He claims that the women were aware the relationship was 'never meant to be anything serious', implying that he set the terms of engagement, regardless of the women's intentions or hopes.

Although Jim denies the sexual assaults that he was incarcerated for, he acknowledged a history of some violence with women, which he nevertheless minimised. Notwithstanding, he maintains the position of being a caring, romantic and loving man, and this is inconsistent with his violence against women and is more related to the demands of maintaining hegemonic masculinity, particularly in the presence of a female interviewer.

T, a young Samoan man, was one of five men who broke into the home of a woman, gang raping her while her children slept in another room.

T (Samoan): One of the blokes, you know, started pulling his pants down ... um and then she started giving him oral sex ... Like I said I just — it just happened ... I wasn't thinking in my head like 'Let's rape this girl', you know, 'Let's rape her'. I wasn't thinking that ... like it,

> yeah, it just happened, like I think, oh, I think I was just following
> everyone else, what everyone else was doing ... but it just happened
> and I just ... just went with it ...

T handed himself in for this crime and thereby demonstrates some responsibility for his offending behaviour. However, he has great difficulty accepting agency in the rape and minimises any sexual deviancy, instead suggesting that he simply went along with his co-offenders when one of them initiated the sexual assault against the woman. This is consistent with Blanchard's (1959) examination of the dynamics involved in youth gang rape. Blanchard suggested that, in his research, there was an identifiable primary leader within groups of youth who were involved in sexual assault. The other youth in the group tended to over-idealise this leader and attribute to him important masculine qualities, which they felt were lacking in themselves. This led Blanchard to suggest that gang rape is, in fact, more about the relationship between the males involved (that is, the performance of masculinity) rather than between the men and the female victim(s). Despite the age of this research, the conclusions are still helpful in current understandings of gang rape, particularly in reference to masculinity.

According to T's account, all five men were engaged in vaginally and orally raping the woman at the same time, with his involvement being precipitated by the actions of others present. He also identifies that this is the first time that any of the offenders had been involved in sexual behaviour or been naked around one another. The men were also not particularly close friends but, rather, tended to drink alcohol together. Such a situation is not unfamiliar within stories of gang rape by offenders and draws on discourses of masculinity and sex that normalise the group sexual behaviour of men. Although women may talk about sex with one another, they do not have the same discourses available to them about sharing sex. Consequently, it seems that engaging in sexual behaviour in front of other men is a means by which men can perform dominant masculinity, particularly in reference to the sexual conquest of a woman using violence, both of which are inherently related to practices of hegemonic masculinity (Kimmel, 1993; Yancey-Martin & Hummer, 1994).

> Interviewer: Do you think you would have sexually assaulted the
> victim if you were on your own?
>
> T: No.

> **Interviewer:** OK, so how was this situation different then?
>
> **T:** I guess just the influence that was there. Just like, like I said when it just happened … it was all of us, you know what I mean? It was … yeah it was all of us, so I just um … so I jumped in yeah.

T's accounting of his involvement in the sexual abuse highlights that the presence of other men allowed him to sexualise the victim and perpetrate violence on her in a way that directly contradicts his moral and personal values. Further to this, by referring to his actions as 'jumping in', T minimises the criminality and violence in this context, placing the emphasis on the other males present, rather than on the female victim.

Drawing on discourses of hegemonic masculinity within a group setting thereby allows for the further distortion of masculinity, often leading to violence against those that are viewed as subordinate, including women. In such situations, violence is about proving masculinity to one's peers and establishing masculine capital in the gendered context of interaction.

Facilitating the Protection of Women

Within discourses on masculinity, particularly those available within antisocial subcultures, there is a taken-for-granted chivalry that dictates women should be protected, as they are weaker and generally dependent on men (Connell, 1995; Mullins, 2006). This is particularly the case for women who are related to a man by blood, as these women hold special status and, as such, are afforded particular privileges.

Iash draws on these discourses in accounting for the fact that he would feel compelled to protect his former wife, even though they were divorced at the time of interview, and this would also include the use of violence in retaliation for any perceived threat to this woman.

> **Iash (Lebanese):** If I'm outside and something happens like that … probably, you know, because now we're divorced and that it doesn't matter, you know what I mean? It doesn't matter at all … she's still the mother of my children … and — I'll be straight up with you, I'll probably kill someone for her, you know? If someone ever raped her, or attacked her or hurt her … I wouldn't leave it in the police's arms to do something about it.

According to Iash, the fact that he was married to this woman, to whom he also had children, implies that the relationship between them continues even after divorce. As such, he suggests that he is still duty-bound to protect this woman. He is invoking this discourse as being seemingly helpful in this situation; however, it is also suggested that such discourse allows Iash to continue to hold his wife accountable for her behaviour due to an ongoing sense of obligation long after their relationship has ended.

The above quote also highlights Iash's antisocial mentality, whereby he 'wouldn't leave it in the police's arms to do something about it'. This underlines an inherent distrust of authority, common within antisocial subcultures (Sim, 1994; Winlow, 2001). However, his statement also serves to highlight his own capability and power, and therefore his masculinity, by implying that he would be capable of dealing with any threat to his former wife independently and without any assistance.

Jim also discusses the need to protect women and this is accounted for in the context of other misogynist beliefs about women and relationships.

> Jim (Anglo): …Because when I come in [to jail], it was all me, me, me … things had [emphasised] to be done the way I wanted, if we went out, it was to where I wanted to go out, you know? … I'm very, very protective, you know, you look at my missus the wrong way, 'I don't care mate', whack! [makes a sound like hitting someone], you know, if you insult my missus, whack! … you insult my mother, whack! [chuckles], you know, I'm very protective of my family and if I'm with a woman, she's my family … no hesitation whatsoever, I'm defending … my kingdom.

This quote highlights Jim's propensity to violence, often with little provocation. Jim conflates his use of violence with being 'very protective', thus minimising any negative impression, but also implying that violence is justified under certain conditions. Jim suggests that it would be appropriate for him to engage in violence should someone look at 'my missus the wrong way'. The term 'my missus' is a derogatory reference to a woman belonging to a man, drawing on antiquated notions of a woman being a man's 'chattel', with which he can do as he pleases. This is further supported by Jim's use of the word 'kingdom' to refer to his family. Moreover, it is important to unpack the notion of what Jim might mean by 'the wrong way'. In this context, Jim is referring to another man looking at his woman sexually, which he implies is 'wrong', presumably according to commonly accepted masculine discourse that stipulates that when a woman is involved with a man, she is 'off limits' to other men, even visually. Such beliefs often place unfair responsibility on women to somehow publicly advertise their unavailability.

In accounting for his behaviour in this way, Jim is implying that women require the protection of men, particularly in response to insults or sexual looks. Thus, Jim is performing dominant discourses of masculinity that see women as being inferior and incapable. Further to this, the presence of women, according to this discourse, is to prop up the masculinity of men, predominantly in public life (Mullins, 2006). Jim claims that the 'one thing' he has learnt from his cultural heritage is that the 'male is dominant and the woman is submissive'. Therefore, Jim suggests that his beliefs have been established through experience of his family and culture, such that he is simply performing what has always been, as it is 'very hard to fight what you've learnt your whole life'. This allows him to separate from any responsibility with respect to these values, including the commission of violence.

Norm was involved in the home invasion and serious physical attack on a man that he heard had assaulted a woman that he knew only indirectly.

> **Norm (Anglo):** When I found out [about the assault] … my thoughts were, I thought it was wrong … Especially, not just because he hit her, because of the age difference. I've always thought, like, a bloke can take care of himself more than what a female can. My feelings was I didn't really know her that well, it didn't really affect me that much … about a week later when I found out that she had a big black eye and bruising and that. At that stage … I felt totally pissed off with him, you know, like someone of his age to do that.

Norm judged the victim's behaviour as being morally 'wrong', when he found out about the alleged physical assault of the woman. In particular, he expressed umbrage as a result of the age difference between the man and the woman he assaulted. Norm referred to the woman as a 'girl', which serves to exaggerate her femininity and vulnerability. As such, Norm is invoking commonly assumed standards of behaviour for both men and women in relation to violence, which are informed by gendered discourse.

Norm accounts for his criminal behaviour as being motivated by the desire to respond to the affront on the female victim. He claims that he has always believed that 'a bloke can take care of himself more than what a female can'. The use of the Australian slang term 'bloke' conjures images of capability and independence, which Norm suggests are not available to women. As such, his own masculinity is highlighted, while diminishing that of his male victim.

Ostensibly, according to Norm, the behaviour of the male victim was constructed in direct violation of important principles that Norm holds as a result of his family and cultural experience: 'My father brought me up that you don't hit women'. Despite these values, Norm suggests that he was not initially affected deeply by hearing about the man's alleged assault of the young woman. However, his anger was particularly inflamed when he was made aware of the extent of the victim's injuries, including a 'big black eye' and 'bruising', thereby presumably increasing the perceived insult perpetrated by her attacker, as well as exaggerating further the man's failed masculinity and, in turn, challenge to Norm's masculine status. Norm responded to this challenge by perpetrating violence on the man, which he suggested was justified by the victim's inappropriate and 'unmasculine' assault of a woman.

The above discussion demonstrates that hegemonic masculinity can become refracted in particular ways within the gendered context of social interaction, such that criminal behaviour and violence become the vehicles by which men may seek to establish and maintain masculinity (Connell, 1995; Mullins, 2006). Violence is naturalised within dominant doctrines of masculinity (Connell, 1987), granting men almost unchallenged access to the use of violence in navigating social interaction. Therefore, men must have some relationship to violence, even if they do not engage in violent practices personally (Winlow, 2001).

This (violent) masculinity is achieved subculturally where other means by which gender is conventionally performed, according to dominant cultural values, are unavailable (Collins et al., 2000; Taylor Gibbs & Merighi, 1994). Such masculinities can become stylised and exaggerated, often in an attempt to compensate for perceived failures in masculinity and this has implications for men's relationships with each other and with women and influences choices in and expressions of criminal behaviour.

The performance of such exaggerated masculinities was suggested to be particularly salient within group contexts, especially in front of other men, where masculinity can be hotly contested and more reliably achieved with the recognition of the group (Messerschmidt, 1994; Mullins, 2006). As such, masculine traits may be reinforced within the group context (Blanchard, 1959), which tends to centre on activities that promote masculinity and involve 'male bonding' (Aumair & Warren, 1994). This may also increase the likelihood of violent offending behaviour in groups (Mullins, 2006), particularly for men of ethnic minority status, who are, socioculturally relegated to positions of subordinate masculinity (Poynting et al., 1998; 2004).

In summary, this analysis of identity in the performance of criminal violence highlights that identity is inherently flexible and related to culture, including ethnic, criminal and masculine culture. Establishing and maintaining identity is important and, in order to achieve this aim, people will draw on whatever capital they have available in social interaction. Such capital is limited in the context of fragile identity, as in the case of confused or bicultural cultural identity, and this has been demonstrated both with respect to ethnicity and masculinity, making the process of 'doing' identity even more complex. In achieving identity in reference to their offending behaviour, offenders drew variously on discourses relevant to ethnic culture, criminal culture and masculine culture, thus highlighting that identity is a resource to be mobilised in social interaction, and culture is implicated to the extent that people draw on whatever resources may be available to them at the time.

In addition to the inherent complexities in and the politically charged nature of identity, interpersonally violent crime fulfils important functions in 'doing' identity, much of which is shaped by the social demands of accounting for crime. Specifically, offenders appear to accomplish and maintain identity through their criminal behaviour and in reference to the 'goods' ascribed by their cultural experience and values. Violence tends to occur in direct response to a perceived threat to identity, including honour and/or reputation, which may not be redressed through other means, depending on the cultural capital available. This is about establishing identity (ethnic, criminal and masculine) and, for those with minority group status and experience of collectivist culture, criminal violence may also relate to the performance of cultural pride and is likely to include the presence of co-offenders, who serve as a collective within which identity is achieved consistent with more collectivist cultural values.

Culturally, interpersonal violence was used as a means of achieving identity, both personally and publicly, with the latter being more salient to those offenders adhering to cultural values that prioritise the group and this occurred in two ways. First, offences were perpetrated in the presence of others, who provided greater access to security in identity. Second, the establishment of cultural pride was important, particularly for those with vulnerable or fragile ethnic identity, on the basis of their cultural experience.

There are, however, three important issues that complicate the assumed relationship between cultural experience and identity. First, culture, like identity, does not simply relate to ethnicity. Rather, discourses located in criminal culture, masculine culture and also migrant culture shape identity and subsequent choices in behaviour for offenders by providing the lens thorough which to interpret experience. In other words, offenders position themselves in relation to culture in order to account for their behaviour and the relationship between salient cultures may at times be complex and even competing.

Further, this analysis suggested that there is a relationship between the influence of collectivist versus individualist ideals in shaping choices in identity and (criminal) behaviour. However, this relationship is contextualised within the multicultural community of Sydney, Australia, whereby Anglo–Australians are the majority and those with 'obvious' ethnicity are relegated to minority status. As such, members of the collectivist cultural groups will experience a degree of uncertainty in ethnic cultural identity that comes from being members of nondominant groups and this may also influence the performance of criminal violence. It is, therefore, suggested that culture is most likely to be invoked in exaggerated ways in accounting for criminal violence for those offenders whose cultural identities were particularly fragile and this was demonstrated in relation to both ethnicity and masculinity. Therefore, vulnerability in cultural identity seems to have particular effects in relation to violent crime.

7

'This is for my people' versus 'It's your fault … leave me alone': cultural meanings of criminal behaviour

IT HAS BEEN ARGUED in previous chapters that cultural experiences influence the development of identity and relationships, such that people from different communities (that vary along the continuum between what has loosely been categorised as collectivism and individualism) can have markedly different experiences of the world, of themselves and of the people with whom they interact. It is further asserted that these cultural processes, too, shape the motivations for and choices in criminal behaviour, particularly in interpersonal violence. It is suggested that this occurs through the mediating influence of construals of Self and of Other, whereby cultural experience affects people's beliefs, which in turn shape motivation for and understanding of criminal violence. These suggested differences will be explored in reference to offenders' stories of their criminal behaviour, including the meanings they make of the motivations for their criminal violence, as situated in culture.

Individualist Cultural Needs

In cultures that subscribe to individualist values, the needs of the individual supersede those of the group (Rhee et al., 1995) and, therefore, when there is conflict between the needs of the group and that of the individual, it is expected that individuals will seek to realise their own needs, even if this is at the expense of the group.

Within individualist communities, positive emotional states are generally those that arise out of situations in which the Self is promoted or enhanced and in which internal personal attributes are expressed (Markus & Kitayama, 1991). Therefore, people with experience of cultures that promote individualism can be expected to be motivated to do what makes them feel good, in order to meet their own needs, and express their own desires, with less focus on the others around them. Further to this, the structure and processes of individualist cultures encourage the expression of self-focused emotions, typically including anger, which result from either the blocking or satisfaction of individual needs (Markus & Kitayama, 1991). A primary focus on the Self, including the expression of self-focused desires and emotions, was strongly present in the accounts of offenders who participate in the dominant Australian community that values practices of individualism.

Hedonism

Nick, an Anglo–Australian man, was 23 years of age at the time of interview and was serving a 12-year minimum term of a 16-year sentence for various charges including murder, armed robbery and discharging a firearm in a public place. Much of the interview focused on the murder, which occurred when, during the process of a bag snatch, Nick struggled with the victim allegedly causing his gun to fire, fatally shooting the victim, who was a middle-aged woman. Prior to this offence, Nick had a long history of involvement in other criminal (generally nonviolent) behaviours and the following quote relates to how Nick first became involved in such antisocial conduct.

> Nick (Anglo): I started (doing crime) when I was about 12 … like the older boys in the area, that do crime, I started driving stolen cars for them. Then I started um helping people sell drugs … I've come from a broken home, my mum never really used to have much money so I um … seen it as a way of getting what I need for myself … Looking after myself … Um … getting for myself what everybody else has.

Nick describes his involvement in crime as generally being associated with a desire for money and material possessions. Nick was raised in a poor and socially disadvantaged single-parent family, and he claimed to have become involved in criminal activity in the context of the desire to provide for himself what he perceived others had access to. As such, Nick justifies his criminal behaviour by seeing himself as entitled to what 'everybody else has', even if he has to obtain what he believes he is entitled to through antisocial means. This sense of entitlement can be strong for many offenders, not just those responsible for violent crimes (Hatch-Maillette, Scalora, Huss, & Baumgartner, 2001). Nick is obviously focused on his own needs and uses the word 'myself' three times in this brief excerpt. The other is very much absent in his account and there is no mention of the people from whom he takes what he believes he deserves. To some extent, Nick's criminal behaviour appears to be a reaction to his socially disadvantaged upbringing in relation to which he would have had little agency.

> Interviewer: Has most of your crime been about money or about possessions?
>
> Nick: Yeah, I suppose so … like, I see a nice looking car and I'll steal it so I can drive it … or I see a nice looking house, I'll break in and see what they got … and take stuff for myself and sell the rest to get money.

Nick claims that he would spend the money on 'clothes … um going out places … um drugs occasionally'. This highlights that, even though Nick was committing crimes for acquisitive reasons, he was not spending the money on daily necessities like food and accommodation, but rather on 'lifestyle' goods, such as drugs and clothing. As such, Nick's offending behaviour is very much driven by the desire to fulfil his own needs, including obtaining material possessions and living an unstructured lifestyle revolving around drug use and partying with friends. Such hedonistic pursuits are prioritised in modern western society and are assumed to motivate behaviour much of the time (Triandis et al., 1988). The only reference to others in this quote relates to Nick's thinking about the property that may be either useful to him or valuable to sell.

Nick acknowledges that his lifestyle is outside of the norm, which he understands in relation to employment.

> Nick: I don't see it, like the way I should, see the way you should work 9 'til 5 … even though it's stupid, but it's the right thing to do.
>
> Interviewer: Why is it stupid?

> **Nick:** Because you waste your time all your life working 9 to 5 to save up to buy stuff when you can, um like half an hour's work and I can get what they earn in a week. Um, half an hour's work, I can get what they earn in a year sometimes.
>
> **Interviewer:** So you're supposed [emphasised] to, in inverted commas, according to our [emphasised] values, work 9 to 5?
>
> **Nick:** According to what the community says, yeah.
>
> **Interviewer:** OK and you're different to that because you don't believe in that?
>
> **Nick:** I believe in it, I just never done it. I just um ... cut corners, took shortcuts ... It was easier ... quicker.

Nick implies that he required the financial and material proceeds from crime in order to meet his needs, because he was unwilling to participate in conventional means of making money. As such, he does not endorse mainstream conservative values that do not support criminal behaviour. He recognised that he 'should' live in a manner that the majority of the community would support; however, living according to criminal values is seen as being 'easier' for Nick and presumably also more likely to bring immediate gratification, thus representing the 'shortcut' to which he refers. Working for one's money and lifestyle goods is seen as being a 'waste' of 'time' to Nick as crime is more lucrative and generally so in the more immediate term. As such, Nick does not appear to see any inherent value in employment (or other mainstream community activities) and, rather, is motivated to follow hedonistic pursuits. It could be argued that Nick presents himself as a product of the 'Lucky Country' (a common reference to Australia); he sees that he has a choice to live legitimately or to engage in criminal endeavours and receive unemployment benefits as funded by the rest of the community to whom he appears to feel little obligation.

Nick was charged with murder after an altercation with a woman when he was trying to steal her handbag. During this incident, he pulled out the gun in order to frighten the woman into submission, a struggle ensued and the gun went off, killing the woman. Nick denied any specific intent in murdering the victim but, rather, focused on his motivation to steal her handbag, as follows.

> **Nick:** When you go, like to arm rob a place, once you step in that door, it's like that's it, you don't um walk up to the counter and go 'No I'm not going to do this', turn around and walk back out — once

you walk through the door, you go for it, you've got to do it ... I tried
to get it [the handbag] off her and like I wasn't going to leave until I
actually got it.

Nick accounts for this offence in the context of his other (nonviolent)
criminal behaviour. He implied that there is a code of 'rules' that
govern such criminal behaviour and, in relation to a bag snatch, he
should not abort without gaining anything for his efforts. He thereby
denies any intent in the murder of the victim but rather he stated that
the victim, in fact, brought about her own demise by not engaging in
the 'rules' of crime appropriately, claiming that the victim would
'hopefully ... let go of it [the handbag] 'cause she's seen ... the firearm
... (B)ut um ... instead of um letting go of her handbag, she's um ...
gone for the weapon instead', causing it to fire.

Even though the death of the victim was not Nick's intent, he
clearly engaged in aggressive and violent behaviour by not only threatening a woman with a gun in order to steal her handbag, but also by
engaging in a physical struggle with the woman for her bag. Nick minimises this and accounts for his criminal behaviour by drawing on discourses of entitlement that serve to silence the other and prioritise his
perceived needs and desires.

Getting One's Needs Met

Jim was born in Australia to an Australian father; however, his mother
was of Hungarian descent. Culturally, Jim identifies as being '50/50',
although it is clear that he subscribes primarily to western individualist values that are consistent with those of the dominant Anglo–
Australian community. It is also noted that European countries and cultures are predominantly individualist in their orientation and practices.

At the time of interview, Jim was 27 years of age and he was
serving his first custodial term for a series of physical and sexual
assault charges. Jim acknowledged a long history of criminally violent
behaviour, which he was willing to discuss in some detail, although he
denied the sexual assault charges, claiming that he had consensual sex
with his partner at the time and, therefore, was not guilty of rape.

Jim offers the following in relation to a discussion of his charges
for violence:

Jim (Anglo): It was a case of the people I cared about hurting me.

Interviewer: So you got the control back?

> Jim: The only way I knew how. Talking didn't help. I'd tried, I warned them three times — you know, 'Please [whistle — as if saying "pull up"] ... Settle down!'

Jim's criminal behaviour appears to be a function of an inability to manage his emotional state, communicate his needs with others and resolve interpersonal difficulties. He articulated feeling hurt by others' behaviour towards him and he responds to this by attempting to take control in the 'only way' he knows, which is by being violent. However, Jim suggested that he warns others of the impending violence, presumably to encourage them to change their behaviour in line with his wishes or expectations. Jim's accounting for his violence suggests that his needs took priority and that there was no option for compromise or recognition of the needs of others. Others are thereby mentioned in his account, but their needs and motivations are downplayed as being secondary to Jim's, and he minimises the impact of his behaviour on others.

Jim engages in violence as a means of controlling the behaviour of others around him in order to meet his own needs and he has insight into the effects of his violence in this way. He describes himself as using violence to teach others 'a lesson', such that he is able to turn 'chaos into peace', which is a much-desired resolution to significant interpersonal conflicts. This description also implies a level of discomfort in such difficult personal situations, which contributes to Jim's perceived need to restore peace and calm, although his idea of this corresponds to others conforming to his own agenda. The following quote relates to Jim's description of this process.

> Jim: Anger, little feelings turn into big feelings, so frustration and more blah, blah, turns into anger and anger turns into rage, rage turns into hate. All of these turn into power and when unleashed physically ... on others, it becomes fear ... Fear brings a desired response ... I'm the one leading, with whatever I was feeling at the time ... and I'm the one using the violence to control the situation. Fear brings the desired result.
>
> Interviewer: Which is?
>
> Jim: I think in this case, they weren't listening, they started listening.

The most salient emotional experience for Jim in relation to this violence is anger. However, there are clearly a variety of other emotions that feed into this anger. Anger is an emotion commonly associated with stereotypical notions of masculinity within western culture (Copenhaver, Lash, & Eisler, 2000; Kinney, Smith, & Donzella, 2001) and may serve a particular self-regulatory function for men, allowing them to diffuse or create distance from vulnerable emotional states, for which they have few coping resources. Jim appears to distort his other feelings, naming them instead as anger, which serves to justify his subsequent violent behaviour. Jim interprets his anger as relating to the fact that others will not conform to his expectations and he responds to this by using violence to 'make' people listen to him. He does not express any appreciation that he is, in fact, terrorising people into doing so.

In relation to the offences that led to his incarceration, Jim describes a build-up of significant events in the period prior to his offending; the most salient of which related to the breakdown of a 5-year relationship after finding his girlfriend in bed with his best friend. As a result of this breakdown, Jim was hurt and engaged in distorted thinking about women in general, including believing that women were untrustworthy.

> Jim: I've always had problems trusting [emphasised] people … I couldn't, so … I asked for the time out. They didn't give it to me, the pressure just, on top of a steam cooker already, you know? … I didn't get the time so when … when the violence happened, it went off …

In the months leading up to the offences, Jim was involved in casual relationships with four women at the one time. He claimed to have experienced this as quite stressful, with an increase in perceived pressure when these women allegedly became more demanding of his time, despite his protestations that the relationships were casual. This precipitated his desire for 'time out'.

Jim acknowledges his emotional vulnerability in this quote, although he places responsibility with his partners to meet his emotional needs, without communicating this effectively to them. Then, if his partners do not comply in this regard — for example by giving him 'time out' — Jim responds with violence when he is no longer able to tolerate the situation, which he experiences like being in a 'steam cooker'.

Jim's accounting for 'the violence' here serves to objectify his behaviour in a way that removes agency, by suggesting that 'it (the violence) went off'. Bohner (2001) refers to this as an 'agentless passive', the use of which obscures responsibility. Jim's use of this language here is a rhetorical strategy designed to navigate blame, suggesting that 'the violence' was a response to an extreme situation and not something that Jim could control.

Jim identifies several intense emotions in response to these afore-mentioned significant events and it was these feelings that culminated in his engaging in violence when he was unable to cope or express himself in any other (more helpful) manner.

> Jim: I don't know how other people take betrayal, but I'd just been betrayed immediately ... this happens, that is automatically placed on top of that ... One big scene of betrayal and that was it ... It's all fucked up ... I couldn't handle it. You know? ... the whole [emphasised] situation was just a big picture, which has got a lot of little things happening. The big break-up, um the arguments with four girls, ah my brother ... my mate ... all come together, so it's now a really big picture ... the situation got bigger than what I could actually handle.

Above, Jim identifies feeling 'betrayed' by a number of important people in his life, most notably relating to his girlfriend having been unfaithful. Jim's account suggests that he coped with this betrayal poorly, contributing to the experience of similar negative emotions, which he describes as being 'fucked up'. Jim acknowledges his inadequacy in managing these difficult emotions, which he resorted to controlling with violence.

In summary, Jim's account of his criminal behaviour suggests that he used violence as a means of controlling his emotional state, in addition to his interpersonal situation, when he felt unable to cope in any other way. Specifically, violence was used as a means of getting his needs met, when others failed to comply with his expectations and demands. Others are present in Jim's account, although only to the extent that they have failed him or caused him emotional concern. As such, others are seen as requiring controlling and he has found violence an effective means of achieving this in order to regain control and re-establish his agenda as the priority. Hence, Jim's story of criminal violence draws on discourses of masculinity, entitlement and power, which have their foundation in individualist notions of Self.

Neutralising Personal Pain

Eloqui was born and raised in rural Victoria and, in many ways, led a fairly insular and unsophisticated existence, through which he was indoctrinated into traditional discourses of masculinity and relationships. Eloqui was allegedly the victim of sexual abuse at the age of 14 and this, in addition to other earlier developmental experiences, had a catastrophic impact on him emotionally, especially in relation to his developing identity and sexuality. In order to perhaps escape or deal with this, Eloqui left his home town and went travelling. At the time of his offending, he was living and working in a sheep shearing shed in an isolated part of rural New South Wales.

Eloqui shot four people, two of whom died, and he was serving an almost 19-year minimum term for two counts of murder, one count of attempted murder and one count of malicious wounding. The victims were two females, both of whom he had had sexual encounters with, a male who was a friend of his and who was also dating one of the female victims, and another male person who was ostensibly unknown to him.

The following quote relates to Eloqui's discussion of his relationship with one of the female victims. Specifically, he is accounting for the way in which their relationship contributed to his offending.

> **Eloqui (Anglo):** I guess it was more about her rejection of me [emphasised] and her treatment of me ... I couldn't handle her ... rejection of me in the way that she did and the name calling, then hating me and not hating and doing all that sort of stuff and ah, the fact that ah, she was in bed with another guy like within a couple of weeks, you know? And here I was, seriously [emphasised] looking for a relationship. Like when she came out to the shed, it was like ... oh ... just all of a sudden there was this safety there ... with her it's like yes I'm OK.

In this quote, Eloqui expresses anger at the victim's perceived rejection of him. However, earlier he suggested that the victim was, in fact, interested in him sexually, but he did not 'pick up on the vibes', which was partly to do with his perceived sexual inferiority and low self-esteem. It appears then that the woman may have felt that her advances were rejected by Eloqui and she responded to this by making jokes about him and accusing him of being homosexual publicly. This was experienced as like 'a dagger in my heart' for Eloqui, especially given his already fragile masculinity and sexuality.

Like Jim, Eloqui acknowledges that he had difficulties managing the emotional aspects of this situation, most especially because of the public 'attack' on his masculinity and sexuality (Mullins, 2006). This 'insult' was further exacerbated when the victim began a sexual relationship with another man (the male victim), thereby further challenging Eloqui's sexuality. Eloqui's account suggests that he placed his emotional wellbeing in the hands of this woman, including his obvious need to feel validated and 'safe', both sexually and emotionally, and this vulnerability facilitated Eloqui's overreaction to this situation.

The second female victim had also slighted Eloqui both sexually and socially.

> Eloqui: So um we'd been together and she was out at that shed and we got together out there but um, the experience that I had with her in bed was, it was a little bit too quick for her ... and she kicked me out. In front of the other woman who was in the same room as her, came in after we'd just finishing what we're doing [laughs] ... oh, it was crushing, you know ... I was gone ... to identify myself sexually was a huge thing. I had to feel OK about it and I was constantly looking for that ... And then because we were working together, well there was a lot of things said ... and the more they joked about it the more I felt that everything was sort of backing on top of me I guess [laughing].

This quote relates to a sexual encounter Eloqui had with this second female victim, in which he ejaculated in a manner that was 'too quick' for his partner, thus failing to satisfy her and adding to his sense of sexual inadequacy. The woman responded to this in a public manner that served to humiliate Eloqui further, most particularly as it was in front of the first female victim. Not surprisingly, this was experienced as 'crushing' for Eloqui, adding to his mounting sense of personal pain, which he described as feeling as if 'everything was sort of backing up on top of me'. It is interesting that Eloqui chooses to laugh at this point. This almost lightens what must have been an intense emotional experience for him, ultimately contributing to his decision to shoot four people.

This perceived challenge to Eloqui's (already fragile) masculinity was then further exacerbated by the presence of the male victim who represented the epitome of masculine success to Eloqui.

> Eloqui: ... um I was jealous of him ... I wanted what he had. He represented everything that I ever wanted, so I was envious.

This man began a sexual relationship with the woman who was initially sexually interested in Eloqui, although he did not realise this at the time.

He perceived that they were flouting their relationship publicly, which added to his sense of insult and inadequacy. Therefore, Eloqui came to identify this man with the success of masculinity, which further reinforced his internalised sense of failure as a man and a lover.

Eloqui began to experience the continued presence of this man and the two women in his life as intolerable and contributing to increasing emotional pain, for which he did not have adequate coping resources. The very public nature of these interpersonal difficulties only exacerbated this for Eloqui and contributed to his emerging desire to kill these people. Starzomski and Nussbaum (2000) argue that, in the context of personal and interpersonal disintegration, self-awareness may become so painful that violence is engaged in as a means of negating the Self and neutralising emotional pain, which is no longer able to be tolerated, and this is relevant to an understanding of Eloqui's criminal violence, as described below.

> Eloqui: [I] opened up the door to where they were and I've got the rifle in my hand and turned on the light and saw them in the room. I turned the light on to see them so I could ... you know ... I think I said a while back that I wanted them to see me [emphasised] like that [emphasised] ... Controlled and ... to dominate the situation.

In committing the crime, Eloqui used a rifle belonging to the male victim, so that the man was shot and killed with his own gun. This was particularly meaningful for Eloqui in being able to assert himself and purge the emotional pain he perceived these people had caused him. This quote creates a very powerful image of Eloqui standing in the doorway in front of the victims while he shot them, so that they would see him and know it was him who had taken their lives. This image exaggerates strength and masculinity, in the face of what had been perceived as a mounting attack for Eloqui. In this sense, he was able to establish the 'ultimate' control over these people who had caused him so much pain and he wanted them to know who was shooting them and why. This behaviour appears to have been designed to establish reputation and masculinity in the eyes of the victims (Mullins, 2006), who, for Eloqui, are the sources of challenge to the same.

The following quote relates to Eloqui's own understanding of his criminal behaviour.

Eloqui: When I was standing at the door, it was … 'How dare youse'
— you know, 'It's your fault I feel the way I do'. 'It's your fault … I'm
not fitting in, just go away, leave me alone.'

Others are strongly present in this quote, although only to the extent
that they are sources of emotional pain for Eloqui. He blames the
victims for how he is feeling and suggests that the only way he will be
placated is through the absence or removal of these people, which will,
in turn, neutralise his pain. In shooting the victims, Eloqui claimed to
have felt relaxed, with a sense of relief, as if he were 'purging I guess in
some way', thus alleviating his pain without consideration for the
other people involved.

In accounting for his crime in this way, Eloqui is clearly describing
how his offending behaviour was couched in individualist notions of
coping with self-focused emotions and confused identity. Eloqui's
story of his offending is rich and multilayered and perhaps the best
example of purist individualism resorting in criminal violence. In
essence, Eloqui engaged in the criminal behaviour because the victims
made him feel bad about himself.

Upholding a Principle

The last theme pertaining to the meanings for criminal violence in the
individualist group relates to the desire to uphold an important principle. In other words, violence was engaged as a means of teaching a
lesson to the victim, who was seen to have wronged the personal standards of the offender.

Norm was born in Australia and raised within conventional Anglo-
centric dominant socialisation practices. He was 34 years of age at the
time of the interview and had a long history of involvement in the criminal justice system, including having spent various periods of time in
custody dating back to his early adolescence. Therefore, in addition to
the cultural influences of mainstream Australia, Norm was also subject
to the cultural ' gaze' of the antisocial or criminal subculture, which also
informs his criminal behaviour and performed identity.

Norm was incarcerated for a home invasion, in which a man was
deliberately targeted and violently assaulted. Norm offered the following
in response to being asked why he believes he committed this offence.

Norm (Anglo): I don't know, just to be one of the boys, the boys
were going so I was going. So, not, not, not peer pressure or nothing

> it was my (emphasised) choice ... I think he deserved it and that. My
> mates were going so I was going ...

Norm has strong values associated with loyalty and mateship, which
are seen as solid Australian values within this community, but are also
morals strongly prized within the criminal subculture. This is relevant
in the sense that he was with friends at the time the offence was committed and he allegedly went along with the suggestion of his friends
to commit the offence as one of them knew the female victim personally. Norm subsequently took the 'rap' for his co-offenders, thereby
maintaining criminal loyalty. Norm was the only one of the offenders
from a culture that prioritises individualist values to have offended in
the presence of others, and while he acknowledges that the presence of
co-offenders gave him the necessary impetus to retaliate against the
victim in the way that he did, he is quick to emphasise his autonomy
and independence, claiming that his own behaviour was motivated
primarily by the desire to uphold a personal principle. As such, he dis-
misses the influence of 'peer pressure', and emphasises that it was 'my
choice' to offend, which he relates to the fact that he believed the
victim was deserving. Therefore, even though the presence of his
friends was important, Norm needs to be seen as independent and
responsible for his own behaviour, consistent with both masculine
and individualist discourses. However, both discourses of loyalty/
mateship and independence/autonomy are salient for Norm in understanding his offending behaviour.

According to Norm, the victim deserved to be violently assaulted
as his behaviour transgressed a principle that was important to Norm.

> **Norm:** ... to actually just go somewhere and kick someone's door in
> and that ... I know it's wrong to do, but if there's a principle behind it
> ... the principle I felt was right.
>
> **Interviewer:** So what's the principle, if you could say it, like succinctly
> in a sentence?
>
> **Norm:** Like the one my father told me. You don't ... hit girls. Like,
> you know? ... see my principle was if you want to bash a female, well
> cop it on the chin when you get bashed back. So, even though it was
> wrong to go there and kick the door in ... part of my, my thoughts
> were it's right that he gets bashed. So, it justified doing it.

This quote relates to Norm's belief that it is inappropriate for a man to
hit a woman. There is a history to this principle in that it was handed

down to Norm by older male relatives. He uses the word 'girls' in articulating this principle and this word renders women to a subordinate
position, where they are seen as being weak and in need of male protection, as discussed in an earlier chapter. Later in this quote, Norm
refers to women as females and the use of this term in this context
serves to objectify women and render them both silent and impotent.

The male other (i.e., the victim) is present in Norm's account,
although he is not imbued with any respect, such that his feelings
should be acknowledged or taken into account. This is the result of his
behaving in ways that are inconsistent with Norm's values. Norm suggests that if a man physically assaults a woman, he should expect physical retaliation from other men. Norm uses this rationale to justify his
criminal behaviour, which he acknowledges as 'wrong', although his
behaviour is considered to be justified by the principle he believes he
is upholding, which overrides any moral code. In behaving this way,
like Eloqui, Norm describes his offending as giving him a sense of
emotional release and 'closure', such that he felt he had acted on the
principles that were important to him.

Norm's criminal violence is, therefore, seemingly motivated by
personal or individualist needs, as he is responding to and performing
his principles, while at the same time constructing a particular identity for himself. This identity is of someone who is strong, capable,
independent, protective, moralistic, loyal and bound by principles.

An examination of accounts of the criminal violence perpetrated
by these offenders suggests that their offending occurred as a means of
meeting personal needs and furthering self-interest. These needs
related to the pursuit of hedonism or personal advantage, including
material possessions and financial resources (significant capital in
individualist cultures), the expression of emotion or resolution of a
personal or interpersonal conflict, in addition to upholding important
personal principles. These categories are not mutually exclusive and it
is argued that the ways in which these men offended and the meanings
that they made of their crime are couched in cultural discourses available within individualist communities, such as Australia.

For many, violence can be used as a means of communication and
is often related to the emotional experience of anger (Howells, 2004),
the expression of which can enable someone to be truly heard
(Phillips, 1998). For some people, particularly men, the experience of

anger may, in fact, be related to a number of other painful or uncomfortable emotions with which they perceive themselves to have few coping resources (Jakupcak, Tull, & Roemer, 2005; Moore & Stuart, 2004). As such, anger and ultimately violence become the expression of what is unable to be communicated through any other means. This also serves the purpose of encouraging others, through fear, to manage their behaviour in such a way that emotional peace for the offender is restored.

Further to this, in modern western society, with its focus on individualism, people are taught that to tolerate is unacceptable and, rather, it is important to voice discontent or negative feelings to relevant others, in an attempt to both develop personally and to heal relationships (Presdee, 2000). By extension, such practices may inadvertently encourage violence, particularly in those who have limited insight and personal coping resources or may otherwise have difficulties communicating by other methods. The words of Poynting et al. (1999) are particularly powerful in describing this process: 'Violence compensates for the words that are not available'.

Engaging in socially coercive behaviour that is designed to meet one's communication and emotional needs (Tedeschi & Bond, 2001) is couched in the principles of individualist culture, where as a by-product of the socialisation process individuals are encouraged to pursue their own needs and actualise their personal attributes, even if this is at the expense of others, who are either absent or silenced in the accounts of offenders' criminal violence.

It is also suggested that criminal violence may also be employed in order to bring about an end to an unpleasant or otherwise confronting situation (James et al., 2002). According to the stories of offenders reviewed here, the degree to which any such situation is experienced as aversive appears to depend on the frustration of individual needs and restriction on personal expression, consistent with individualist cultural values. To some extent, this may be a function of the experience of social disadvantage, which, in competitive modern western culture, can engender a sense of powerlessness (Presdee, 2000). Further, James, Seddon and Brown (2002) suggested that in western society individuals may use violence as a means of counteracting this powerlessness and neutralising the personal pain associated with a lack of meaning and agency.

To this end, violence may be used as a way to restore order, enact retribution or create justice. Justice is a powerful human motive (Staub, 2003), and has been invoked throughout history as a justification for violence or aggression (Bond, 2004), such as in public riots, the War on Terror, or vigilante crimes. According to social interactionist theory, coercive behaviour (including aggression and violence) is one of the means by which people achieve social control and justice (Tedeschi & Bond, 2001). This is likely to be even more salient in situations in which interpersonal relationships are at issue, where in order to achieve one's aims, other people must be negotiated.

Often the use of aggression or violence is a short-term solution to an immediate problem for which the person seeks relief but lacks other means of achieving their set goals. This may be especially powerful for offenders who tend to be lacking in social and self-regulation skills that provide the material, personal, social and psychological resources to get their needs met through other means (Browne & Howells, 1996; Day, Howells, Heseltine, & Casey, 2003). Such practices are also couched in modern individualism, whereby social bonds are weakened and coercive tactics are encouraged in the pursuit of individual gratification, which is prioritised as a function of cultural understandings (Bond, 2004).

Collectivist Cultural Needs

In contrast to the above cases, within cultures that espouse collectivist values, the needs of the group are seen to overrule those of the individual (Rhee et al., 1995). The group is idealised (Westen, 1985) and seen as the means by which people realise their needs of identity and belonging. As such, harmony is prized and people are expected to behave in ways that facilitate greater social goals, often to the detriment of individual pursuits (Andersen & Chen, 2002; Markus & Kitayama, 1991). As such, in more collectivist societies, violence, coercion and aggression are inhibited, as they typically relate to self-interest (Tedeschi & Bond, 2001), which is inconsistent with the values of such cultures.

Within group-oriented communities and cultures, individuals are driven to action that facilitates relationships and connectedness with others (Markus & Kitayama, 1991). Typically these others are members of the person's in-group, and those in the out-group can be treated quite harshly. Therefore, people from more collectivist cultures are motivated by other-focused emotions, such as sympathy, shame and communion, which have their foundation in interpersonal relationships. People subscribing to these cultural values are thus more likely to sublimate behaviours that prize the expression of individual needs in deference to acting in ways that are consistent with the collective norms of their internalised community or group. This may be true even for those who, through migration, have settled in countries with significantly different value systems, and it may even be true for those who were born in Australia to migrant parents.

Given the social foundations of collectivist cultures, the depth and quality of relationships differs considerably from those in cultures prioritising individualism, and important relationships, including friendships, are typically highly intimate and long-standing (Triandis et al., 1988). Further to this, because of the nature of the relationships and the intense bonds and obligations that develop, individuals may engage in criminal behaviour that has important cultural meanings within the group (Maris & Saharso, 2001). At times, criminal behaviour can be perpetrated by individuals who see themselves as representative of the group (Wetherell & Potter, 1992), and who ostensibly experience the goals of the group as being their own.

In sum, individuals in collectivist cultures interpret and make meaning of their behaviour in reference to their obligations, responsibilities and relationships with others, and this is true also for criminal violence. Following is a discussion of the ways in which offenders from collectivist cultures made sense of their criminal violence. Specifically, violent crimes were committed in order to stand up for the group, fulfil obligations to important others or to save face in front of important others.

Standing Up for the Group

Richarn was born in New Zealand and came to Australia as an adolescent. Living in New Zealand, he identified culturally as a New Zealander, although he maintained some distance from the White majority in that country. Richarn described being able to connect more strongly with his parents' Samoan cultural heritage when he relocated to Australia, seemingly in response to the difficulties he experienced adjusting to Sydney's multicultural landscape as a member of a minority group. It was within this context that he spoke of experiencing cultural 'pride', in addition to a desire to know more about and experience more of the Samoan culture.

Not long after arriving in Australia, Richarn was involved in the bashing murder of a Lebanese taxi driver, whom he claimed had been making racist comments about Pacific Islander peoples. The offence was committed in the presence of two co-offenders, also of Samoan descent, who supported Richarn in his attack on the victim. Following, is an extract from Richarn's account of the context in which this violence occurred.

> **Richarn (Samoan):** Before we jumped in … he started mumbling about how Islanders kept running away from him um every time they drop them off at the destination and … he started taking it out on us — he started making racial comments where Islanders are too poor … we didn't mind it we just let that one go … and then he kept going, kept going, about being 'Look youse are coconuts, coconuts are stupid' … and then I pulled out my money, I threw it at him, and I go, 'Look you can have the money', and then he kept going about Islanders, 'Look youse are bad people' — that's when things started getting out of hand — you know, the first time that someone's actually being racist … and it didn't really hurt as much but the more I thought about it like I kept saying to myself … look … this is my [emphasised] pride, this is my, my people. You know, we didn't do anything wrong …

Richarn suggests that the victim made a series of derogatory comments towards him and his co-offenders that implied that all Pacific Islanders were poor people and, moreover, were immoral people who cheated on their fares. Richarn claims that the victim referred to he and his co-offenders as 'coconuts', which was experienced as a disparaging term referring to people of Pacific Islander descent.

Richarn made repeated reference to the fact that the victim allegedly 'kept going' in his verbal abuse, thereby increasing Richarn's ire. This is further cemented by the fact that Richarn suggests he let the initial insults slide, implying a certain degree of graciousness in his interaction with the victim. However, despite specific requests to desist, Richarn claimed that the taxi driver continued in his alleged barrage of racist comments about Pacific Islanders. It is, however, noted that Richarn was also inebriated during this incident and, therefore, his recollection of events may be questionable. Regardless, this is the way in which he has made sense of his criminal behaviour.

In the context of this purported abuse, Richarn equates himself with all Samoans, making reference to 'my pride' and 'my people', suggesting that he internalised the greater Samoan (and Pacific Islander) community as being constitutive of his own identity, thereby motivating his violence. As such, it appears that Richarn felt compelled to act against the taxi driver, in order to stand up for his people and right the perceived injustice levelled against them by the victim's behaviour. Further to this, during the attack, Richarn made racist comments to the victim, referring to him as a 'rag head' and a 'camel fucker', presumably in an effort to dehumanise and objectify the victim by pushing his racist agenda, thereby making it easier to behave in a violent and abusive manner (Ressler et al., 1993; Turvey, 1999).

As stated, Richarn committed the crime in the presence of two Samoan co-offenders and the following quote relates to his perception of the role these people played in his offending.

> Richarn: I didn't want to do it … but yet I was sort of torn between, look my friends are here and I didn't want to look like an idiot, and not do anything … and basically it was just about doing the cool thing instead of the right thing … and it's also like a sense of belonging, I wanted to belong.

Richarn acknowledges that the presence of his co-offenders went some way to encouraging him to violence and this was motivated by his desire to be liked and accepted by these people, who were also members of his cultural community. The connection with the Samoan culture and community had taken on increasing importance for Richarn in the period leading up to his offending and, therefore, feeling as if he belonged to a group of Samoan youths went some way to facilitating Richarn's sense of cultural pride. In this excerpt, Richarn also identifies another powerful motive for his criminal behaviour, which relates to his desire not to look like an 'idiot' in front of his co-offenders. Although meeting Richarn's needs, this can also be conceptualised as a group-oriented motive, as Richarn's expressed desire to belong was more related to his need to be identified culturally with other Samoans, which helped him establish cultural pride, than it did with social motivations relating to the need to identify with a network of peers.

In summary then, Richarn is suggested to have engaged in criminal violence as a means of protecting the perceived identity of his cultural community, who were a significant part of his own performed identity.

Lucky was born and raised in Fiji and came to Australia in 1996. At the age of 22 years, Lucky, and several co-offenders also of Fijian descent were involved in the murder of an Indian taxi driver who was violently assaulted and stabbed. Lucky's account of his offending is complex and suggests that there were several layers of meaning for him in the offending. First, his crime was partly motivated by the desire to protect his younger cousin.

> **Lucky (Fijian):** I was ah … more standing up for my cousin — I mean 'cause I don't care what happens to me, you know what I mean? … I thought more for my blood than myself …

Lucky claims that he became violent with the victim in response to observing the taxi driver threaten his younger cousin. In accounting for this behaviour, Lucky draws on culturally relevant discourses of supporting and protecting one's family members. Specifically, he implies that his behaviour was motivated by a selfless desire to protect one's 'blood', whose needs are seen to take priority over one's own. Such an account highlights kinship responsibilities, as Lucky has been taught culturally that one should 'never leave your countrymen behind'. This notion of 'blood' extends beyond family and also relates to the entire Fijian community, for which Lucky feels some responsibility and obligation. This is relevant in understanding Lucky's motivation for criminal violence. The following quote relates to the importance of the Fijian culture in his offending.

> **Lucky:** I know this sounds bad but, I mean, I'll be straight up with you — you may not know — things that happen back home in Fiji … But um … not only once, twice, a couple of times Indians just try to take over Fiji, know what I mean? … 'cause I knew he was Indian … and I knew I was Fiji, no way, they didn't take my land and no way he wouldn't take my pride …

Lucky identifies the culture of the victim early on in the interview. On specific questioning, Lucky asserts that the culture of the victim was irrelevant in relation to his offending behaviour; however, later, he goes on to discuss in some depth, how Indian people have disadvantaged native Fijians and attempted to take over Fiji on many occasions, suggesting that his fight with the victim had a history that long superseded their coming face to face. If left unavenged, Lucky perceived that the victim's behaviour would have negated his cultural pride and somehow diluted the integrity of 'his' land and 'his' people. Lucky's comments to this effect are powerful and suggest that his personal identity became conflated with that of his entire cultural community, much like Richarn. As such, Lucky felt a powerful need to stand up for all Fijians and retaliate against this Indian taxi driver, not only for the slight on his family or his masculinity, but for the history of Indians taking over Fiji. Lucky referred to refusing to let the victim take 'my pride', which was important on a number of levels in this situation. Therefore, like Richarn, Lucky accounts for his violence as being motivated by the desire to maintain group pride and integrity. This was especially salient for Lucky, given the fragility of his cultural identity, which was compromised by his being 'half-blooded'.

Kadr's accounting for his criminal violence is not discussed separately here, as his story was somewhat 'thin'. However, succinctly, Kadr suggested that he engaged in violence in order to communicate his dissatisfaction at allegedly being referred to as 'fucking wogs' by a group of 'Aussies', who then told him that he should 'go back to your country'. Engaging in violence in this way is not dissimilar to Jim's accounting of violence as a means of communication and problem-solving. Taking a culturally situated perspective on Kadr's account, it is suggested that, given his fragile cultural identity in the context of perceived entrenched and systemic racism, Kadr felt compelled to act in order to re-establish his sense of group/cultural identity. In other words, through his actions, Kadr perceived he could resist the influence of racism on behalf of his cultural community, whom he claimed had been scapegoated and disenfranchised as a result of certain political and world events, such as the War on Terror and the Tampa Boat Crisis (Poynting et al., 2004; Saxton, 2003).

To summarise, the criminal violence of these men appeared to occur in response to a perceived need to stand up for their (ethnic/cultural) group in order to maintain the integrity of their people in the face of perceived attack. In these situations, both Lucky and Richarn conflated their individual identities with those of their larger cultural group, such that they felt the need to respond on behalf of the group. This was particularly powerful as the ethnic cultural identities of these men were inherently fragile, therefore requiring greater (public) demonstration and recognition.

Fulfilling Obligations

Genuine was born in Vietnam and came to Australia as a young child, after having fled his home country as a refugee in a boat, with the crossing killing the majority of his family. Genuine speaks with some affection about Australia and he identifies himself as being Vietnamese–Australian culturally. However, he is clearly more strongly aligned with Vietnamese and Asian cultures and, in fact, goes some way to actively separate himself from 'Australians', whom he imbues with negative qualities.

Genuine appears to have had somewhat of a difficult home life and, during his adolescent years, he became increasingly estranged from his family and involved in a peer network of delinquent Asian youths, with whom he participated in a gang. He describes this gang as taking on the emotional cadence of a family for him, such that he experienced a sense of connection and obligation with his gang 'brothers'.

Along with several co-offenders, also from the same gang, Genuine was involved in a violent offence perpetrated in retaliation for an attack on a friend, who was also a fellow gang member.

> **Genuine (Vietnamese):** A friend of mine, that day, got bashed, real damaged, physical damage … and I wasn't happy — how I felt for not being there and helping … I came to fix it up.

Genuine's words carry a strong sense of obligation and duty to those important people with whom he has a connection; in this case, a friend of his who also participated in the same gang. As a consequence of Genuine's felt duty to this person, he believes he should have been there to help his friend in his time of need and Genuine claims that he perceived a need to 'fix it up' for this person, such that he could perform this obligation.

The experience of his friend being physically assaulted has resonance with other previous experiences in Genuine's life in which he felt as if he was unable to fulfil his obligations to important others. In the following quote, Genuine describes how his younger brother was shot some years ago when Genuine was in custody.

> **Genuine:** [long pause] … I knew I had to do something, like I was more … arked up [upset and angry] than anyone else, you know … I remember when I was in jail, my little brother got shot — my blood brother — my little brother got shot in the leg … even though it was only a .22 bullet that shot him in the ankle, I wasn't happy, you know,

> I didn't deal with it very good ... I was in boys home, I couldn't do
> nothing ... So when something happened again, I didn't take it too
> good ... it's like all over for me again, you know what I mean? It
> happened again, but this time I can [emphasised] do something
> about it.

As a result of being incarcerated at the time his brother was shot,
Genuine was unable to either protect his brother or to respond in
retaliation on his behalf and this was clearly very difficult for him.
Therefore, when his friend was injured, there were parallels for
Genuine that contributed to his decision to offend in this situation.
Genuine appears to equate his friend and fellow gang member with a
'blood' brother, thus extending his sense of responsibility and obligation to this person even though he is outside of the family per se.
Genuine appears to have experienced a sense of shame at having not
been there to protect this person, thereby motivating his subsequent
violence. In this way, others are strongly present in Genuine's account
and it is essential to appreciate the importance of these relationships
in his life in order to understand Genuine's criminal violence. These
relationships also include the wider group to which Genuine is connected, which in this case refers to his gang.

> Genuine: [long pause] ... It's pride ... because words get around, you
> know what I mean? You don't want to put a bad impression on ...
>
> Interviewer: On your group?
>
> Genuine: Yeah because ... if something happened to someone, you
> know, you don't often hear the good thing that happened to them ...
> you only hear the bad thing. If someone got shot, if someone got
> stabbed, you will hear who and why, and they'll have their ideas of
> who did it, you know what I mean? More action than words gets
> around ...

Genuine describes how he gains a sense of pride from furthering the
reputation of his group, although this also relates to the sense of pride
and identity that he gains as an individual who is accepted by the
group. Importantly, for Genuine, this pride engenders a sense of obligation and duty to those also involved in this gang and this is an
important motivation for group-oriented behaviour, including criminal violence (Aumair & Warren, 1994; Staub, 1988). He believes that
'actions speak louder than words' within his (subcultural gang) community and, therefore, Genuine's involvement in violent offending can

be understood as being motivated by the desire to fulfil his obligations to important others in his life, which include not only his friend and fellow gang member, but the gang as a whole.

Ngahau was born in Australia to parents of Tongan origin and he reportedly spent much of his childhood in Tonga, returning to Australia intermittently. He identifies strongly with the Tongan cultural community and expresses pride in his ethnic cultural heritage.

Ngahau has a long history of involvement in antisocial activity and has a well-established criminal identity, revolving around a consistent network of antisocial peers. Ngahau was serving a jail sentence for two separate series of offences and he accounted for these differently. While to some extent Ngahau has clearly internalised materialistic and individualist values that have motivated his criminal behaviour, at least superficially Ngahau also accounts for his offending by referring to discourses of loyalty and obligation to friends, consistent with values of collectivism.

> **Ngahau (Tongan):** The first one I was with some um, some friends … ah one of my mates, he spotted some blokes in a car that … I don't know, he had troubles with or something. I don't know what happened. I just seen him run over … and I ran over too to see what's going on, he started yelling at the bloke … things happened, worse come to worse and I just pulled the bloke out and just bashed him … Took his keys out of his car so he wouldn't be able to drive it … I don't know what the full story was but 'cause of my mate, I'm loyal to my friends …

In this quote, Ngahau identifies a strong sense of loyalty and commitment to his friends, such that he would respond with violence in support of his friends, without even knowing 'what the full story was'. This suggests that Ngahau's loyalty is unconditional and unquestioned and, in this case, motivates his engagement in criminal behaviour in order to protect the rights of his internalised group members.

Ngahau's use of the phrase 'worse come to worse' is interesting here, as it suggests that the violence was undesirable. However, to Ngahau, violence is obviously acceptable in certain situations, one of which is clearly related to performing loyalty through defending a friend's honour. This suggests that 'normal' moral standards may be overruled in some circumstances, particularly where duty and obligation are implicated. This has its foundation in collectivist cultural values that prioritise important relationships and connectedness, the maintenance of which is assumed to be an important motivation for behaviour (Markus & Kitayama, 1991; Triandis et al., 1988), including interpersonal violence.

Saving Face

In addition to criminal violence occurring as a means of promoting or protecting the needs of the wider group or fulfilling important obligations, offenders from collectivist cultures also identified engaging in criminal behaviour in order to 'save face' in front of the group, whether actual or perceived. To contextualise the following discussion, Genuine provides a good description of being aware of the need to save face (see Goffman, 1959; Sanko, 1994).

> **Genuine (Vietnamese):** You know, family — the value — the way you carry yourself, you know what I mean? You eat to please yourself but you dress to please others ... even our Asian community, you don't want to walk down the street and see your relatives looking at you, 'Oh look at him, what he's wearing is wrong, he's living on the street', you know what I mean? 'Cause that going to reflect back to your mum and dad ... worst [emphasised] case is, you will not want them to say, you know, oh, they can look down at you.

Genuine's words identify an awareness of the impact of one's behaviour in relation to important and connected others. He feels the need to maintain a certain level of behaviour and appearance, as social judgment is assumed to be pervasive and also applied to others with whom one is associated. In this context, saving face refers to behaving in a manner that honour and obligation are fulfilled, and the reputation of others is maintained.

Iash was born in Australia, but identifies strongly with his Lebanese cultural heritage. Iash actively distances himself from the mainstream Australian community at times, suggesting that he is no longer comfortable in this country due to perceived systemic racism and concern over the global anti-Muslim sentiment that has arisen post-September 11. These beliefs allow Iash to perceive aggressive intent in social interaction and to justify retaliatory aggression in his interaction with others (Bradley, 2003).

In relation to the criminalisation process Iash experienced, he describes having come from a socially disadvantaged family, who struggled financially to provide for a large number of children. Therefore, as Iash transitioned into adolescence, he became involved

in antisocial behaviour as a means of making money and buying possessions — an inherently individualist motive. However, much of
Iash's antisocial sentiment and criminal behaviour is couched within
the discourses made available to him through his family and cultural
community, which are predominantly collectivist in nature. Following
is Iash's account of his initial crimes, which relate to his avenging a
man who refused to pay him money owed for illegal business activities. Iash and several Lebanese co-offenders kidnapped this man and
another person and then 'tortured' and physically assaulted them
before Iash took the man's car.

> **Iash (Lebanese):** It was all about like reputation and that, you know?
> ... Like, I've had a reputation growing up — nobody mucks around
> with us, nobody rorts us, nobody talks shit about us, you know, and if
> people ever tried to, they know what will happen to them ... and
> people start to think twice if they ever tried to rob me or rob my
> family or, you know, tried to rort me or my family members and that.
>
> **Interviewer:** So whose reputation were you thinking of? Was it just
> your own or your own and your family?
>
> **Iash:** Oh it was mine, my cousin's, was my uncle's ... my brother's, you
> know? ... because I come from a real large background Lebanese
> family ... with uncles and cousins and all that ... Because a lot of them
> are incarcerated as well and for them to hear that 'Oh yeah, [Iash's last
> name suppressed] got ripped' ... and it rubs off in a bad way on them
> too. You know like 'Oh yeah look at him, he's nothing, he's a gronk
> [weak idiot], let's rob him', this sort of stuff ... So I wasn't just thinking
> about me, I was thinking about them as well at the time.

Iash identifies his offending as being motivated by the desire to preserve reputation. However, for Iash, his personal reputation also
relates to that of his extended family and important others to whom
he is connected. As such, others are strongly present in Iash's account
and contribute to a motivation for violence. Specifically, Iash expresses
an awareness that his reputation and behaviour impacts on the wider
group. He claims that if he is to be 'ripped' — that is, taken advantage
of by others — his reputation, and that of his family, will be sullied
within their (cultural and antisocial) community. In this situation, he
suggests that he will be seen as a 'gronk', which is a derogatory term
used within the jail culture to refer to a weak idiot who is not deserving of respect. Again, this term will implicate other members of his
family and encourage people to take advantage of him and his family.

Iash's account suggests that he was aware of this complexity of reputation and relationship in making a decision to engage in violence against the victim.

T also offended in order to save face in front of the group, although in this case, the group at issue was his co-offenders. T was born in New Zealand but identifies as Samoan, consistent with the ethnic cultural heritage of his parents. T was serving time for a serious sexual assault that was perpetrated on an adult woman in the context of a home invasion initially motivated by the desire to obtain money to spend on drugs and alcohol. Around the time of the offences, T was using illicit drugs heavily and had been associating with antisocial peers. He had been drinking in the presence of his co-offenders, most of whom were also Pacific Islanders, on the night of the offence and, although T did not know his co-offenders particularly well, he was drawn into the sexual assault of the victim when his other co-offenders allegedly started to rape the woman.

> **T (Samoan):** ... well, one of the blokes just started pulling his pants down ... and that's how it started. He pulled his pants down ... and then he got her to orally, orally um orally sex and shit and um ... and another bloke jumped in and then ... we jumped in ... It just um ... like it, yeah, it just happened, like I think oh ... I was just following everyone else, what everyone else was doing, but yeah it, it just happened and I just ... just went with it.

The sexual offending was very difficult for T to talk about, as evidenced by his ineloquent account, frequent pausing and conversation fillers, such as 'um'. He required considerable prompting to be able to discuss these issues at interview. T denies any sexual intent in his behaviour but rather accounts for his offending as occurring in the context of the desire to conform to the expectations of his co-offenders and thereby save face in their presence. That is, he claims to have experienced a pressure to become involved in the sexual abuse of the victim because of the other men present at the time. This was an implicit pressure that also draws on issues of masculinity and identity for T.

T was so disgraced by his offending behaviour that he gave himself up to police not long after the rape. He did not disclose the identities of his co-offenders to police as this would be against the normative criminal code (subcultural values). The following quote refers to T's decision to hand himself into authorities.

> T: Oh, it's disgraceful, I feel disgraced and that ... disgraced for my family, sad for my culture and my people and I just feel ... sad for what I did to the lady ... I was feeling a bit ... just giving my family a bad name ... and giving Samoans a bad name.

In addition to engaging in criminal violence as a function of his connection to a group of peers, T's post-offence behaviour also revealed an awareness of group consistent with values that are more collectivist in nature. T describes finding his offending *'disgraceful'*, presumably in relation to his own moral values about appropriate behaviour. However, further to this, T expresses sadness at the potential impact of his behaviour on both his family and entire cultural community. His family are the priority, followed by an obligation to the Samoan culture and the female victim appears to take the least priority in T's account of his sexual offending behaviour. In this sense, groups of others are seen to take precedence over individuals and it is the sense of shame he feels at challenging the 'face' of his family and his people that prompted T to hand himself into police.

Sammy was born in Australia and identifies as a Turkish–Australian, acknowledging the cultural legacy of his family. Sammy generally aligns himself with both Turks and/or Middle Eastern Muslims and, at times, he actively distances himself from mainstream 'Australians'. In addition to being acutely aware of his cultural allegiance to Turkey and to Muslims, Sammy has also internalised the cultural obligations of the criminal community in prison, thus describing himself as having been 'institutionalised' after having spent so many years in custody.

Sammy was initially incarcerated for break and enter, and armed robbery charges; however, while in jail he was involved in the murder of another inmate who had threatened him in relation to the supply of drugs in the jail. Sammy offended in partnership with another Turkish inmate, and the victim was identified as having been Australian, as was the victim's support person in the altercation. The following quote relates to Sammy's account of the antecedents to this violence.

> Sammy (Turkish): Well, they come up, they smashed my window, they called me a dog [informant] and in jail you get called a dog you can't walk away from that, you have to go and face them and usually it leads to a knife ... Well they called me a dog in front of the whole unit ... and the jail ... the way it's set up, you have to go out on the main walkway to go and get your buy-up. You can stay in your wing

and hide out, but you're not going to get your buy-up, you're not
going to get your cigarettes and you may as well be in the bone yard
on protection. Well I weren't going to do that, you know what I mean?

Sammy claims that he was referred to as a dog by the other inmates
and the social impact of this has been discussed earlier. However, the
important issue for Sammy here is that the insult was offered in the
presence of 'the whole unit', thus, challenging his 'face' in front of his
community in jail. This insult has particular effects on his reputation
in jail, which also implicates Sammy's cultural community.

The most salient community for Sammy in relation to his murder
of the victim was the jail community, which, given a history of incarceration, served to function as his primary cultural community. Sammy's
account highlights his awareness of the issues of 'face' within the jail
community. In considering retaliation with violence, he comments 'I'm
not a weak cunt, I've done nothing to deserve it and I'll go out and deal
with it'. As such, he is aware of the potential social repercussions for him
and his relationships with others, should he not respond to the challenge laid down by the other inmates who referred to him as a dog.

Sammy's offending behaviour is suggested to be the direct result
of cultural influence on identity and relationship, and can be
explained in reference to certain taken for granted assumptions or
cultural values that provide the foundation for his behaviour. These
relate to Sammy having killed the victim in order to save face within
his cultural community — that is, jail — as well as the community of
Muslim and Middle Eastern inmates, and his extended family
network in the community. This behaviour is designed to save face
and maintain honour, and has a history in Turkish society (Maris &
Saharso, 2001), although it is not clear to what extent this contributed
to his involvement in the murder. To construct this story, Sammy
draws on notions of war, including discourses of provocation and survival, suggesting that he had no other choice but to retaliate physically
against the victim who ostensibly set him up by engaging certain rules
for violence.

There are various layers of group relevant for Sammy that operate
on him over and above that of the individual, consistent with his cultural values prioritising collectivism over individualism. Sammy talks
at length about issues of group and, more particularly, issues of group
identity that are distinguished along cultural lines between Turks and

non-Turks (insiders and outsiders), but also between Muslims and non-Muslims, between officers and 'crims', and between people he trusts and those he doesn't. There are many such dichotomies in his narrative, suggesting that for Sammy, identity comes from the groups in which he is involved. The following quote relates to the impact of these various group relationships and obligations.

> Sammy: ... a lot of Turks do respect me because they know I've been in jail a long time; like, a Turk will come to jail and automatically their family will ring my family and say 'Listen my son's come to jail, could you please talk to your son and make sure he's alright' ... a lot of them know me, like especially the Turkish [unintelligible] room, where my dad is all the time, a lot of the blokes, the elder blokes ... in there, they all know what I've done in jail, they know how long I've been inside and they've all got a respect for me ... I walked the line that I walked and ... I didn't shit myself and run like a little girl, and I've become a man [emphasised] in their eyes, you know what I mean?

Sammy's account indicates that he experiences a sense of cultural obligation to other Turks, particularly within the criminal justice system. Further, he implies that his murder of the victim allowed him to command the respect of others, particularly within his cultural community. He describes his offending as also allowing him to gain masculine credibility with cultural elders and this draws on stereotypical masculine images of strength, fortitude and tenacity in the sense that he was directly challenged by other men and responded with decisive violent action that neutralised the threat. Sammy directly juxtaposes his (masculine) action with the assumed weakness of 'shitting himself' and running 'like a girl'.

With respect to the murder, Sammy accounts for his behaviour as being motivated by the significant issue of group identity, such that he was not prepared to be seen by others in his community as failing to conform to cultural values; for example, by being weak, unmasculine, a dog and so on. Sammy is also aware of the impact that his behaviour in jail has on his cultural relationships within the community and this is important to him. Sammy's criminal violence has also enabled him to establish culturally sanctioned identity and validity.

In summary, the accounts of violence offered by Sammy, T and Iash suggest that their offending was motivated, at least in part, by the desire to save face in the presence of their internalised community, whether that be cultural, criminal or peer. As such, these men were aware of the implications of their behaviour for others to whom they are connected in important ways.

The above analysis of the accounts offenders from cultural groups valuing collectivist ideals gave of their criminal violence suggests that their offending was primarily motivated by group-related values. Specifically, violence is suggested to be motivated by a desire to promote or protect the interests of the group, to fulfil obligations to salient others or to save face in front of the wider collective. These offenders account for their behaviour in a way that minimises the role of the individual and, rather, prioritises the group, such that the individual takes on the emotional experience and social responsibility for the whole group and this, in turn, is manifest in the meaning offenders make of their violence.

People from primarily collectivist cultures are dependent on their connections with others for their sense of identity and understanding of the social world. They feel obligated to others and are motivated by their interpretation of group goals. There are a variety of groups that might be relevant to the individual and these may include the family unit (usually extended), a peer network or a larger collective, such as a cultural or community group.

In examining the accounts of criminal violence from offenders who have been raised with more collectivist cultural values, it was apparent that much of their criminal behaviour was motivated by the desire to stand up for the group and assert the group's needs or rights, whether this be in relation to the family, peer or other social group. This is consistent with the rather porous and inclusive Self that is hypothesised for individuals from such cultural communities (Brewer & Gardner, 1996; Triandis et al., 1988).

These offenders appealed to higher (group) loyalties or obligations in justifying their criminal behaviour. Accounting for criminal violence in this way served to further reinforce negative stereotypes of out-group members (Markus & Kitayama, 1991), and facilitate both aggression and violence. At times, these beliefs can become patterned or ritualised within a culture, such that they become a taken for granted, often contributing to acts of group violence (Staub, 1988).

Consistent with an increased awareness of and responsibility to others, offenders from collectivist cultures demonstrated a recognition of the impact of their behaviour on others, although this did not typically include the victim but rather members of salient groups, including family and community. In order to maintain these obligations and commitments, people must behave in ways that facilitate 'face saving', not only for the individual, but also for important others. Mullins (2006) suggests that a social actor is 'out of face' when he or she presents images that are inconsistent with internalised values and externalised social expectations of the group and for men, particularly, the potential loss of face may be a strong contributor to acts of violence (Sanko, 1994).

In summary, it is argued that the accounts of criminal violence offered by these offenders prioritised group obligations, all but disregarding individual need, to the extent that at times personal goals were experienced as group goals, and individual identity was confused with group identity. Criminal violence, in these cases, was seen as an extension of group responsibility and obligation, and was perpetrated in such a way that group identity and needs were publicly demonstrated.

The above analysis reveals that offenders do account for their criminal behaviour in terms of culturally situated motivations and understandings. These cultural understandings, including conceptions of Self and Other, and the complexities in connection between the two, shaped offenders' understandings of and justifications for criminal violence in important ways. Specifically, those offenders from individualist cultures prioritised their own needs and desires, and appeared to engage in criminal violence in order to meet personal needs, which included coping with difficult interpersonal situations. Those offenders from more collectivist cultures offended in order to publicly defend the group, to discharge important group-oriented obligations, which also included 'saving face', both for the individual and the relevant group.

Over and above, however, there was an apparent fragility in identity for many offenders that also contributed to their motivations for and accounts of criminal violence. Specifically, for those from more collectivist cultures, this fragility appears to be seen in predominantly cultural terms, whereas for other offenders from cultures that prioritise individualist values, the fragility in identity may be constructed in personal terms, such as relating to masculinity. Taking into account offenders' stories of their crimes, it appears that cultural motives and understandings for violence may be particularly salient for those men for whom cultural identity is fragile. This may be more powerful for those from minority groups who have experienced challenges to cultural identity, either through migration or through the perception of cultural impurity. For these people, cultural pride is especially salient.

It is also worth considering the issue of cultural pride versus individual honour in accounting for the motivations in criminal violence. In response to a perceived challenge, offenders from collectivist cultures behaved in a manner that facilitated or maintained cultural pride. However, those from more individualist cultures offended in order to maintain individual honour within culture, which related variously to material status, ability to control both the Self and Others, and in relation to behaving in a manner consistent with important moral principles. Although this refers to situated cultural meaning, for the offenders from individualist cultures, this appeared to be more a function of cultures of masculinity, criminality and individualism that prioritise the Self, in contrast to ethnic cultural discourses of collectivism that focus on relatedness and social obligation.

8

'I just lost it': offenders' rationalisations for criminal violence*

THE IDEA OF RESPONSIBILITY has long been central to the judicial process, in which it is considered crucial in terms of assigning punishment in sentencing. As Wells (2001) argued, attributions of responsibility and blame in constructions of events, such as crimes or accidents, and in determining innocence or guilt, are 'the life blood of a legal system' (p. 40). The limits of responsibility, in terms of mental illness and age, for example, have long been the stuff of legal battle; indeed, the attribution of responsibility has become crucial to recognising the socially constructed nature of crime (Roberts & Golding, 1991). Furthermore, over recent decades, there has been an increasing focus on getting offenders to 'take responsibility' for their crimes in alternative ways, rather than by just being punished. Interest in notions of restorative justice, conferencing and mediation, victims' rights, and the use of victims' statements in court are all evidence of this increasing emphasis (Braithwaite, 2002). Yet, in the context of 'moral panics' around ethnicity and crime, a resurgent conservative discourse of responsibility has

---

* This chapter was co-authored with Dr Greg Noble

often focused both on individual responsibility (thereby resisting the 'social' explanations of crime) and on the responsibility of an ethnically defined 'community', which pathologises crime as culturally determined (Collins et al., 2000). In this context, the ways offenders themselves construct responsibility is central both because it has practical implications for these alternative forms of justice, and also because, as will be suggested here, it has consequences for thinking through the relationship between crime, identity and agency.

This chapter will show that much of the rhetorical work by offenders was consistent with the literature in terms of the types of excuses and rationalisations used to negotiate responsibility both publicly and privately. However, the main focus of this chapter will be to explore two ways in which offenders navigated personal responsibility for criminal violence that have not been addressed in detail in the literature. The first of these relates to invoking the notion of a threshold, which, when breached, results in irrational and criminal behaviour that is suggested to be outside of the control of the offender. This idea is well known within forensic practice and draws on moral accounting for criminal behaviour, which has as its foundation in community discourses about crime and about criminals. For some offenders, the notion of threshold was also related to culture and this will be discussed in some depth. Second, this chapter will explore how the idea of culture is drawn on by some offenders in justifying their criminal violence, an aspect which has not been addressed adequately in the literature, but which emerges strongly when taking a culturally situated perspective on violence. Several of the offenders whose backgrounds were in cultures that prioritised values of collectivism utilised notions of culture in explaining their criminal behaviour, particularly those offenders with fragile ethnic identity as a function of migrant experience. In other words, culture is one way in which offenders may seek to negotiate personal responsibility for criminal violence. This is consistent with the increasing perception in Australia of a link between culture and crime, such that offenders are suggested to be drawing on readily available community discourses about culture and crime in accounting for their offending. In contrast, accounts of offenders from individualist-oriented cultures were generally culture absent and tended to draw on different, predominantly individualised values for understanding their experiences and explaining their behaviour.

The Need to Justify

Criminal behaviour is seen to contravene the fabric of morality that holds a community together and, as such, crimes are labelled as being deviant and are classified as such within a criminal code and a legal system that seeks to penalise wrongdoers and protect the community (Heath, 1984; Smith & Pollack, 1994). Social groups, such as communities, have dominant discourses about crime and criminals, and offenders are positioned through and according to these discourses. Consequently, offenders must navigate the social and moral consequences for their crime, against simple judgments of their behaviour, as being immoral or deviant. As such, offenders need to find ways of presenting a positive self-image, as well as defend against feelings of guilt (Hudson, 2005). This process also allows them the possibility of maintaining an identity and place *within* the community. To this end, offenders offer *accounts* of their crimes that seek to rationalise, justify or normalise their criminal behaviour (Adler & Alder, 1994; Palmer, 2003), and the more deviant the behaviour is considered, the greater the pressure to engage in this process, both publicly and privately.

According to Felson and Ribner (1981), accounts are social acts that seek to align the speaker to the listener within commonly accepted social order. Such acts take on special significance if the speaker has violated this order, thus motivating a need for social acceptance. Accounts are activated whenever the actions of the speaker have been called into question and are subject to evaluation within available social practice and discourse (Scott & Lyman, 1968). In other words, offenders are motivated to portray themselves as being 'normal' (Hudson, 2005) and this is as much for their own sense of Self, as for their relationships with Others. As such, accounting for crime is always inherently a negotiation of identity (Scott & Lyman, 1968), both personally and interpersonally.

Attempts to rationalise, justify or normalise offending will be particularly salient in social interactions where offenders are asked to directly account for their criminal behaviour, although they may also develop as part of the process an offender goes through in order to make sense of their behaviour psychologically (Potter & Wetherell, 1987). If a person believes that their behaviour is within their control, they may be held responsible and allocated blame; however, if the person is somehow able to reduce the perceived agency in their behaviour, then social responsibility is limited, as is the expectancy of punishment (Sampson, 1988). For many offenders, this is unrelated to their experience of the criminal justice system.

The process of navigating responsibility for crime is often complex and relates to the experience of guilt and shame (Hudson, 2005; Ward et al., 1997). Experiencing guilt and shame is a common response to the knowledge that one has caused pain to another (whether emotional, physical or material), and thereby engaging in rationalisations or excuses allows offenders to feel better about themselves and their behaviour through neutralising this guilt or shame.

There are two primary means by which offenders may navigate responsibility and these are in offering either *excuses* or *justifications* for their behaviour. With an excuse, offenders admit to the wrongdoing but distance themselves from responsibility by seeking to explain it in terms of reference to causal factors unrelated to the offender personally (Adler & Adler, 1994; Scott & Lyman, 1968). In contrast to excuses, justifications are those discursive acts that seek to align the offender with commonly accepted social norms. Through this process, offenders acknowledge responsibility but seek to have this responsibility negated by reference to other factors supposed to account for the wrongdoing. In other words, the behaviour is acknowledged as unacceptable but is justified within the context of particular information (Adler & Adler, 1994; Felson & Ribner, 1981).

Strategies That Negotiate Responsibility
Victim Blame
Most of the offenders sought to place some blame with the victim of their offences and this is a common strategy employed by offenders to negotiate personal responsibility for criminal violence (Doherty & Anderson, 2004; James et al., 2002; Hudson, 2005). This strategy may have its foundation in common community discourses about offenders and victims that often seek to place blame with victims of criminal acts (Egerton, 1995; Tedeschi & Bond, 2001). By invoking discourses that blame the victim for acts of violence, offenders can separate themselves from responsibility and rather, construct their behaviour as an understandable response to the acts of another (Mummendey, Linneweber, & Loschper, 1984; Wetherell & Potter, 1992).

According to Walster (1966), it is common practice for people in the community to feel compelled to assign responsibility for wrong-doing and this increases with the severity of the offending act. Further, the manner in which people allocate blame is a function of social experience, in addition to the available discourses within a community (Tedeschi & Bond, 2001). Without this attribution of responsibility, both community and personal anxiety is increased, because it appears that such acts of misfortune are haphazard and random and, therefore, unable to be anticipated or controlled (Janoff-Bulman, 1992).

A poignant example of victim blame comes from Lucky's account of his offending. Lucky was involved in the bashing murder of an Indian taxi driver. The violence started when the taxi driver allegedly took Lucky and his co-offenders 'the long way' home and then attempted to charge them for this.

> **Interviewer:** So things changed pretty much when he wouldn't take the money?
>
> **Lucky (Fijian):** Yeah ... well ... he took the money all right, but he wanted more money ... I was pissed off and ... that just topped if off, you know what I mean? ... we wouldn't have done that if ... he took the money.

In this quote, Lucky blames the victim by suggesting that he was at fault for trying to charge Lucky and his co-offenders an unreasonable amount of money for the fare. Lucky made statements that blamed the victim throughout the interview, suggesting that the victim's behaviour caused the violence to escalate; for example, by brandishing the knife that was subsequently used against him. In this way, Lucky minimised his own responsibility in claiming that the offence would not have occurred if the victim had charged them appropriately. In this way, the victim's behaviour is seen as contributing to his death.

Nick also sought to place blame on his victim, although he achieved this in a way not usually heard in work with offenders. Nick, a young Anglo–Australian man, was involved in the murder of a woman, which occurred in the context of a bungled bag snatch.

> **Nick (Anglo):** I never thought I would even um ... have to fire a firearm in my entire life ... most people in most things that I've done, as soon as they see a firearm they will — their job is to give you the cash ... and meet the armed robber's demands and um make everything go smoothly.

Nick brandished a gun in attacking the victim and seeking to steal her handbag although, as stated above, he had no intention of using the gun but rather was showing it to the victim in order to scare her into submission. The victim, however, engaged in a struggle with Nick for the handbag, causing the gun to fire, ultimately shooting and killing the victim. What is interesting in Nick's account is that he seeks to excuse his behaviour by referring to crime as being a stylised form of human interaction, in which both the offender and the victim have a set role that dictates certain rules and obligations in behaviour. By accounting for his offence in this way, Nick draws on assumed knowledge by inferring that the victim should have known the rules of this social engagement and therefore she was complicit in her death by behaving in a manner that breached the taken-for-granted roles in this situation. By doing this, Nick reduced his responsibility by indicating that his intent was not to shoot the victim, who should have behaved according to her 'job' and therefore she would not have died.

Dehumanising the Victim

In addition to blaming the victim, another means by which offenders can avoid the distress associated with acknowledging having hurt someone is to dehumanise or objectify their victim (Ressler et al., 1993; Turvey, 1999).

Ngahau has a long history of involvement in antisocial and violent practices, which are often targeted at specific people for perceived wrongdoings. He made the following statement in relation to the people he has abused through his criminal violence.

> **Ngahau (Tongan):** To me they're … just like rubbish … You know what I mean, drifting down the street … Like nothing at all.

Ngahau's description of his victims is powerful and allows him to disregard his victims, reducing any sense of empathy or guilt in relation to his criminal behaviour that has caused obvious pain to others. In fact, Ngahau claimed that he enjoyed hurting others, as it made him feel good.

> **Interviewer:** What made you feel good?
>
> **Ngahau:** Um [laughs].
>
> **Interviewer:** Why are you laughing?

> **Ngahau:** It's just, you know what I mean … going back then … ah I
> don't have any feelings at all. I didn't feel sympathy for people … to
> me … it's like a joke. Even if you got done [arrested], it was like a joke
> … so … it was like nothing to me, I mean jumping on a fella's head
> was nothing to me.

In thinking about his crime in this way, Ngahau minimised his violence and refers to it as a 'joke'. In other words, he was able to perpetrate extreme acts of violence without considering his behaviour as being serious or causing harm to others, even if he was arrested and charged for these acts. It is suggested that seeing victims in this way negates the emotional experience of offenders and therefore also the subsequent guilt at recognising the pain of others. As such, the 'human' element of the crime is minimised, rendering the behaviour somehow less offensive.

Poor Me

In addition to negating responsibility by making reference to the victim and their behaviour, offenders may also justify their offending by suggesting that they, in fact, are the victims of the particular situation that resulted in criminal action (Milsom, Beech, & Webster, 2003). By invoking 'poor me', offenders often attempt to portray themselves in a favourable light and reduce accountability for crime.

Jim, an Anglo–Australian man, was serving a custodial sentence for a series of violent crimes, including sexual assault, and he has a long history of interpersonal violence. Jim suggested that his offending was the result of a series of difficult situations in which he was taken advantage of, disrespected and dismissed by important Others in his life.

> **Jim (Anglo):** … it was more of, I looked after everybody and when I
> needed looking after, nobody was there … I'd just been shit on by
> the world … So I just got mega shit on and then I'm trying to
> organise my life so that it's getting back to normal and I keep getting
> shit from everywhere … 'Why me?'. 'Poor me'.

Jim describes the experience of interacting with others in the lead-up to the offence as if he had been 'shit on'. Further to this, there was seemingly a series of such interactions, which Jim described as 'mega shit', implying that the effect of these experiences was cumulative and extreme. This suggests that he was unfairly treated and is deserving of

both sympathy and support. Taking this position allowed Jim to minimise the severity of his subsequent violence, as well as undermine the
position that others may take in holding him accountable.

'It Just Happened'

A further way in which offenders seek to negotiate responsibility is to
minimise the extent of planning in relation to their offending, by
claiming that the crime 'just happened'. This limits obvious criminality as well as minimising intent, thereby constructing a different sce-
nario socially to acknowledging a crime was committed after careful
planning, which in turn exaggerates antisociality and portrays the
offender as both callous and dangerous. Conventionally, spontaneous
offences are seen as being less reprehensible than those that are
planned and premeditated, and this also has obvious social and psychological implications for the offender.

None of the offenders suggested that there was any planning
involved in their violence but rather their offending was claimed to be
reactive to the situation. Perhaps the most poignant example of this
was T's account of his involvement in the violent gang rape of a
woman in the context of a break and enter.

> **T (Samoan):** ... one of the blokes, you know, started pulling his pants
> down ... um and then she started giving him oral sex ... I was drunk
> and ah I just joined in ... Like I said, it just happened ... I wasn't
> thinking in my head like 'let's rape this girl', you know,' let's rape her',
> I wasn't thinking that ... it just happened ... oh I think I was just
> following everyone else, what everyone else was doing ... but ... it
> just happened and I just ... went with it.

T's account of the sexual violence suggests that the abuse was initiated
by one of his co-offenders by pulling down his pants, which somehow
prompted the victim into 'giving' his co-offender oral sex. T does not
account for the connection between these two events and this also
diminishes the assumption of criminality and deviance on behalf of
the offenders. This notion of 'giving' undermines the obvious threat
and force that would have been present in this situation, and his story
of events also minimises any direct manipulation or coercion engaged
in by the offenders in order to force the victim into sexual behaviour.

T claims that he simply 'jumped in' and imitated the behaviour of
his co-offenders and this places responsibility with his co-offenders for

initiating the assault, also minimising his own agency and initiative in the offence. He made repeated references throughout his account to the rape 'just happening' and, to some extent, this was likely motivated by the fact that T was obviously uncomfortable in discussing the sexual assault, as highlighted by his use of stilted language, frequent pauses and regular conversation fillers, such as um and ah.

Use of Passive Voice

Offenders may also choose to navigate personal responsibility by using language that removes agency or is passive in nature (Bohner, 2001; Lamb, 1991). This is slightly different to implying that criminal behaviour 'just happened', as discussed previously, although as a linguistic move it serves similar ends.

Norm was involved in a violent home invasion in which a man was seriously injured and he used passive language in various places in his account.

> Norm (Anglo): ... my friend said he had a baseball bat in the car ... So, um, that's what was used and ... at the time, like basically the security door got ripped off, the front door got kicked in ... two people went running in there, and ah one of them attacked him with the bat, um, I'd walked in the door after that was finished basically. Oh, I grabbed the bat and I hit him a couple of times with the bat ... and then we just left ... it wasn't like you know, there was no robbery, there was nothing taken ... or anything like that, it was just ... wanting to hit the bloke.

There are various examples of passive voice in this quote: 'that's [the baseball bat] what was used', 'the security door got ripped off' and 'the front door got kicked in'. The impact of this language is to reduce Norm's agency, as well as that of his co-offenders, by implying that these behaviours occurred without their active initiation. In other words, Norm and his co-offenders cannot be held accountable for what they did not initiate and could not control.

Norm claimed that his co-offenders initiated the physical assault on the victim while he was outside of the premises. He stated that he came into the home after the violence was ostensibly finished; however, he added that he, too, assaulted the victim, almost as an afterthought. Norm described how the purpose of the offence was to assault the victim and, therefore, no property was taken and the victim was not robbed. The rhetorical impact of these statements is to minimise the severity of the offence by inferring that somehow their behaviour would have been worse had they engaged in these other offences. This is an example of a linguistic strategy offenders often use in order to create a hierarchy of offending, which then implies particular personality characteristics of offenders (see Hudson, 2005). In accounting for his offending in this way, Norm suggested that he is not 'as bad' as the type of person who would engage in such violence as well as robbing the victim.

Temporary Aberration

Through the deployment of excuses and justifications, offenders attempt to absolve their responsibility for violent crime. Another of the strategies by which responsibility may be negotiated is by suggesting that the crime was precipitated by a temporary aberration in character and judgment, for example, brought about by the ingestion of drugs or alcohol, or by transitory mental illness (Hudson, 2005). This is consistent with public accounting for crime that often draws on individual pathology as a reason for offending (Ericson, Baranek, & Chan, 1991; Farrington, 1996), seeing criminals as somehow crazy either by an act of will (drug use) or by nature (mental illness). The use of such excuses allows offenders to consider their behaviour idiosyncratic rather than diagnostic (Scully & Marolla, 1994) and to see their 'will' as having been compromised by inadequate knowledge, distorted information or reduced capacity for judgment (Scott & Lyman, 1968).

Many of the offenders referred to being under the influence of alcohol and/or illicit drugs at the time of their offending, which served to either limit their memory or impair their ability to think clearly or rationally.

> **T (Samoan):** There's no way in the world, if I was straight ... there's no way in the world I would have done that crime ... I think it [drugs] just blinded me, sort of ... blinded what I was doing ... I was blinded like on how serious it was, you know?

T claims that he was using a great deal of illicit drugs in the period leading up to the offending, in response to which he described himself as having been 'a wreck', such that he was rendered 'mentally unstable', including suffering from symptoms of a drug-induced psychosis. As a result of this heavy drug use, T claimed that he was 'blinded' to the seriousness of his actions and he referred to this three times even within this brief excerpt. The use of this word is powerful, as it suggests that T was literally unable to 'see' or appreciate the nature of his illegal behaviour. By invoking the effects of drugs and alcohol, T suggested that his criminal violence was the result of a temporary suspension of rationality and 'normal' human control, implying that he cannot be held accountable for this behaviour. This may serve both public and private purposes.

Normalising/Appealing to Positive Social Values

According to Hudson (2005), even individuals who have been stigmatised by the community as deviant or otherwise abnormal wish to portray themselves as conforming to the generally accepted social values of their community. This is about saving face and also relates to constructing an identity that will allow one to participate actively in the community, which is seen as essential to psychological and personal wellbeing (Staub, 2003). In order to achieve this, offenders may appeal to commonly accepted social values that serve to normalise their deviant and violent behaviour.

Perhaps the clearest example of negating responsibility by reference to positive social virtues is Iash. Iash has a long history of involvement in antisocial behaviour, which has included operating a criminal enterprise. The following quote is offered by Iash in accounting for his criminal behaviour in general, rather than the specific violent offences that precipitated his incarceration.

> **Iash (Lebanese):** I've never ever, ever stolen in my own backyard, like there's a saying, don't ever, ever shit in your own backyard . . .You know what I mean, and I never did … I mean I had plenty [emphasised] of opportunity to shit in my own backyard, but I never. So whatever I did steal, it was like from people and I used to think 'Yeah sucked in' — you know what I mean — 'You deserve it' … stupid people used to leave, you know, three, four, five, $6000 in their shop, in the back of their shop. Why leave it there? Go bank it! Put it away! … So they deserved that kind of thing … so I justified myself by doing that … 'cause where I grew up, that was my [emphasised] community, that was my [emphasised] home … my home was already shit [emphasised] as well … So for me to make it even worse by maybe robbing this shopkeeper and then taking him out of business and then it closes down and then all of a sudden, you know, a lot of shit stuff happens and families got to travel a lot longer to get to their certain places and food and all that sort of stuff … I'd never do that.

Iash made reference here to a saying that has influenced his criminal enterprise: not 'shitting' in one's backyard, and this implies awareness that crime has a negative impact on the community. As such, Iash portrayed himself as someone with empathy for others, although this empathy is obviously selective (Fisher, Beech, & Browne, 1999; Hanson, 2003; Miller & Eisenberg, 1988), as he expressed distaste for people who leave themselves vulnerable to crime. Therefore, Iash is able to place some blame with his victims, who are seen as being deserving of and perhaps even initiating the crimes against them, although this ignores Iash's own criminal behaviour in these situations.

Iash has made a great deal of money out of his criminal 'business' over the years and he drew on a Robin Hood archetype to suggest that his offending was justified by the fact that he was robbing from the rich to give to the poor, who constituted his family and local cultural community. Consequently, he claimed that he was giving back to his community through crime, which he suggested was especially important given the disadvantages his community has faced. Again, this ignores the self-gratification involved in Iash's offending and focuses instead on the community, which performs the work of face-saving and positive impression management through highlighting his positive qualities, which are consistent with community discourses about 'moral' behaviour (Goffman, 1959).

Invoking the Notion of Threshold

An analysis of the strategies that offenders used to distance themselves from criminal responsibility revealed a particular strategy that has not been well addressed in the forensic psychological or criminological literature. This refers to invoking the notion of a threshold that, when breached, results in irrational, unpredictable and violent behaviour, in relation to which the person has little control. Such excuses are commonly offered within forensic psychological practice and draw on discourses of moral accounting for crime that see criminal behaviour as both deviant and abnormal (Hopkins Burke, 2005; Sanders & Lyon, 1995). Despite being accepted conventionally, the literature does not address this form of rationalisation succinctly. Notions of threshold appear to be invoked most often in relation to threats to identity, including masculine, ethnic and criminal identity and, as suggested earlier, this demonstrates that criminal violence is one way in which offenders respond to such challenges, thus restoring their identity both publicly and privately. In this way, this threshold is also related to notions of culture, as mediated by identity.

The ways in which offenders invoked this threshold notion related to a perceived inability to cope or a temporary suspension of 'normal' reasoning or control. For example, Kadr offered the following statement in relation to an offence involving his brandishing a gun in order to scare a group of seemingly 'Australian' youths, who were allegedly making racist comments towards Kadr and his co-offender.

> Kadr (Lebanese): ... as we've gone back to the car, they've gone, you know, 'Come have a go you wogs' — this, that ... I couldn't handle it no more. You know what I mean? I went all mental and that.

Kadr blamed the victims for initiating the offence by referring to him and his co-offender as 'wogs', who should 'go back to your country', and he experienced this in racist terms. Kadr's language implied that he experienced a build-up of emotions in response to the behaviour of these people, which directly challenged his sense of ethnic identity and legitimacy in Australia, an affront Kadr perceived as both undeserved and intolerable. Kadr then seemingly reached a hypothetical point at which he was unable to cope any longer, such that he 'went all mental'. This notion of being 'mental' implies the suspension of reason and normality that comes with insanity, and this is commonly accepted as causal in crime, according to discourses of mental illness and abnormality (see Foucault, 1975, as cited in Davidson, 1999).

Jim, an Anglo–Australian man, also accounted for a build-up of emotions in response to interpersonal difficulties, which resulted in a breach of hypothetical threshold, such that he 'lost control' and engaged in violence.

> Jim (Anglo): At the point of explosion, my last words to them were, 'This is my house, have some fucking respect' . So it was a more of ... 'What's going on?', do you know what I mean? I didn't understand the how or why and then all of a sudden it just, I don't know, I just saw red and that was it ... I didn't have the capability to ... control it.

Like Kadr, Jim blamed the victims for his experience of intense and difficult emotions, which occurred in response to behaviour that was perceived as disrespectful, with the implication being that the victims acted in ways that were inconsistent with commonly accepted social norms.

Further to this, however, this behaviour also threatened Jim's perceived sense of control, in addition to the primacy of his agenda socially.

Jim utilised the metaphor of an 'explosion' to describe his violence and this suggests a level of pressure and force, in relation to which it is difficult to exercise control. This was further reinforced by his assertion that this occurred 'all of a sudden', such that there was no warning that would have afforded him the opportunity to act differently. Therefore, Jim implied that he cannot be seen as responsible for his violent behaviour, which is constructed as a response to extreme circumstances, initiated by others, and about which he could not control. Jim described this process as his 'brain' saying 'fuck it', again reinforcing the notion of a suspension of rationality and reason.

Jim further reinforced this notion of threshold through the use of colourful metaphors that highlight concepts of pressure and explosion, causing a response that was outside of his control.

> Jim: ... the pressure just, on top of a steam cooker already, you know? ... it went off ... The lid just flew off ... the steam cooker exploded ...

> Jim: It was just a big bomb that went boom [makes a sound like an explosion] ... The stove was too hot ... the kettle too small, boom.

Accounting for his violence in this way reinforced Jim's performed identity of being someone who is caring and supportive and who is thus forced into violence by the actions of others; and hence justifying his violence also refers to the maintenance of identity, as discussed previously. The personal responsibility he might assume for this criminal violence is thereby limited and this also achieves the work of face saving and positive impression management (Goffman, 1959).

There is some support in the literature for the notion of violence occurring in response to a perceived build-up of intolerable emotions. In their Australian research on domestic violence perpetrators, James et al. (2002) suggested that offenders offered excuses for their violence by implying that they could no longer cope with difficult emotions. Adams, Towns, and Gavey (1995) found similar arguments used by domestic violence perpetrators to justify their violence against women. Specifically, these authors suggested that perpetrators implied people 'just snap' in acts of violence and, often, this is in response to a build up of emotional pressure. It is worth noting that offenders, in general, experience difficulties regulating their emotional state

(Jakupcak et al., 2005; Krueger, Schmitte, Caspi, Moffitt, Campbell, & Silva, 1994) and therefore are perhaps more likely to experience intense and negative emotions as intolerable, thereby contributing to acts of violence.

Richarn also clearly accounted for his violence as being the result of a breach of threshold beyond which he was unable to cope and exercise reason. Richarn was born in New Zealand, but identified ethnically as Samoan. Not long after moving to Australia, during his teenage years, he was involved in the murder of a taxi driver, whom he perceived was making racist comments against Pacific Islanders.

> Richarn (Samoan): ... he [victim] started making racial comments where Islanders are too poor so ... and we didn't mind it we just let that one go ... and then he kept going, kept going, about being 'look youse are coconuts, coconuts are stupid' ... and then I pulled out my money, I threw it at him ... and I go look you can have the money and ... then he kept going about Islanders, 'look youse are bad people' and ... that's when things started getting out of hand.

Richarn's account suggested that he was prepared to let the alleged initial insult by the victim pass without response, seemingly because he was able to tolerate such a minor act of verbal abuse. However, the 'pressure' in this situation increased for Richarn as the victim made repeated insults, despite the reportedly obvious displeasure of Richarn and his co-offenders. Richarn stated several times that the victim 'kept going' in his attack on Pacific Islanders, and he acknowledged that this behaviour was bringing him close to the threshold where he was no longer able to cope and he described this as the situation 'getting out of hand', meaning that it was approaching a state of being uncontrollable.

Richarn was almost incredulous that the victim persisted in his barrage of insults, despite the repeated requests of Richarn and his co-offenders to desist. Accounting for his violence in this way ostensibly served to normalise Richarn's extreme violence, which resulted in the death of a man, as an understandable response to an abnormal set of circumstances, brought about by the victim's inappropriate and racist behaviour.

Genuine was involved in a series of violent offences that were committed in retaliation for the assault of a friend and fellow gang member. Like others, Genuine suggested that his behaviour was the result of a build-up of extreme emotions that resulted in the perceived experience of a loss of control and reason associated with violence. He offered the following in response to being asked how he was feeling at the time he heard about the assault on his friend and fellow gang member.

> Genuine (Vietnamese): [sighs] ... very intense at that moment, very intense. Filled up for emotion, mostly rage ... but rage within ... not much reasoning, you know, just rage.

Genuine describes having been 'filled up' by emotions, suggesting that there was no room left for anything else. The most significant emotion for him at the time was rage and, according to Phillips (1998), rage is a powerful emotion that is associated with a perceived loss of control, such that the person is rendered helpless. This rage serves to compromise Genuine's ability to reason and think clearly, which, again, draws on notions of mental insanity and a loss of 'normal' human capacity for control, which is used to justify violence.

The previous discussion outlines the ways in which offenders attempted to negotiate personal responsibility for criminal violence by suggesting that their behaviour was a response to a breach of a hypothesised threshold, beyond which they were unable to exercise 'normal' human control. Generally, this breach is argued to occur in response to a build-up of intolerable emotions, the responsibility for which is placed on others, often the victims of such crimes. Further, it appears that for many offenders, this hypothetical threshold is breached in the context of perceived challenges to identity, including that related to ethnicity, masculinity and criminality. Such challenges and their relationship to criminal violence have been discussed in an earlier chapter, which argued that the performance of criminal violence is one way in which offenders may respond to these challenges, such that their identity, both public and private, is maintained. It has been argued, for example, that involvement in criminal gangs and violence provides a source of a sense of empowerment, status, honour and responsibility for some young men in the face of experiences of marginalisation (Monti, 1994). In particular, it may be that these challenges are most salient to those offenders whose identities are inherently fragile, either with respect to their ethnic status, masculinity or adherence to criminal values. In other words, it is these offenders who are most likely to experience such challenges as intense and confronting, which, in turn, causes extreme emotional states that may be expressed through violence.

Offenders' accounts suggest that once this hypothetical threshold is breached, they are unable to effectively cope any longer and engage in criminal violence as an expression of their emotional state, and this is experienced as both irrational and uncontrollable. This serves to justify criminal violence in two ways: first, by placing blame for the events that gave rise to the violence outside of the perpetrator; and second, by minimising the personal responsibility of the offender by invoking discourses of irrationality and mental illness.

Drawing on this notion of a threshold breach implies that the 'average' person can be expected to respond with criminal violence under abnormal circumstances. As such, violence can be seen as a latent potential in all people that is, rather, controlled on an ongoing basis for most people, most of the time (Potter & Wetherell, 1987). In this way, offenders can naturalise their violence and seek to establish a shared understanding with others who, they suggest, would respond similarly under such extreme circumstances. This achieves the work of positive impression management (Goffman, 1959) and, further to this, allows the offender to maintain the identity of someone who is not inherently abnormal or evil (Hudson, 2005), and this is important both publicly and privately.

It is worth noting that in order to construct their offending in this way, offenders are drawing on commonly accepted community discourses about crime and about criminals, which often see criminal violence as a result of character aberration, weakness or mental infirmity (Hopkins Burke, 2005; Sanders & Lyon, 1995). In other words, the excuses offered for criminal violence are in part provided by the wider community, of which offenders are a part.

Newman's (1998) distinction between instrumental and expressive violence has achieved some currency within the criminal justice literature and forensic practice. Instrumental violence occurs in situations in which violence is used as an instrument to achieve a particular end (see also Sanko, 1994). For example, the majority of armed robberies would be considered instrumental violence, whereby violence is used as a means of exercising control in order to obtain money. Expressive violence, in contrast, is that which occurs as an expression of emotion and this tends to capture more of the inherently violent offences, such as assaults.

It appears that this notion of a threshold breach is related to accounting for expressive violence more so than instrumental violence, which is most likely due to the connection that this violence has to extreme emotional states and also to community attitudes about violence. Specifically, expressive violence may be more normatively accepted, and the perpetrator seen as less responsible, not only socially but also legally, due to the extreme nature of the emotional experience that precipitated the violence. Instrumental violence, in contrast, is more likely to be considered callous and diagnostic of a disordered and antisocial personality and is therefore less easily accepted or tolerable socially.

In summary, the examination of offenders' accounts of criminal violence demonstrated that many offenders drew on understandings of crime occurring in response to a perceived threshold breach, as contextualised in community discourses about crime and about criminals. This hypothetical threshold appeared to relate to the experience of difficult emotions that at some point become seemingly intolerable and unmanageable, often in response to a perceived challenge to identity, which is suggested to be most difficult for those whose identities are inherently fragile. Responsibility for these circumstances tends to be placed outside of the offender and, often, with the victim. Once this threshold has been breached, offenders suggest that they engage in criminal violence, which is constructed as being irrational and out of control. As such, offenders attempt to navigate responsibility and identity in a way that maintains a positive self-image.

Ethnicity as Rationalisation

It was apparent that some offenders invoked notions of ethnic culture as an excuse for violent crime. This was particularly the case for offenders with experiences of cultures that prioritise collectivism. In contrast, ethnicity was largely absent in the accounts of offenders from individualist cultures. This is particularly significant for two key reasons: on the one hand, there has been a tendency in recent years for the media and politicians to engage in 'law and order' debates, which often attribute responsibility for criminal activity to the cultural backgrounds of offenders, often pathologising those cultures as prone to criminal behaviour (Collins et al., 2000). On the other hand, the 'cultural defence' has sometimes been invoked at court — most notably by the defence lawyer in a high profile rape case involving young Muslim men — to 'explain' and excuse the criminal behaviour of men (Dagistanli, 2007). In both cases, the rhetorical use of culture relies on a problematic reduction and even pathologisation of whole ethnic communities, yet the voices of offenders are rarely heard in these debates.

Following, it will be argued that offenders will draw on whatever means they have available to them in negotiating responsibility, and issues of culture are likely to be more salient to those from nondominant groups in the community, which is partly a function of community discourses about culture and crime. The fragility in identity that is engendered through migrant experience may also facilitate engaging in justifying violence through the lens of ethnic culture.

Richarn was raised in New Zealand, but identified more with his Samoan cultural heritage. As stated earlier, he was involved in the murder of a taxi driver, not long after arriving in Australia. In justifying his violence, Richarn implicated ethnic culture as follows.

> Richarn (Samoan): Yeah I sort of remember look this is, you know the first time that someone's actually being racist … and it didn't really hurt as much. but the more I thought about it like I kept saying to myself … look … this is my [emphasised] pride, this is my, my people … You know, we didn't do anything wrong ….

Richarn experienced the victim's behaviour as racist and he took offence to this, suggesting that the victim was attacking his sense of cultural pride, as well as the status of his cultural group generally. Richarn accounted for this as justifying his involvement in killing the taxi driver.

> Richarn: I think it was just that particular circumstance because um … he was being racist … I'm not the one that really goes out and really starts something for no reason.

Here, Richarn suggests that he is not an inherently aggressive person but, rather, he claimed that the murder occurred in a situation that caused him to act in ways that would normally be against his character; that is, in response to a perceived racist attack on his cultural group by the alleged verbal abuse of the victim. This is significant, in contrast to other uses of culture/ethnicity that entail cultural pathologisation, Richarn is responding to the hidden injuries of racism (Collins et al., 2000, p. 137), rather than explaining criminal behaviour in terms of ethnicity per se. This sense of injured identity is not unusual for someone from a marginalised group in the community. As has been discussed elsewhere, Richarn's sense of ethnic cultural identity was particularly fragile in response to his having lived a culturally disconnected lifestyle in New Zealand. After migrating to Australia, Richarn made a more deliberate effort to connect with his cultural heritage, in part as a response to the identity challenges posed by migration (Fisher & Sonn, 2002), and this caused him to feel an increased pressure to demonstrate his Samoan identity, particularly to others. Hence, being the perceived victim of racism was experienced as intolerable for Richarn, and resulted in his feeling the need to overtly and deliberately maintain the status of the group, especially in the presence of his co-offenders, with whom he shared ethnic culture.

Lucky also has a particularly fragile ethnic cultural identity, which may have precipitated his use of culture as a rationalisation for engaging in criminal violence. Lucky described himself as being 'half-blooded' and consequently he challenged the legitimacy of his claim to Fijian cultural identity. This contributed to Lucky's perceived need to demonstrate his commitment to Fiji and its culture, most significantly to others, whom he believed overlooked or disregarded him at times, as a function of his supposed impurity.

Like Richarn, Lucky was involved in the murder of a taxi driver. However, rather than making overtly racist remarks, the victim, an Indian man, was argued to have tried to cheat Lucky and his co-offenders by overcharging them.

> **Lucky (Fijian):** ... it wasn't the first experience of um ... especially Indian taxi drivers um taking the guys, you know what I mean, taking people around long ways and all that, because they want to ... get more money.

Lucky assumed that the victim's behaviour was a result of the inherent greed of Indian people, with whom he allegedly has some experience, thus invoking notions of ethnic culture to explain the victim's assumed socially inappropriate behaviour. This is much closer to the pathologisation of culture we've seen in media accounts of crime that provide explanations in ethnic terms. However, further to this, Lucky accounted for his involvement in the crime as being a function of his own ethnic identity and, specifically, a history of conflict between Fijians and Indians over land.

> **Lucky:** Not only once, twice, a couple of times Indians just try to take over Fiji, know what I mean? ... 'cause I knew he was Indian ... and I knew I was Fiji, no way, they didn't take my land and no way he wouldn't take my pride ....

Lucky justified his involvement in criminal violence by suggesting that, culturally, he was obliged to stand up for Fijians and respond to yet another 'attack' by an Indian. To this end, Lucky invoked notions of ethnic culture to explain his criminal behaviour, which was informed not only by relationships between Indians and Fijians, but also by Lucky's felt need to demonstrate publicly his inherent 'Fijianness', including a commitment to protecting the interests of the group. This is suggested to be a function of the fragility of his cultural identity, given Lucky's understanding that his being of mixed blood compromised his claim to ethnic culture.

Iash was born in Australia, but identified strongly with the Lebanese cultural heritage of his family. He has a long history of involvement in antisocial activities, which have been both modelled and normalised for him by his extended family and local area network. However, in accounting for his involvement in criminal activities, Iash blamed the government of this country, in addition to the entire mainstream Australian community, by suggesting that through systemic practices of racism, Lebanese and Muslim people have been rendered powerless and recruited into positions of antisociality through social disadvantage.

> **Iash (Lebanese):** Oh that's all I knew ... Like the government didn't care about me, you know what I mean? ... The government didn't care about my family, they were just happy to give my father whatever he needed, welfare payments, just enough for us to live and then ... whoever it was at the time, I think it was Paul Keating at the time, ended up saying 'yeah consider yourself lucky that you're getting that' ... Because they don't care about us and ... there was a lot of Lebanese families in my community at that time too, all they were receiving was just enough to live ... I think it was more like um doing the crime and then reaping the rewards. Like doing that crime and then realising 'Oh yeah mad [clicks fingers], I'm going shopping now and I'm going to do this now, I'm going to do that now, I'm going to do that now'.

In contrast to Richarn's use of interpersonal racism, Iash suggested that entrenched or institutionalised racism was responsible for the criminalisation of his people, as a result of the government only providing 'just enough' for Lebanese people 'to live on' through welfare payments. It is unclear what Iash believed would have been fair of the government in this situation, but it is argued that.in making such statements, Iash is globalising in seeking to portray the Anglo–Australian community in a negative light, while maintaining a positive identity for Lebanese Muslims in this community, who he sees have been unfairly treated. Such practices have an established history in racist discourse (van Dijk, 1987; 1993).

In accounting for his crime in this way, Iash justified his behaviour on the basis of social need. Importantly, he is also seeking to extend this justification to his entire ethnic community. However, cultural discourse for Iash is somewhat confused. As a result of the alleged social disadvantage created for Lebanese Muslims by the racist practices of the government in this country, Iash suggested that his criminal violence was motivated by the desire to obtain material possessions, which he believes were unavailable to him through other means. However, at interview, he stated that he also provided for members of his extended family through crime. This served to justify his behaviour, as does the fact that he was taking from Anglo–Australians — others outside of his local community, who were seen as contributing to the 'problem' for him and his people.

Iash drew on a sense of the hidden injuries of racism to explain his antisocial behaviour, which he suggested was the result of the unfair and systematic exclusion of Lebanese Muslims from opportunities for social advancement and success in this country, such that Iash and his people 'couldn't get a fair go'. The notion of a 'fair go' is one that has a long history in Australia and is seen as being somewhat foundational to the 'Australian' culture, perhaps exacerbating Iash's negative comments directed at this community, in which he claimed that he no longer feels comfortable or accepted. His offending is excused as being the product of social disadvantage and his inability to negotiate the 'temptation' present in the Australian lifestyle and values, which are constructed in contrast to those of Lebanese/Muslim culture.

Kadr, an Australian-born Lebanese man, was involved in a series of events that gave rise to a manslaughter charge, in addition to charges of affray and possession of a firearm. His accounting for these offences was generally irresponsible and included repeated references to the actions of the victims, which he claimed caused the offences. Specifically, he implied that the victims made racist comments towards he and his co-offenders, by calling them 'wogs' and telling them to 'piss off'. Kadr appeared to blame his 'obvious' ethnicity for this and he contextualised the victim's behaviour in the generally racist practices that are reportedly well entrenched within the Australian community. As such, Kadr tended to actively separate himself from the mainstream Australian community and identify himself with a subcommunity of Lebanese and Muslim people, many of whom he claimed to be involved in criminal behaviour.

Several times, Kadr discussed how he believes he has been treated unfairly by the criminal justice system, which he attributed to his being of Lebanese descent. Moreover, Kadr expressed repeated concerns about the way in which Lebanese and Muslim people have been treated in Australia and many of Kadr's rationalisations for violence are couched within racist discourse, suggesting that he was the victim of systemic racism, which he perceived as intolerable.

Like Iash, Kadr accounted for his criminal violence by suggesting that he was provoked by the racist actions of 'Australians', as a result of his being of Middle-Eastern origin. While to some extent Kadr may certainly have been the victim of such practices, the salient issue is the way in which he uses this to account for his involvement in violent crime. As such, he paints himself as a helpless victim of racism, who has no avenue for recourse other than to engage in violence as a means of protest.

> Kadr: ... do you see Australian, the racial against other cultures, not just Lebanese, I mean other cultures? ... See who are you supposed to see for that? Who do you tell? You can't tell no one about it, you can't do nothing about it.

Central to these accounts is a sense of being disrespected by 'Australian' or mainstream society, both individually and collectively as a culture. This echoes the common insight that the masculine preoccupation with honour and reputation is a frequent feature of violent and criminal behaviour. This is often understood in terms of class (Monti, 1994; Winlow, 2001) and sometimes sexuality (Tomsen, 2003), but the accounts of offenders confirms an emerging claim about the specifically ethnicised nature of honour and the consequences of experiences of racism in young marginalised men, and the recourse to particular actions in order to reclaim status and honour (Noble, 2007).

Unlike the accounts of violence offered by some of the offenders from collectivist cultures that drew deliberately on notions of racism and ethnicity as a rationalisation, offenders from cultures prioritising individualism tended to be silent on issues of ethnic culture. This is consistent with conventional notions of culture that see it as belonging only to the other, nondominant sections of Anglo-centric western communities (Moreton-Robinson, 2000).

Jim was the only one of the offenders from individualist cultures who drew on ethnicity in accounting for his criminal violence. Jim tended to endorse attitudes of masculinity and misogyny, which he claimed are a function of his ethnic cultural heritage and experience.

> Jim (Anglo): My European side come over as free men ... out of both sides, I've learnt one thing, the male is dominant ... My mother's only five foot and I've seen a beautiful move, whack [makes a sound as if hitting someone], land the old man on his ass ... I loved it but at the end of the day, the male is dominant and the woman is submissive ... It's very hard to fight what you've learnt your whole life.

Jim suggests that he was recruited into misogyny from observing his father's violent practices, particularly in relation to his mother. Jim claimed that his father's behaviour taught him that men are dominant over women, which he attributed to cultural values, and the domestic violence that occurred within the family home was taken as proof of this. Jim is a first generation Anglo–Australian in that his mother was born in Hungary and, although Jim's father's family had been in this country for several generations, he drew on the assumed Anglo-European heritage of his father's family as impacting on his father's violence. As such, he implicated migrant identity here, although this migrant experience was further removed than for other offenders. Jim used this to justify his engagement in violent practices, claiming that it is 'hard to fight what you've learnt your whole life'.

Even though Jim is able to acknowledge and discuss his use of violence as couched in ethnic cultural learning, he generally minimised his involvement in violence directed against women. Where Jim did acknowledge such violence, he tended to blame the female victim by suggesting that they engaged in behaviour that was disrespectful towards him and dismissive of his needs, although this is somewhat inconsistent with an ethnic cultural excuse.

It is particularly interesting that Jim raised issues of ethnic culture in accounting for his criminal violence, as Jim expressed surprise when he was asked about his culture, claiming that he had 'no idea' about what was meant by the term culture in reference to his experience and identity. This highlights the confusion surrounding ethnic identity for Jim and this is probably so for many Anglo–Australians, particularly those with ancestors from other countries who have come to Australia since European settlement.

The previous discussion highlighted how some of the offenders drew on notions of racism and ethnicity to explain and justify criminal violence. This was more common for offenders from cultures with experience of collectivism and is suggested to be a function of migrant experience to some extent. Specifically, membership of nondominant community groups brings with it certain challenges to identity, which may particularly impact on ethnic cultural identity (Fisher & Sonn, 2002). It has been suggested elsewhere that the resultant fragility in identity can contribute to criminal violence in particular ways, which have their foundation in fundamental cultural values and principles. Drawing on ethnic culture is one way in which offenders may gain social capital used to navigate the complexities of interpersonal interaction, particularly where they are asked to account for their involvement in crime. For those with migrant experience, whose ethnic identities are less stable, ethnic culture may be particularly salient in terms of accounting for behaviour and establishing identity.

Ethnic culture was generally silent in the accounts of offenders from cultures that prioritise individualism and this is consistent with notions that culture belongs to the non-dominant sections of the community (Moreton-Robinson, 2000). There was one exception to this, whereby an Anglo–Australian man attempted to justify his violent practices in the context of cultural learning. His use of ethnic culture in this way was somewhat confused and may also load on migrant experience, as this participant was first generation Australian and, therefore, cultural identity would have been somewhat more fragile and uncertain for him than for others whose histories are more entrenched in this country.

Criminal behaviour is understood as behaviour that is outside of conventional social norms (Heath, 1984; Smith & Pollack, 1994) and community discourses about crime typically consider criminals somehow immoral, infirm or insane (Foucault, 1975, as cited in

Davidson, 1999; Sanders & Lyon, 1995). As such, offenders are motivated to account for their criminal behaviour in ways that maintain
apparent normalcy (Hudson, 2005) and facilitate social acceptance
(Goffman, 1959). In order to achieve this, offenders offer excuses and
rationalisations for their criminal violence that seek to explain, neutralise or justify their violence based on mitigating circumstances that
either blame others or create a social alignment that encourages
empathy and understanding (Adler & Adler, 1994; Felson & Ribner,
1981). If this work is successful, offenders can reduce their personal
responsibility for crime and alleviate the guilt associated with an awareness of having caused pain to another and Hudson (1995) refers to this
as distancing.

Consistent with the extant literature in this area, many of the
offenders here actively sought to negotiate personal responsibility by
seeking to excuse their criminal violence through blaming victims,
dehumanising or depersonalising victims, or claiming that they should
be seen as victims themselves. Further to this, offenders also suggested
that their offences were spontaneous, or the result of a temporary aberration in character, such as that caused by substance intoxication.
Responsibility was also reduced by discussing the violence in passive or
agentless language or by appealing to prosocial values that sought to
establish a positive social alignment with the interviewer. These tactics
used by offenders have been reliably established within forensic practice
and have been accounted for in the literature.

Examination of the accounts of offenders for criminal violence suggested that personal responsibility for their violence was navigated in
two ways that have not been well documented previously in the literature. The first of these related to invoking discourses that construct
criminal violence as behaviour that occurs following the breach of a
hypothetical threshold, beyond which a person is described as behaving
in irrational ways that cannot be controlled. This process is accounted
for as being akin to mental illness and seeks to negotiate responsibility
in similar ways by challenging assumed rationality and agency. This
hypothesised threshold is suggested to be breached by the build up of
strong emotions (Adams et al., 1995; James et al., 2002), which tend to
arise in response to the inappropriate behaviour of others in interaction. Often this occurred in response to direct challenges to identity,
including criminal, ethnic and masculine identity, and, consistent with

that discussed elsewhere, challenges that are related to culture appear to have been experienced as less tolerable by those whose identities were most fragile.

Last, several offenders also utilised discourses of racism and ethnicity in accounting for their criminal violence and this has not been discussed in the extant literature. It was clear that ethnicity, or experiences of racism and marginalisation based on ethnic identity, was used to justify criminal violence by some of the offenders, more likely those from cultures that prioritise collectivist values. However, rather than this necessarily being a function of culture per se, it appears that ethnic culture was invoked by those offenders for whom issues of ethnic culture were more salient social capital. This is suggested to be a function of insecurity in identity, or the consequence of particular experiences of discrimination, consistent with that discussed in other chapters. In this way, it is suggested that justifications for violence that draw on notions of ethnic culture are one of many possible justifications that offenders may use, dependent on social context. Such strategies of rationalisation may be more available to those for whom ethnicity is more salient both through migrant experience and membership of nondominant cultures.

Australian media and politicians often 'blame' culture for crime and this provides the foundation for much of the racist practices alluded to by some offenders. As such, the community offers discourses of ethnic culture to offenders in order to justify criminal violence and this is perpetuated through the influence of the media and other state institutions. Such practices are powerful enough to be utilised by those in positions of dominance culturally who, at other times, would not necessarily position themselves in relation to culture.

In summary, exploring the rationalisations and excuses offered by offenders for criminal violence supports the value of taking a culturally situated position in understanding crime. In part, cultural experience shaped the ways in which offenders account for crimes, most especially as a function of identity, thus highlighting the salience of culture, particularly for those people whose migrant status created specific challenges to the security of ethnic cultural identity.

9

the way forward

THE JOURNEY OF THIS BOOK has as its foundation the premise that dominant community discourses seek to blame culture for crime. It is argued here that it is far more useful to take a more nuanced approach to the role of culture in understanding criminal violence that goes beyond basic assumptions of causality and, rather, explores the complexities in the ways culture is related to crime through identity, gender, experience and so on.

Examining the stories of offenders about their criminal violence has allowed for the development of a richer and more nuanced understanding of crime and violence as situated within culture. Specifically, offenders' accounts of criminal violence suggested that interpersonal violence is one of the ways that offenders can achieve identity, particularly within situations in which other, more conventional means of achieving identity are limited. In this way, crime becomes social capital by which offenders can establish and maintain identity, particularly within subcultural groups (such as criminal gangs). Moreover, the particular ways in which identity was performed through violence were also informed by cultural experience, with offenders from more individualist cultures engaging in criminal behaviour that facilitated personal identity, whereas those from cultures emphasising collectivism offended in ways that cultural pride was facilitated, identity within the group was highlighted, as was the salient group identity as a whole.

The relationship between identity and culture, however, was obviously complex in that it was apparent that culture was, in fact, broader than ethnicity and encapsulated other facets that also informed identity, including criminality, 'group-ness' and masculinity, all of which shape violent crime through the provision of particular ways of being and specific norms through which to interpret action and social interaction. Furthermore, the particular effects of fragility in identity, with respect to acts of interpersonal violence, was highlighted. Specifically, the performance of identity through violence was especially salient for those offenders for whom identity was most fragile, as a function of their personal and social experiences. This fragility was constructed differently for those offenders from more individualist societies, compared with those with experience of cultures that prioritise collectivism. For this latter group of offenders, fragility in identity was constructed primarily in ethnic terms and appears to have been particularly influenced by migrant experience, in addition to the specific cultural and personal challenges that this poses (e.g., Fisher & Sonn, 2002). For those offenders from individualist cultures, fragility in identity was constructed in more personal terms, such as in reference to masculinity or sexuality. This is consistent with culturally mediated understandings of Self (Markus & Kitayama, 1991; Triandis et al., 1988). As such, crime may become an especially potent source of social capital, which can facilitate interpersonal violence in relation to the source of fragility (i.e., ethnicity, masculinity etc.).

In reference to the motivations for criminal violence offered by offenders, those from individualist cultures perpetrated violent crime in ways that promoted self-interest through the pursuit of hedonism and getting one's needs met, including the neutralisation of personal pain and the promotion of important personal principles. Offenders from cultures that were more collectivist in nature were argued to offend for group-oriented reasons, which included standing up for the perceived group, fulfilling important interpersonal obligations or 'saving face', which also involved an inherent awareness of the effects of one's behaviour on salient others, including extended family and community. These differences in culturally situated motivations for criminal violence had their foundation in notions of Self and Other, which are constructed differently according to cultural experience. As a result of the implication of Self, fragile identity was also relevant to this issue, with assumed ethnic motivations for violence having particular importance for those with migrant status. Further to this, cultural identity appeared to take on more salience for those offenders whose identity was fragile. This also drew on notions of cultural pride and individual honour.

Offenders also drew on issues relating to culture in justifying their violence. Specifically, it seems that offenders may invoke the notion of a threshold, the breach of which often occurred in relation to culture resulting in violence. Further, ethnic culture was invoked as a rationalisation for criminal violence by some of the offenders with collectivist cultural experience and, again, particularly those with fragile ethnic identity. However, for those offenders from cultures prioritising individualist values, culture was either noticeably absent in their accounts of crime, or it was present, but only to the extent that it implicated the individual, such as in reference to masculine or criminal cultural capital.

It is argued that taking a culturally situated approach to violence engenders psychologically 'deeper' and 'richer' narratives of crime, which speak to the lived experience of offenders with respect to their motivations for violence. This has implications in a number of areas.

Clinical Implications

The field of psychology has applications in working with criminal behaviour, both empirically and clinically, because of the inherently interpersonal nature of crime (Ainsworth, 2001). Listening to the stories of offenders in relation to violence has important clinical implications within the practice of forensic psychology. First, this highlights the value of understanding criminal violence within the context of culture, particularly for those people whose cultural identity is inherently fragile, for example through the experience of dislocation and migration. Therefore, clinicians should be encouraged to be mindful of cultural experience and its impact, and to listen for stories of culture in offender's accounts of their violence, as this will often be important to the offender in terms of understanding and conceptualising their behaviour, in addition to setting a context for therapeutic change.

Second, being sensitised to issues of culture implies that it would be fruitful for clinicians to ask questions of offenders that prioritise culture in order to develop psychologically 'rich' stories about crime, rather than the typically 'thin' and culturally absent stories that are developed through the criminal justice process (e.g., James et al., 2002). Examples of such questioning may include, 'To what extent are issues of culture relevant in your offending?' 'In what ways do you think your cultural experiences contributed to how you thought and behaved in that situation?' 'Do you think someone from a different cultural background may have responded differently? Why or why not?' In Australia, the criminal justice process encourages narratives of individual responsibility through interviewing by police and other representatives of the legal system, which is often designed to elicit a confession or evidence that may be used at court against an offender (Baldwin, 1993; Kassin & Gudjonsson, 2004; Williamson, 1993). Whilst such interviews no doubt elicit important information for the criminal justice process, they may not engender stories that capture the essential meanings of criminal violence for offenders. This being the case, forensic treatment may miss important avenues by solely focusing on individualist and culture-absent accounts, especially for those offenders from nondominant groups.

Another obvious implication is for clinicians to work in culturally sensitive ways with offenders within the forensic treatment process and this may even include working collaboratively with cultural representatives in order to develop a more responsive treatment process (Andrews & Bonta, 2007). It is important that cultural experience and values are recognised for clients, even for those offenders who are born and raised in Australia, but who are second generation Australians with their parents being born overseas. It appears that it is these offenders whose cultural experience is most confused and, therefore, they are perhaps the most vulnerable with respect to identity and this will be especially salient in their understandings of and motivations for criminal violence. Succinctly, those offenders whose identity and cultural connection are inherently fragile may be more likely to engage in exaggerated demonstrations of cultural pride and allegiance through criminal violence.

An extension of this point relates to the inclusion of culture and culturally relevant issues as treatment targets in forensic practice. For

example, addressing issues of identity, pride and group allegiance may
be useful avenues to pursue in working with offenders to address their
criminogenic needs. Specifically, it may be useful to introduce a com-
ponent on identity to the treatment process, whereby offenders are
encouraged to think about who they are and how they have come to
develop this identity. Further to this, thinking through the importance
of others in their lives and the extent to which these people have
shaped their identity is also important. However, crucially with respect
to offence-specific treatment, offenders should be encouraged to
develop an understanding of the ways in which this identity has
informed their behaviour and, moreover, to develop skills by which they
may make other, more prosocial choices in offence situations, particularly those that challenge identity. Given the stories of the offenders,
such treatment will likely extend the effectiveness of traditional forensic
practices that tend to focus on individual responsibility, including
addressing the individual antecedents to crime, such as substance abuse,
distorted thinking and poor personal problem solving or social skills
(McMurran, 1996; Towl & Crighton, 1996; Ward et al., 1997).

Theoretical Implications

Chapter 3 provides a general overview of existing theories about
crime. These theories focus variously on individual pathology, either
biological or psychological; social variables that facilitate crime, such
as poverty and family breakdown; or interactional theories, which
suggest that criminal behaviour is a function of the complex interplay
of both individual and social vulnerabilities, giving rise to the consideration of criminal propensity as a balance of both risk and protective
factors (Andrews & Bonta, 1997).

Hopkins Burke (2005) argued that there have been three 'waves' of
theory seeking to explain the development of crime, all of which are
essentially western focused and have their foundations in individualist
values. The first of these 'waves' related to the 'rational actor', suggesting that individuals have free will to 'choose' to engage in behaviour,
including crime. Part of the assumed inherent rationality of human
beings prioritised the pursuit of pleasure (i.e., hedonism) and crime
was hypothesised to occur when an individual single-mindedly
pursued pleasure, without thinking about the consequences of their
actions on others, including the community. This theory had obvious

limitations in failing to account for the lack of criminal acts committed by those who were, by definition, 'irrational', such as children and those suffering from an intellectual disability or mental illness, in addition to accounting for the fact that most individuals desist from crime, despite the obvious benefits of such behaviour (e.g., money).

The next 'wave' of criminological theory proposed the notion of a 'predestined actor', which was couched in positivist understandings of determinism. In other words, the criminal was someone who was 'destined' to be so, either through personal vulnerability (biological or psychological) or through a particular combination of social experiences. This approach undermines free will and argues that the criminal has little control over their developmental trajectory, and it cannot explain how certain individuals with similar experiences and vulnerabilities 'choose' to behave differently.

Finally, and most recently, theory has shifted to propose the 'victimised actor' model of crime. This suggests that the criminal is someone who is unfairly prejudiced by social vulnerabilities, which have contributed to their antisocial behaviour. In other words, social inequalities, racism and limited opportunity can facilitate engagement in crime.

It is argued here that existing criminological theory does not go far enough in considering the 'bigger picture' of crime, which includes the experience of culture and how this shapes sociocultural and psychological factors, such as identity. Consequently, a fourth 'wave' to criminological theory is offered, extending that offered by Hopkins Burke (2005), and this is of the criminal as a 'culturally situated actor'.

Ferrell et al. have argued for a process of cultural criminalisation (e.g., Ferrell, 1995; 1998a; Ferrell & Sanders, 1995; and also Presdee, 2000), which highlights that crime is an inherently cultural process. This body of work highlights that notions of deviance and crime are socially and culturally constructed (see also Adler & Adler, 1994; Cohen, 1972) and, further, that cultural and subcultural processes may shape the performance of crime in particular ways.

It is argued that the development of the criminal is a complex process that combines personal vulnerabilities (e.g., low intelligence, poor attachment, exposure to abuse), with social disadvantages (e.g., poverty, poor role modelling, lack of educational opportunity), the effect of which is to remove avenues of social capital by which to achieve important personal needs. In this context, crime becomes a means by which a person can achieve social capital. However, the importance of culture in shaping identity, personal and interpersonal responsibility and experience is ignored in this, and the stories of offenders explored here speak to the salience of culture in shaping the performance of criminal violence. Therefore, the 'culturally situated actor' is one who experiences personal vulnerability and social disadvantage within the complex rubric of culture, which facilitates an interpretation of these experiences in ways that may encourage criminal behaviour. This appears to be particularly salient for those offenders whose identity is inherently fragile, especially in the context of cultural confusion and the dislocation caused by migration.

Understanding criminal behaviour in culturally situated ways facilitates a deeper and richer understanding of crime, and especially violence, which speaks to offenders' lived experience of crime and may facilitate more 'responsive' forensic treatment, as outlined above.

Criminal Justice Implications

As stated, the interviewing of offenders within 'taken for granted' criminal justice processes can shape offenders' stories in particular ways (e.g., James et al., 2002). Specifically, these accounts privilege notions of individual responsibility, which may not speak to the deeper motivations behind criminal violence, particularly for those offenders whose experience is of collectivism, or who are migrants raised in nondominant cultures.

The accounts of offenders typically engendered by criminal justice interviewing are unlikely to facilitate the courts having an accurate understanding of the antecedents to an offender's crime, which are so important in court dispositions of offenders, including sentencing and treatment recommendations.

Given what we now know, it is suggested that being mindful of culture in seeking to understand criminal violence is important, and therefore criminal justice representatives would also be well served to prioritise issues of culture in shaping their interactions with offenders through the criminal justice process. For example, police officers may be wise to ask offenders about their relationships with any co-offenders, as well as their understandings of obligation and relationship in making the decision to engage in crime. Alternatively, offenders might be asked what the meaning of their crime was for them in order to explore the more contextually relevant motivations for violence. In sum, it is suggested that, similar to the suggestions of Wetherell (1998), offenders might be asked to account for their crime, rather than simply describe the actions that they engaged in with respect to acts of crime, even in being interviewed by police.

Community Implications

Crime prevention has been an important public agenda for some time and issues of law and order, at least in Australia, have been prioritised in the public forum in recent years. The aforementioned implications for forensic treatment with offenders would be conceptualised as strategies for the tertiary prevention of crime, which is working with already identified offenders to reduce their risk of recidivism. However, the community has a responsibility in both the primary and secondary prevention of crime (Brantingham & Faust, 1976), which addresses the issues relevant to the development of crime from a community perspective. Typically, such prevention strategies are not of particular interest to the community, who would rather blame criminals for crime than thinking about other variables, which may influence crime and for which the community can be responsible (Collins et al., 2000; Goode & Ben-Yehuda, 1998; van Dijk 1987; 1993).

It has been argued that one of the ways in which deviance and, therefore, crime may be reduced is through the protection and promotion of community, in such a way that relationships and connectedness between people are encouraged (e.g., Hazelhurst, 1987; Staub, 1988; 2003).

Part of the journey is necessarily in thinking about the meaning we can make from the stories of offenders in relation to the community, particularly in Australia, where we are faced with many of the social challenges engendered by the uneasy practice of multiculturalism (e.g., Ang et al., 2002; 2006; Fisher & Sonn, 2002; Saxton, 2003). In taking a culturally situated understanding of criminal violence, it is important that we consider, as a society, how we are managing our community and in particular, developing and maintaining relationships with minority and migrant groups, who continue to be marginalised and disenfranchised. Listening to offenders and their stories of violence raises a number of important questions about how the fabric of modern western multicultural society may be facilitating certain forms of violence. It is not suggested that people from minority groups offend more than those from the dominant cultural majority, but it is suggested that perhaps there are ways in which we as a society deal with minority groups that facilitates disharmony and instability, which in turn may facilitate interpersonal violence and this is worth considering further.

Perhaps there are ways in which our society may prioritise connectedness and obligation to Others that might restrain violence. Furthermore, perhaps the promotion of competitive, self-focused 'dog eat dog' individualism contributes to acts of criminal violence (e.g., Colvin et al., 2002). Are there ways that values of collectivism could be encouraged within the community and would this reduce acts of violence?

In conclusion, it is suggested that it is important to take a culturally situated approach to understanding and working with criminal violence, from all angles of the criminal justice process, through the community, the legal system and the 'front line' practitioners who work to reduce an offender's risk to the community. Ward (2004) talks about taking a positive approach to working with offenders, such that 'good lives' are facilitated through the realisation of important needs, which meet positive personal goals. Working with offenders within a positive framework is important and has far greater effectiveness in treatment and management than taking a pathologising and pejorative perspective on crime and criminals. It is argued that acknowledging culture and identity as important personal needs, the challenge to which may restrain a 'good life', is helpful and may facilitate a more meaningful understanding of crime and violence.

I opened this book by discussing some of the ways in which my work developed the ideas that encouraged me to interview violent offenders about their crimes. I want to close similarly. In completing the journey of this research, I was asked to assess a teenage client for the purposes of sentencing at court. This young man was born in the Philippines and, in the years leading up to his offending, had been well entrenched within a criminal gang, the majority of whom were also of Asian background. He discussed these gang connections as facilitating a sense of family and belonging that was lacking in his life as a result of dysfunction within his family. In particular, one of his gang associates, also his co-offender, had taken him in and provided for him at times when his family had failed to do so. This client was involved in the stabbing murder of another Asian man, who allegedly had conflict with his co-offender, most likely as a result of inter-gang relationships. The young man discussed the motivations for his involvement in the murder as relating to the desire to protect his co-offender, who was being physically assaulted by the victim. Further to this, even though he was frightened in the situation, the client talked about feeling a strong sense of obligation to his co-offender who had taken care of him in times of need and, therefore, had established a close bond with him that brought with it important obligations and commitments. Understanding this client's crime within the context of culture, identity and relationship was crucial for the courts, particularly as he was likely to receive a lengthy sentence that would take him well into his adult years. Therefore, I highlighted these issues in my report for court, so that in sentencing the client the court would have a clear picture of the meaning of the crime for the offender and hopefully offer him an appropriate sentence that would also facilitate his important treatment needs. Apparently, this other perspective on the crime was gratefully received by the court.

So, in real terms, this research has shaped my perspective of crime and violence, and has impacted on my practice in such a way that I might be able to work to better facilitate the needs of clients and to encourage the criminal justice process to take a therapeutic and psychological perspective on crime. Moreover, I think both the criminal justice system and the community as a whole can work better with crime, and I believe that listening to the stories of offenders about their criminal behaviour is the most fruitful source of information about what we need to know in working with crime in more helpful ways.

appendix:
methodological approach

FOLLOWING IS AN OUTLINE of the methodological approach taken in this research that entailed interviewing violent offenders about their criminal behaviour. Theoretically, this research was founded on the premise that culture is implicated in the choices offenders make in interpersonally violent crime. Specifically, this was assumed to occur through the mediating influence of sense of self and sense of other. Therefore, the aim of interviewing offenders and analysing their stories in depth was to explore interpersonal violence from a culturally situated perspective, paying particular attention to Self (identity) and to Other (relationships). Specifically, this process sought to:

- explore offenders' understandings of their interpersonally violent criminal behaviour, with a view to culture
- explore the meanings of any differences in the ways offenders from collectivist versus individualist cultures understand and make meaning of their interpersonally violent offending
- explore the meaning of any differences in the motivations that offenders from collectivist versus individualist cultures have for interpersonally violent offending

- explore issues of identity and relationship within offenders' accounts of their criminal violence and investigate whether these can be conceptualised within a framework of culture.

Given the aims of this research, qualitative methods of inquiry were considered richer, because they allowed the flexibility to explore the social construction of culture and crime without ordering the data in specific ways or limiting it through the use of quantitative methods (see McLeod, 2001; Willig, 2001).

The process of Modified Analytic Induction (MAI) was chosen as the particular method with which to explore and analyse the interview data. The aim of MAI is to develop theory from an inductive examination of the data. This theory is inherently descriptive (Bogdan & Biklen, 1998) and seeks to make statements about the relationships between and patterns in the variables of interest (Gilgun, 1995). Further to this, the importance of the inductive method allows for novel ways of understanding when there is little extant literature or information about the area of study (Varallo, Berlin Ray, & Hartman Ellis, 1998).

A new area of research that has recently burgeoned within the social sciences with respect to crime is that of cultural criminology (see Ferrell, 1998a; Ferrell & Sanders, 1995a; 1995b; Presdee, 2000). This field brings with it exciting new developments in understanding crime as a cultural and subcultural process; couching an understanding of crime within available discourses on culture, deviance, power and inequality. Ferrell, one of the seminal authors in the field of cultural criminology, identifies that researchers in this area develop 'criminological verstehen' (Ferrell, 1999; Ferrell & Hamm, 1998), which refers to the subjective appreciation or understanding about criminal behaviour that guides research. This understanding forms the frame through which events are interpreted and this will intimately affect any research outcomes.

MAI allows for the use of 'criminological verstehen' in that the induction process is assumed to begin from general hypotheses that the researcher has developed prior to coming into the data analysis. Hewson, Germanos and Faine (2003) refer to this as embracing the sensitivity of the researcher at the time of data collection, rather than during the analysis stage (Gilgun, 1995; 2001). For the present purposes, within MAI, culture becomes a sensitised concept with which to approach an understanding of criminal violence and is thereby drawn on in both interviewing participants and in analysing the data.

Through the process of MAI, individual cases are reviewed and analysed for their fit with the research hypotheses and emerging theory. As analysis progresses, the original hypotheses are refined and developed, and this continues until a 'saturation' point is reached, such that new cases no longer contribute to the development of theory in novel ways. In this case, rather than being solely data driven in a nondirective sense, the analytical work of MAI is purposeful and data is selected that adds to the developing theory (see Bogdan & Biklen, 1998).

According to Gilgun (1995, 2001), who has researched and published using MAI both theoretically and clinically, the analysis process begins with the researcher 'wading' into the data and testing their hypotheses against the data, engaging in theory-building as this progresses. This is referred to as the 'constant comparative method' and continues until the research hypotheses are able to 'stand alone' without further revision or refinement (Whitehead & Carpenter, 1999). This process is, at least partly, inductive in nature in that it moves from the specific to the general, building understandings from *a priori* knowledge that is brought into the analytic process by the researcher (Gilgun, 1995; Mullins, 2006).

The aim of the analytical process in MAI is the development of theory. This theory is not necessarily causal but descriptive and may, at its simplest level, relate to making statements about the relationship between at least two events or variables of interest (Bogdan & Biklen, 1998; Gilgun, 2001). These theories are not held as being universal, compared with those of quantitative research paradigms, but are, rather, situationally bound and contextually relevant, in a social constructionist sense (Burman & Parker, 1993; Willig, 2001), such that new information or new experience may change the theories in important ways. In other words, through engaging in MAI, the researcher is only offering one interpretation of the data, of many possible and equally valid interpretations, based on the literature reviewed, the researcher's experiences and beliefs, and the stories of particular participants interviewed. In this case, the aim was to add to existing criminological theory by offering an understanding of criminal violence that was couched in culture, including that related to ethic culture, masculine culture and criminal culture.

This Research

The Participants

The participants in this research were comprised of convicted and incarcerated violent offenders within one major correctional centre in New South Wales, Australia. This centre also housed the Violent Offender Treatment Programme (VOTP), where many of the participants were undergoing treatment for their offending.

In order to be a potential participant, offenders had to be sentenced on charges of an interpersonally violent nature. Interpersonal violence was defined as an act of violence in which a person was deliberately targeted and hurt (e.g., murder, aggravated sexual assault, malicious wounding, assault occasioning actual/grievous bodily harm). Acts of violence that were directed against an object (e.g., bank robbery) were not included, as it was in the relationship between victim and offender that the influence of culture was anticipated to be most salient.

In order to select potential participants, ethnic cultural experience was distinguished according to individualism and collectivism. Acknowledging that in reality culture probably exists on a continuum between individualism and collectivism, specific definitions of cultural status were drawn on in order to make distinctions viable in selecting potential participants. The individualist group was comprised of people of Anglo descent, who were born in Australia, as were at least one of their parents. Collectivism was defined in relation to group-oriented cultures, and offenders from Asian, Pacific Islander and Middle-Eastern communities were selected. These three groups were identified not as being primary or perfect examples of collectivism or group-oriented cultures, but because they are the most significantly represented in the criminal justice system of the possible collectivist cultural groups. In other words, these cultural/geographic areas were selected as a means of operationalising the ethnic cultural distinction of interest, rather than being considered definitive of ethnicity or culture. In order to maximise the ethnic cultural experience in the collectivist groups, offenders who were either born overseas, either in Asia, the Middle East or the Pacific Islands, or who were first generation Australians, and whose parents were born in the aforementioned areas, were selected as potential participants in the collectivist group.

All participants were males aged between 18 and 35 years. The majority of interpersonally violent offenders are 'young' and 35 years was set as a ceiling for 'young'. Further to this, it was hoped to exclude potentially confounding variables associated with age, gender or development.

Potential participants were recruited from both the VOTP and the surrounding units in the correctional complex. As mentioned previously, the sampling process involved in MAI is purposeful and participants are recruited whose stories allow for an in-depth exploration and understanding of the research question (Patton, 2002). The recruitment process used involved targeting males between the ages of 18 and 35 years, who were serving a custodial sentence for an interpersonally violent crime (as defined earlier). Further to this, for the aforementioned reasons, negative cases were not actively recruited but, rather, examples of contradictory or disconfirming data were explored within the interviews of participants. Recruitment continued until new cases no longer added to, but continued to thicken, the developing theory and ideas, thereby, suggesting 'saturation' had been reached (Bogdan & Biklen, 1998; Gilgun, 1995, 2001).

There were 15 participants recruited, four of whom were from the individualist group and 11 from the collectivist group. Of the latter, there were four from Pacific Islander cultures, five from Middle-Eastern cultures and two from Asian cultures. In the final analysis, three of these participants were excluded; one Middle-Easterner and one Asian offender were excluded due to their denials of the offence, rendering their interviews 'thin' in relation to the issues of interest, and a further man of Middle-Eastern origin was excluded because his English was very poor and difficult to understand for the purposes of transcription.

All of the participants were offered the option of selecting a pseudonym to be referred to throughout the interview and analysis. Some took up this offer, while others referred to themselves by their first name. The surnames of offenders, as well as any other potentially identifying details were not recorded in the transcription of interviews in order to protect identity.

The Interview

The interviews were of between 45 minutes and an hour and a half duration and were semistructured. That is, the interviews were framed by various questions that asked participants for their account of the charges for which they were sentenced, in addition to their understandings of and motivation for their criminal behaviour. Further to this, participants were asked about their cultural experience. Consistent with the comments of Wetherell (1998), questions asked of participants required them to both describe events and to account for events, the latter of which is particularly interesting in understanding the meaning-making process.

With respect to the interviews in this study, it is important to note that the veracity of offenders' accounts of their criminal violence was not at issue. Rather, the interest was in how offenders accounted for their crimes, what justifications, excuses and rationalisations they used and how they made sense of their abusive behaviour (Hudson, 2005). How this correlates to the facts was not important. Other research using the accounts of offenders has highlighted similar issues, particularly in relation to inconsistencies and exaggerations that may be present in such interviews. However, as Mullins (2006) suggests, it is the 'microdynamics' of the interviews in the context of the social interaction with the researcher that are of interest and yield valuable information about the larger sociocultural variables under study. Further to this, if offenders take the opportunity to distort or otherwise misrepresent their experience or behaviour at interview, this, in itself, is valuable information for research.

In qualitative research, the text is treated as the source of data (Parker, 1999) and it is analysed with reference to what it says about the rhetorical and social practices the speaker engaged in (Billig, 1996). Reading and analysing text is inherently an active process (Parker, 1999) that reproduces and/or transforms the text at the same time an analysis of the text is offered (Parker & Burman, 1993), and therefore data analysis is an interactive process whereby the distinction between data collection and analysis is blurred (Friedlander et al., 1994). According to the directions of Wetherell and Potter (1987), all interviews were audiotaped and transcribed verbatim by either the researcher or a paid and professional transcriber. In addition to the words spoken, particular attention was paid to any nuances in speech or nonverbal behaviour (such as laughter), as this also provides important information about interaction and intention.

references

Adams, P.J., Towns, A., & Gavey, N. (1995). Dominance and entitlement: The rhetoric men use to discuss their violence towards women. *Discourse and Society, 6*(3), 387–406.

Adler, P.A., & Adler, P. (1994). *Constructions of deviance: Social power, context and interaction.* Belmont, CA: Wadsworth Publishing Company.

Ainsworth, P.B. (2001). *Offender profiling and crime analysis.* Devon, UK: Willan Publishing.

Andersen, S.M., & Chen, S. (2002). The relational self: An interpersonal social-cognitive theory. *Psychological Review, 109*(4), 619–645.

Anderson, K.L., & Umberson, D. (2001). Gendering violence: Power in men's accounts of domestic violence. *Gender and Society, 15*(3), 358–380.

Andrews, D.A., & Bonta, J. (2007). *The psychology of criminal conduct.* Cincinnati, OH: Anderson Publishing.

Ang, I., Brand, J., Noble, G., & Sternberg, J. (2006). *Connecting diversity: Paradoxes of multicultural Australia.* Artarmon, Australia: Special Broadcasting Service.

Ang, I., Brand, J.E., Noble, G., Wilding, D. (2002). *Living diversity: Australia's multicultural future.* Sydney, Australia: Special Broadcasting Service.

Aumair, M., & Warren, I. (1994). Characteristics of juvenile gangs in Melbourne. *Youth Studies Australia, 13*(2), 40–45.

Australian Bureau of Statistics. (2002). *Census Data 2001*. Canberra, Australia: Australian Federal Government.

Baldwin, J. (1993). Police interview techniques: Establishing truth or proof? *British Journal of Criminology, 33*(3), 325–352.

Bandura, A. (1986). *Social foundations of thought and action: A social cognitive theory.* Upper Saddle River, NJ: Prentice Hall.

Barker, P. (1998). *Michel Foucault: An introduction.* Edinburgh, UK: Edinburgh University Press.

Ben-David, S., & Silfen, P. (1993). Rape death and resurrection: Male reaction after disclosure of the secret of being a rape victim. *Medicine and Law, 12*(1–2), 181–189.

Billig, M. (1996). *Arguing and thinking: A rhetorical approach to social psychology.* Cambridge, UK: Cambridge University Press.

Bischof, G.P., Stith, S.M., & Whitney, M.L. (1995). Family environments of adolescent sex offenders and other juvenile delinquents. *Adolescence, 30*(117), 157–170.

Blanchard, W.H. (1959). The group process in gang rape. *The Journal of Social Psychology, 49,* 259–266.

Bogdan, R.C., & Biklen, S.K. (1998). *Qualitative research for education: An introduction to theory and methods.* Needham Heights, MA: Allyn & Bacon.

Bohner, G. (2001). Writing about rape: Use of passive voice and other distancing text features as an expression of perceived responsibility of the victim. *British Journal of Social Psychology, 40,* 515–529.

Bond, M.H. (2004). Culture and aggression — From context to coercion. *Personality and Social Psychology Review, 8*(1), 62–78.

Bor, W., Najman, J.M., O'Callaghan, M., Williams, G.M., & Anstey, K. (2001). *Aggression and the development of delinquent behaviour in children* (Trends and Issues in Crime and Justice, No. 207). Canberra, Australia: Australian Institute of Criminology.

Bradley, P. (2003). A war on violence? How western societies are reacting to terrorism. *In Psych, 25*(1), 11–13.

Braithwaite, J. (2002). *Restorative justice and responsive regulation,* New York: Oxford University Press.

Brantingham, P.J., & Faust, F.L. (1976). A conceptual model of crime prevention. *Crime and delinquency, 22*(3), 284–296.

Brewer, M.B., & Gardner, W. (1996). Who is this 'we'? Levels of collective identity and self representations. *Journal of Personality and Social Psychology, 71*(1), 83–93.

Browne, K., & Howells, K. (1996). Violent offenders. In C.R. Hollin (Ed.), *Working with offenders: Psychological practice in offender rehabilitation.* Chichester, UK: John Wiley & Sons.

Bruner, J. (1990). *Acts of meaning.* Cambridge, MA: Harvard University Press.

Burman, E., & Parker, I. (1993). *Discourse analytic research: Repertoires and readings of texts in action.* London: Routledge.

Burt, M.R. (1980). Cultural myths and support for rape. *Journal of Personality and Social Psychology, 38*, 217–230.

Cohen, S. (1972). *Folk devils and moral panics: The creation of the Mods and Rockers.* London: MacGibbon & Kee.

Cole, M. (1997). *Cultural psychology: A once and future discipline.* Cambridge, MA: The Belknap Press of Harvard University Press.

Collins, J., Noble, G., Poynting, S., & Tabar, P. (2000). *Kebabs, kids, cops and crime.* Annandale, Australia: Pluto Press.

Colombo, M., & Senatore, A. (2005). The discursive construction of community identity. *Journal of Community and Applied Social Psychology, 15*, 48–62.

Colvin, M., Cullen, F., & Ven, T.V. (2002). Coercion, social support, and crime: An emerging theoretical consensus. *Criminology, 40*(1), 19–24.

Connell, R.W. (1987). *Gender and power: Society, the person and sexual politics.* Sydney, Australia: Allen & Unwin.

Connell, R.W. (1995). *Masculinities.* Sydney, Australia: Allen & Unwin.

Copenhaver, M.M., Lash, S.J., & Eisler, R.M. (2000). Masculine gender role stress, anger, and male intimate abusiveness: Implications for men's relationships. *Sex Roles, 42*(5/6), 405–414.

Corben, J. (2006). *NSW inmate census, 2006: Summary of characteristics,* Statistical Publication 28. Sydney, Australia: NSW Department of Corrective Services.

Dagistanli, S. (2007). 'Like a pack of wild animals': Moral panics around ethnic gang rape. In S. Poynting & G. Morgan (Eds.), *Outrageous: Moral panics* (pp. 181–196). Hobart, Australia: Australian Clearing House of Youth Studies.

Davidson, A.I. (Ed.). (1999). *Michel Foucault: Abnormal, lectures at the College De France, 1974–1975.* New York: Picador.

Davies, B., & Harre, R. (1990). Positioning: The discursive production of selves. *Journal for the Theory of Social Behaviour, 20*(1), 43–63.

Day, A., Howells, K., Heseltine, K., & Casey, S. (2003). Alcohol use and negative affect in the offence cycle. *Criminal Behaviour and Mental Health, 13*(1), 45–58.

De Cilla, R. Reisigl, M., & Wodak, R. (1999). The discursive construction of national identities. *Discourse and Society, 10*(2), 149–173.

Doherty, K., & Anderson, I. (2004). Making sense of male rape: Constructions of gender, sexuality and experiences of rape victims. *Journal of Community Applied Social Psychology, 14*, 85–103.

Egerton, M. (1995). Emotions and discursive norms. In R. Harre, & P. Stearns (Eds.), *Discursive psychology in practice.* London, UK: Sage Publications.

Ericson, R.V., Baranek, P.M., & Chan, J.B.L. (1991). *Representing order: Crime, law and justice in the news media.* Toronto, Canada: University of Toronto Press.

Farrington, D.P. (1991). Psychological contributions to the explanation of offending. *Issues in Criminological and Legal Psychology, 1*(17), 7–19.

Farrington, D.P. (1996). Criminological psychology: Individual and family factors in the explanation and prevention of offending. In C.R. Hollin (Ed.), *Working with offenders: Psychological practice in offender rehabilitation.* Chichester, UK: John Wiley & Sons.

Felson, R.B., & Ribner, S.A. (1981). An attributional approach to accounts and sanctions for criminal violence. *Social Psychology Quarterly, 44*(2), 137–142.

Ferrell, J. (1995). Style matters: Criminal identity and social control. In J. Ferrell, & C.R. Sanders (Eds.), *Cultural criminology*. Boston, MA: Northeastern University Press.

Ferrell, J. (1998a). Culture, crime and cultural criminology. In S.E. Anderson, & G.J. Howard (Eds.), *Interrogating popular culture: Deviance, justice, and social order*. Guilderland, NY: Harrow and Heston Publishers.

Ferrell, J. (1998b). Criminalising popular culture. In F.Y. Bailey & D.C. Hale (Eds.), *Popular culture, crime, and justice*. Belmont, CA: West/Wadsworth Publishing Company.

Ferrell, J. (1999). Cultural Criminology. *Annual Review of Sociology*, 395- 418.

Ferrell, J., & Hamm, M.S. (1998). *Ethnography at the edge: Crime, deviance and field research*. Boston, MA: Northeastern University Press.

Ferrell, J., & Sanders, C.R. (1995a). Culture, crime, and criminology. In J. Ferrell & C.R. Sanders (Eds.), *Cultural criminology*. Boston, MA: Northeastern University Press.

Ferrell, J., & Sanders, C.R. (1995b). Toward a cultural criminology. In J. Ferrell, & C.R. Sanders (Eds.), *Cultural criminology*. Boston, MA: Northeastern University Press.

Fisher, D., Beech, A., & Browne, K. (1999). Comparison of sex offenders to non-offenders on selected psychological measures. *International Journal of Offender Therapy and Comparative Criminology, 43*(4), 473–491.

Fisher, A.T., & Sonn, C.C. (2002). Psychological sense of community in Australia and the challenges of change. *Journal of Community Psychology, 30*(6), 597–609.

Flynn, T. (2005). Foucault's mapping of history. In G. Gutting (Ed.), *The Cambridge companion to Foucault* (2nd ed.). Cambridge, UK: Cambridge University Press.

Forsyth, D.R. (1999). *Group dynamics* (3rd ed.). Belmont, CA: Wadsworth Publishing Company.

Friedlander, M.L., Heatherington, L., Johnson, B., & Skowron, E.A. (1994). Sustaining engagement: A change event in family therapy. *Journal of Counselling Psychology, 41*(4), 438–448.

Gardner, W.L., Gabriel, S., & Lee, A.Y. (1999). 'I' value freedom, but 'we' value relationships: Self-construal priming mirrors cultural differences in judgement. *Psychological Science, 10*(4), 321–326.

Gilgun, J.F. (1995). We shared something special: The moral discourse of incest perpetrators. *The Journal of Marriage and Family, 57*, 265–281.

Gilgun, J.F. (2001). *Case-based research, analytic induction and theory development: The future and the past*. Paper presented at the 31st Annual Theory Construction and Research Methodology Workshop of the National Council on Family Relations, Rochester, New York.

Goffman, E. (1959). *The presentation of self in everyday life*. New York: Anchor Books.

Goode, E., & Ben-Yehuda, N. (1998). Enter moral panics. In G.W. Potter, & V.E. Kappeler (Eds.), *Constructing crime: Perspectives on making news and social problems.* Long Grove, IL: Waveland Press.

Goodey, J. (1997). Boys don't cry: Masculinities, fear of crime and fearlessness. *British Journal of Criminology, 37*(3), 401–419.

Gottfredson, M.R., & Hirschi, T. (1990). *A general theory of crime.* Palo Alto, CA: Stanford University Press.

Grabosky, P. (1977) *Sydney in ferment.* Canberra, Australia: Australian National University Press.

Greer, C. (2003). *Sex crime and the media: Sex offending and the press in a divided society.* Portland, OR: Willan Publishing.

Hall, S. (1996). Who needs identity? In S. Hall & P. Du Gay (Eds.), *Questions of cultural identity.* London: Sage Publications.

Hanser, R. (2001). A cross-cultural examination of domestic violence. *Crime and Justice International, 17,* 10–11.

Hanson, R.K. (2003). Empathy deficits of sexual offenders: A conceptual model. *Journal of Sexual Aggression, 9*(1), 13–23.

Hatch-Maillette, M.A., Scalora, M.J., Huss, M.T., & Baumgartner, J.V. (2001). Criminal thinking patterns: Are child molesters unique? *International Journal of Offender Therapy and Comparative Criminology, 45*(1), 102–117.

Hazelhurst, K.M. (1987). *Migration, ethnicity and crime in Australian society.* Canberra, Australia: Australian Institute of Criminology.

Heath, L. (1984). Impact of newspaper crime reports on fear of crime: Multimethodological investigation. *Journal of Personality and Social Psychology, 47*(2), 263–276.

Hewson, D., Germanos, L., & Faine, R. (2003). *Episodic stress responses model and the experience of people living with multiple sclerosis and their carers: A qualitative research project.* Report for the MS Society of NSW Research Committee.

Hirschi, T., & Gottfredson, M.R. (1995). Control theory and the life-course perspective. *Studies on Crime & Crime Prevention, 4*(2), 131–142.

Hope, T., & Sparks, R. (2000). *Crime, risk and insecurity: Law and order in everyday life and political discourse.* London: Routledge.

Hopkins Burke, R. (2005). *An introduction to criminological theory* (2nd ed.). Portland, OR: Willan Publishing.

Howells, K. (2004). Anger and its links to violent offending. *Psychiatry, psychology and the law, 11*(2), 189–196.

Hudson, B.A. (1996). *Race, crime and justice.* Dartmouth, UK: Aldershot.

Hudson, K. (2005). *Offending identities: Sex offenders' perspectives of their treatment and management.* Devon, UK: Willan Publishing.

Innes, M. (2003). *Understanding social control: Deviance, crime and social order.* Berkshire, UK: Open University Press.

Jakubowicz, A., Goodall, H., Martin, J., Mitchell, T., Randall, L., & Seneviratne, K. (1994). *Racism, ethnicity and the media.* Sydney, Australia: Allen & Unwin.

Jakupcak, M., Tull, M. T., & Roemer, L. (2005). Masculinity, shame, and fear of emotions as predictors of men's expressions of anger and hostility. *Psychology of Men and Masculinity, 6*(4), 275–284.

James, K., Seddon, B., & Brown, J. (2002). 'Using it' or 'losing it': Men's constructions of their violence towards female partners. *Australian Domestic and Family Violence Clearing House: Research Paper.*

Janoff-Bulman, R. (1992). *Shattered assumptions: Towards a new psychology of trauma.* New York: The Free Press.

Jenkins, A. (1990). *Invitations to responsibility: The therapeutic engagement of men who are violent and abusive.* Adelaide, Australia: Dulwich Centre Publications.

Kane, S.C. (2004). The unconventional methods of cultural criminology. *Theoretical Criminology, 8*(3), 303–321.

Kassin, S.M., & Gudjonsson, G.H. (2004). The psychology of confessions: A review of the literature and issues. *Psychological Science in the Public Interest, 5*(2), 33–67.

Kimmel, M.S. (1993). Clarence, William, Iron Mike, Tailhook, Senator Packwood, Spur Posse, Magic ... and us. In E. Buchwald, P. Fletcher, & M. Roth (Eds.), *Transforming a rape culture.* Minneapolis, MN: Milkweed Editions.

Kinney, T.A., Smith, B.A., & Donzella, B. (2001). The influence of sex, gender, self-discrepancies, and self-awareness on anger and verbal aggressiveness among U.S. college students. *Journal of Social Psychology, 141*(2), 245–275.

Kobayashi, J., Sales, B.D., Becker, J.V., Figueredo, A.J., & Kaplan, M.S. (1995). Perceived parental deviance, parent-child bonding, child abuse, and child sexual aggression. *Sexual Abuse: A Journal of Research and Treatment, 7*(1), 25–43.

Krueger, R.F., Schmitte, P.S., Caspi, A., Moffitt, T.E., Campbell, K., & Silva, P.A. (1994). Personality traits are linked to crime among men and women: Evidence from a birth cohort. *Journal of Abnormal Psychology, 103*(2), 328–338.

Lamb, S. (1991). Acts without agents: An analysis of linguistic avoidance in journal articles on men who batter women. *American Journal of Orthopsychiatry, 61*(2), 250–257.

Little, M., Jordens, C.F.C., & Sayers, E.J. (2003). Discourse communities and the discourse of experience. *Health: An interdisciplinary journal for the social study of health, illness and medicine, 7*(1), 73–86.

Loeber, R., Stouthamer-Loeber, M., Farrington, D.P., Lahey, B.B., Keenan, K, & White, H.R. (2002). Three longitudinal studies of children's development in Pittsburgh: The Developmental Trends Study, the Pittsburgh Youth Study, and the Pittsburgh Girls Study. *Criminal Behaviour and Mental Health, 12,* 1–23.

Lupton, D. (1999a). Dangerous places and the unpredictable stranger: Constructions of fear of crime. *The Australian and New Zealand Journal of Criminology, 32*(1), 1–15.

Lupton, D. (1999b). *Risk.* London: Routledge.

Lupton, D. (1999c). *Risk and sociocultural theory: New directions and perspectives.* Cambridge, UK: Cambridge University Press.

Mackey, E. (1999). Constructing an endangered nation: Risk, race and rationality in Australia's native title debate. In D. Lupton (Ed.), *Risk and sociocultural theory: New directions and perspectives*. Cambridge, UK: Cambridge University Press.

Maris, C., & Saharso, S. (2001). Honour killing: A reflection on gender, culture and violence. *The Netherlands' Journal of Social Sciences, 37*(1), 52–73.

Markus, H.Z., & Kitayama, S. (1991). Culture and the self: Implications for cognition, emotion, and motivation. *Psychological Review, 98*(2), 224–253.

McLeod, J. (2001). *Qualitative research in counselling and psychotherapy*. London, UK: Sage Publications.

McMurran, M. (1996). Alcohol, drugs and criminal behaviour. In C.R. Hollin (Ed.), *Working with offenders: Psychological practice in offender rehabilitation*. Chichester, UK: John Wiley & Sons.

Mean, L. (2001). Identity and discursive practice: Doing gender on the football pitch. *Discourse and Society, 12*(6), 789–815.

Merton, R.K. (1966). Social problems and sociological theory. In R.K. Merton & R. Nisbet (Eds.), *Contemporary social problems*. New York: Harcourt Brace Jovanovich.

Messerschmidt, J.W. (1993). *Masculinities and crime: Critique and reconceptualisation of theory*. Lanham, MD: Rowman & Littlefield Publishers Inc.

Messerschmidt, J.W. (1994). Schooling, masculinities, and youth crime by white boys. In T. Newburn, & E.A. Sanko (Eds.), *Just boys doing business: Men, masculinities and crime*. London: Routledge.

Miedzian, M. (1993). How rape is encouraged in American boys: And what we can do to stop it. In E. Buchwald, P. Fletcher, & M. Roth (Eds.), *Transforming a rape culture*. Minneapolis, MN: Milkweed Editions.

Miller, P.A., & Eisenberg, N. (1988). The relation of empathy to aggressive and externalising/antisocial behaviour. *Psychological Bulletin, 103*, 324–344.

Milsom, J., Beech, A.R., & Webster, S.D. (2003). Emotional loneliness in sexual murderers: A qualitative analysis. *Sexual Abuse: A Journal of Research and Treatment, 15*(4), 285–296.

Monti, D. (1994). *Wannabe: Gangs in suburbs and schools*, Oxford, UK: Blackwell.

Moore, T.M., Scarpa, A., & Raine, A. (2002). A meta-analysis of serotonin metabolite 5-HIAA and antisocial behaviour. *Aggressive Behaviour, 28*(4), 299–316.

Moore, T.M., & Stuart, G.L. (2004). Effects of masculine gender role stress on men's cognitive, affective, physiological and aggressive responses to intimate conflict situations. *Psychology of Men and Masculinity, 5*(2), 132–142.

Moreton-Robinson, A. (2000). *Talkin' up the white woman: Indigenous women and feminism*. Brisbane, Australia: University of Queensland Press.

Mukherjee, S. (1999). Ethnicity and crime. *Trends and issues in criminal justice, Australian Institute of Criminology, 117*, 1–6.

Mullins, C.W. (2006). *Holding your square: Masculinities, streetlife and violence*. Portland, OR: Willan Publishing.

Mummendey, A., Linneweber, V., & Loschper, G. (1984). Actor or victim of aggression: Divergent perspectives — Divergent evaluations. *European Journal of Social Psychology, 14,* 297–311.

Negy, C., Shreve, T.L., Jensen, B.J., & Uddin, N. (2003). Ethnic identity, self-esteem, and ethnocentrism: A study of social identity versus multicultural theory of development. *Cultural Diversity and Ethnic Minority Psychology, 9*(4), 333–344.

Newman, G. (1998). Decoding the violence of popular movies. In F.Y. Bailey, & D.C. Hale (Eds.), *Popular culture, crime, and justice.* Belmont, CA: West/Wadsworth Publishing Company.

Newman, G. (Ed). (1999). *Global report on crime and justice,* New York: Oxford University Press.

Noble, G. (2007). Respect and respectability. *Journal of Intercultural Studies, 28*(3), 345–360.

Oktar, L. (2001). The ideological organisation of representational processes in the presentation of us and them. *Discourse and Society, 12*(3), 313–346.

O'Sullivan, C. (1993). Fraternities and the rape culture. In E. Buchwald, P. Fletcher, & M. Roth (Eds.), *Transforming a rape culture.* Minneapolis, MN: Milkweed Editions.

Palmer, E. (2003). An overview of the relationship between moral reasoning and offending. *Australian Psychologist, 38*(3), 165–174.

Parker, I. (1992). *Discourse dynamics: Critical analysis for social and individual psychology.* New York: Routledge.

Parker, I. (1999). Tracing therapeutic discourse in material culture. *British Journal of Medical Psychology, 72,* 577–587.

Patton, M.Q. (2002). *Qualitative research and evaluation methods* (3rd ed.). Thousand Oaks, CA: Sage Publications.

Petrunik, M.G. (2002). Managing unacceptable risk: Sex offenders, community response, and social policy in the United States and Canada. *International Journal of Offender Therapy and Comparative Criminology, 46,* 483–511.

Phillips, A. (1998). *The beast in the nursery.* London: Faber and Faber.

Polk, K. (1994). Masculinity, honour, and confrontational homicide. In T. Newburn, & E.A. Sanko (Eds.), *Just boys doing business: Men, masculinities and crime.* London, UK: Routledge.

Potter, J., & Wetherell, M. (1987). *Discourse and social psychology: Beyond attitudes and behaviour.* London, UK: Sage Publications.

Potter, J., Wetherell , M. Gill, R., & Edwards, D. (1990). Discourse: Noun, verb or social practice? *Philosophical Psychology, 3*(2), 205–217.

Poynting, S., Noble, G., & Tabar, P. (1997, October). 'If anyone called me a wog, they wouldn't be speaking to me alone': Protest masculinity and Lebanese youth in western Sydney schools. Paper presented at the Fifth International Literacy and Education Research Network Conference, Alice Springs, Australia.

Poynting, S., Noble, G., & Tabar, P. (1999). 'Intersections' of masculinity and ethnicity: A study of male Lebanese immigrant youth in western Sydney. *Race, Ethnicity and Education, 2*(1), 59–77.

Poynting, S., Noble, G., Tabar, P., & Collins, J. (2004). *Bin Laden in the suburbs: Criminalising the Arab other.* Sydney Institute of Criminology Series, 18, Sydney, Australia: The Sydney Institute of Criminology.

Presdee, M. (2000). *Cultural criminology and the carnival of crime.* London: Routledge.

Quinn, W.H., Sutphen, R.M., & Marcia, G.J. (1994). Juvenile first offenders: Characteristics of at-risk families and strategies for intervention. *Journal of Addictions and Offender Counselling, 15*(1), 2–23.

Raine, A., & Buchsbaum, M.S. (1996). Violence, brain imaging and neuropsychology. In D.M. Stoff, & R.B. Cairns (Eds.), *Aggression and violence: Genetic, neurobiological, and biosocial perspectives.* Mahwah, NJ: Lawrence Erlbaum Associates.

Raine, A., & Liu, J.H. (1998). Biological predispositions to violence and their implications for biosocial treatment and prevention. *Psychology, Crime and Law, 4*(2), 107–125.

Random House (Ed.), (1997). *Webster's Unabridged Dictionary.* New York: Random House.

Ressler, R.K., Douglas, J.E., Burgess, A.W., & Burgess, A.G. (1993). *Crime classification manual.* London: Simon & Schuster.

Reynolds, K.J., & Turner, J.C. (2001). Prejudice as a group process: The role of social identity. In M. Augoustinos & K.J. Reynolds (Eds.), *Understanding prejudice, racism, and social conflict.* London: Sage Publications.

Rhee, E., Uleman, J.S., Lee, H.K., & Roman, R.J. (1995). Spontaneous self-descriptions and ethnic identities in individualistic and collectivistic cultures. *Journal of Personality and Social Psychology, 69*(1), 142–152.

Roberts, C.F., & Golding, S. (1991). The social construction of criminal responsibility and insanity. *Law and Human Behaviour, 15*(4), 349–376.

Rouse, J. (2005). Power/knowledge. In G. Gutting (Ed.), *The Cambridge companion to Foucault,* (2nd Ed.). Cambridge, UK: Cambridge University Press.

Sampson, E.E. (1988). The debate on individualism: Indigenous psychologies of the individual and their role in personal and societal functioning. *American Psychologist, 43*(1), 15–22.

Sampson, E.E. (1993). Identity politics: Challenges to psychology's understanding. *American Psychologist, 48*(12), 1219–1230.

Sampson, E.E. (2000). Reinterpreting individualism and collectivism: Their religious roots and monologic versus dialogic person-other relationship. *American Psychologist, 55*(12), 1425–1432.

Sanders, C. R., & Lyon, E. (1995). Repetitive retribution: Media images and the cultural construction of criminal justice. In J. Ferrell, & C.R. Sanders (Eds.), *Cultural criminology.* Boston, MA: Northeastern University Press.

Sanko, E.A. (1994). Challenging the problem of men's individual violence. In T. Newburn, & E.A. Sanko (Eds.), *Just boys doing business: Men, masculinities and crime.* London: Routledge.

Saxton, A. (2003). 'I certainly don't want people like that here': The discursive construction of 'asylum seekers'. *Media International Australia Incorporating Culture and Policy, 109,* 109–120.

Scott, M., & Lyman, S.M. (1968). Accounts. *American Sociological Review, 33*(1), 4–62.

Scully, D., & Marolla, J. (1994). Convicted rapists' vocabulary of motive: Excuses and justifications. In P.A. Adler, & P. Adler (Eds.), *Constructions of deviance: Social power, context and interaction.* Belmont, CA: Wadsworth.

Seidler, K. (2010). Community management of sex offenders: Stigma versus support. *Sexual Abuse in Australia and New Zealand, 2*(2), 34–37.

Sheehan, P. (2006) *Girls like you.* Sydney, Australia: Macmillan.

Sim, J. (1994). Tougher than the rest? Men in prison. In T. Newburn & E.A. Sanko (Eds.), *Just boys doing business: Men, masculinities and crime.* London: Routledge.

Smith, A.B., & Pollack, H. (1994). Deviance as crime, sin, and poor taste. In P.A. Adler & P. Adler (Eds.), *Constructions of deviance: Social power, context and interaction.* Belmont, CA: Wadsworth Publishing Company.

Smith, G. (1992). Dichotomies in the making of men. *Dulwich Centre Newsletter, 3–4,* 9–23.

Starzomski, A., & Nussbaum, D. (2000). The self and the psychology of domestic homicide-suicide. *International Journal of Offender Therapy and Comparative Criminology, 44*(4), 468–479.

Staub, E. (1988). The evolution of caring and nonaggressive persons and societies. *Journal of Social Issues, 44*(2), 81–100.

Staub, E. (2003). Notes on cultures of violence, cultures of caring and peace, and the fulfilment of basic human needs. *Political Psychology, 24*(1), 1–21.

Stewart, A. (2001). Grief of the abused male. In D.A. Lund (Ed.), *Men coping with grief.* Amityville, NY: Baywood Publishing Co.

Street, M.D. (1997). Groupthink: An examination of theoretical issues, implications, and future research suggestions. *Small Group Research, 28*(1), 72–93.

Tajfel, H. (1978). *Differentiation between social groups.* London: Academic Press.

Taylor Gibbs, T., & Merighi, J.R. (1994). Young black males: Marginality, masculinity, and criminality. In T. Newburn & E.A. Sanko (Eds.), *Just boys doing business: Men, masculinities and crime.* London, UK: Routledge.

Tedeschi, J.T., & Bond, M.H. (2001). Aversive behaviour and aggression in cultural perspective. In R.M. Kowalski (Ed.), *Behaving badly: Aversive behaviours in interpersonal relationships.* Washington, WA: American Psychological Association.

Teo, P. (2000). Racism in the news: A critical discourse analysis of news reporting in two Australian newspapers. *Discourse and Society, 11*(1), 7–49.

Tomsen, S. (2003). 'A gross overreaction': Violence, honour and the sanctified heterosexual male body. In S. Tomsen & M. Donaldson (Eds.), *Male trouble* (pp. 91–107). Melbourne, Australia: Pluto.

Towl, G.J., & Crighton, D.A. (1996). *The handbook of psychology for forensic practitioners*. London: Routledge.

Triandis, H.C., Bontempo, R., Villareal, M.J., Asai, M., & Lucca, N. (1988). Individualism and collectivism: Cross-cultural perspectives of self-ingroup relations. *Journal of Personality and Social Psychology, 54*(2), 323–338.

Tunnell, K.D. (1998). Reflections on crime, criminals and control in newsmagazine television Programmes. In F.Y. Bailey & D.C. Hale (Eds.), *Popular Culture, Crime, and Justice*. Belmont, CA: Wadsworth.

Turner, J., & Brown, R. (1978). Social status, cognitive alternatives and intergroup relations. In H. Tajfel (Ed.) *Differentiation between social groups*. London: Academic Press.

Turvey, B. (1999). *Criminal profiling: An introduction to behavioural evidence analysis*. San Diego, CA: Academic Press.

van Dijk, T.A. (1987). *Communicating racism: Ethnic prejudice in thought and yalk*. Newbury Park, CA: Sage Publications.

van Dijk, T.A. (1993). *Elite discourse and racism*. Newbury Park, CA: Sage Publications.

van Dijk, T.A. (1999). Critical discourse analysis and conversation analysis. *Discourse and Society, 10*(4), 459–460.

Varallo, S.M., Berlin Ray, E., & Hartman Ellis, B. (1998). Speaking of incest: The research interview as social justice. *Journal of Applied Communication Research, 26*(2), 254–271.

Vermeiren, R. (2003). Psychopathology and delinquency in adolescents: A descriptive and developmental perspective. *Clinical Psychology Review, 23*, 277–318.

Walster, E. (1966). Assignment of responsibility for an accident. *Journal of Personality and Social Psychology, 3*(1), 73–79.

Ward, T. (2002). Good lives and the rehabilitation of offenders: Promises and problems. *Aggression and Violent Behaviour, 7*(5), 513–528.

Ward, T., & Brown, M. (2004). The good lives model and conceptual issues in offender rehabilitation. *Psychology, Crime and Law, 10*(3), 243–257.

Ward, T., Hudson, S.M., & Marshall, W.L. (1996). Attachment style in sex offenders: A preliminary study. *Journal of Sex Research, 33*(1), 17–26.

Ward, T., Hudson, S.M., Johnston, L., & Marshall, W.L. (1997). Cognitive distortions in sex offenders: An integrative review. *Clinical Psychology Review, 17*(5), 479–507.

Ward, T., Hudson, S.M., & McCormack, J. (1997). Attachment style, intimacy deficits and sexual offending. In B.K. Schwartz & H.R. Cellini (Eds.), *The sex offender: New insights, treatment innovations and legal developments*. Kingston, NJ: Civic Research.

Webster's New World (2003). *Medical dictionary*. Indianapolis, IN: Wiley Publishing.

Wells, C. (2001). *Corporations and criminal responsibility*. New York: Oxford University Press.

Westen, D. (1985). *Self and society: Narcissism, collectivism, and the development of morals.* Cambridge, MA: Cambridge University Press.

Wetherell, M. (1998). Positioning and interpretive repertoires: Conversation analysis and post-structuralism in dialogue. *Discourse and Society, 9*(3), 387–412.

Wetherell, M., & Potter, J. (1992). *Mapping the language of racism discourse and the legitimation of exploitation.* London: Harvester Wheatsheaf.

White, M. (1992). Deconstruction and therapy. *Experience, contradiction, narrative and imagination: Selected papers of David Epston and Michael White, 1989–1991.* Adelaide, Australia: Dulwich Centre Publications.

Whitehead, P.C. & Carpenter, D. (1999). Explaining unsafe sexual behaviour: Cultural definitions and health in the military. *Culture, Health and Sexuality, 1*(4), 303–315.

Williamson, T. (1993). From interrogation to investigative interviewing: Strategic trends in police questioning. *Journal of Community and Applied Social Psychology, 3*(2), 89–99.

Willig, C. (2001). *Introducing qualitative research in psychology: Adventure in theory and method.* Buckingham, UK: Open University Press.

Willig, C. (2003). Discourse analysis. In J.A. Smith (Ed.), *Qualitative psychology: A practical guide.* London: Sage Publications.

Wilson, R.J., Picheca, J.E., & Prinzo, M. (2007a). Evaluating the effectiveness of professionally-facilitated volunteerism in the community-based management of high-risk sexual offenders: Part 1 — Effects on participants and stakeholders. *The Howard Journal, 46*(3), 289–302.

Wilson, R.J., Picheca, J.E., & Prinzo, M. (2007b). Evaluating the effectiveness of professionally-facilitated volunteerism in the community-based management of high-risk sexual offenders: Part 2 – A comparison of recidivism rates. *The Howard Journal, 46*(4), 327–337.

Winkel, F.W. (1990). Crime reporting in newspapers: An exploratory study of the effects of ethnic references in crime news. *Social Behaviour, 5,* 87–101.

Winlow, S. (2001). *Badfellas: Crime, tradition and new masculinities.* Oxford, UK: Berg.

Woo, D. (2004). Cultural 'anomalies' and cultural defenses: Towards an integrated theory of homicide and suicide. *International Journal of the Sociology of Law, 32*(4), 279–302.

Yourell, A.M., & McCabe, M.P. (1988). The motivations underlying male rape of women. *Australian Journal of Sex, Marriage and Family, 9*(4), 215–224.

www.ingramcontent.com/pod-product-compliance
Lightning Source LLC
Chambersburg PA
CBHW050708280326
41926CB00088B/2871